Multilingualism

How do children and adults become multilingual? How do they use their languages? What influence does being multilingual have on their identities? What is the social impact of multilingualism today and how do societies accommodate it? These are among the fascinating questions examined by this book. Exploring multilingualism in individuals and in society at large, Stavans and Hoffmann argue that it evolves not from one factor in particular, but from a vast range of environmental and personal influences and circumstances: from migration to globalisation, from the spread of English to a revived interest in minority languages, from social mobility to intermarriage. The book raises important issues about multilinguals' language competence and multilinguals' literacy development and it highlights educational trends that challenge traditional approaches to language education rooted in monolingual outlooks. A clear and incisive account of this growing phenomenon, it is essential reading for students, teachers and policymakers alike.

ANAT STAVANS is a Professor in Applied Linguistics at Beit Berl College and a researcher at the Institute for Innovation in Education at the Hebrew University in Jerusalem, Israel.

CHARLOTTE HOFFMANN was Reader in Sociolinguistics at the University of Salford, UK.

KEY TOPICS IN SOCIOLINGUISTICS
Series editor: Rajend Mesthrie

This new series focuses on the main topics of study in sociolinguistics today. It consists of accessible yet challenging accounts of the most important issues to consider when examining the relationship between language and society. Some topics have been the subject of sociolinguistic study for many years, and are here re-examined in the light of new developments in the field; others are issues of growing importance that have not so far been given a sustained treatment. Written by leading experts, the books in the series are designed to be used on courses and in seminars, and include useful suggestions for further reading and a helpful glossary.

Already published in the series:

Politeness by Richard J. Watts
Language Policy by Bernard Spolsky
Discourse by Jan Blommaert
Analyzing Sociolinguistic Variation by Sali A. Tagliamonte
Language and Ethnicity by Carmen Fought
Style by Nikolas Coupland
World Englishes by Rajend Mesthrie and Rakesh Bhatt
Language and Identity by John Edwards
Attitudes to Language by Peter Garrett
Language Attrition by Monika S. Schmid
Writing and Society: An Introduction by Florian Coulmas
Sociolinguistic Fieldwork by Natalie Schilling
Multilingualism by Anat Stavans and Charlotte Hoffmann

Multilingualism

ANAT STAVANS AND CHARLOTTE HOFFMANN

CAMBRIDGE
UNIVERSITY PRESS

CAMBRIDGE
UNIVERSITY PRESS

University Printing House, Cambridge CB2 8BS, United Kingdom

Cambridge University Press is part of the University of Cambridge.

It furthers the University's mission by disseminating knowledge in the pursuit of education, learning and research at the highest international levels of excellence.

www.cambridge.org
Information on this title: www.cambridge.org/9781107471481

First published 2015

Printed in the United Kingdom by Clays, St Ives plc

A catalogue record for this publication is available from the British Library

Library of Congress Cataloguing in Publication data
Stavans, 'Anat, author.
Multilingualism / Anat Stavans and Charlotte Hoffmann.
    p.   cm
Includes bibliographical references and index.
ISBN 978-1-107-09299-0 (hardback) – ISBN 978-1-107-47148-1 (paperback)
1. Multilingualism–Social aspects.   2. Second language acquisition–Social aspects.   3. Multilingualism–País Vasco (Spain)   4. Multilingualism–Pays Basque (France)   5. Sociolinguistics.   I. Hoffmann, Charlotte, author.   II. Title.
P115.45.S83 2014
404'.2–dc23
2014032052

ISBN 978-1-107-09299-0 Hardback
ISBN 978-1-107-47148-1 Paperback

For our families – three generations of multilinguals.

Contents

Figures and maps

Tables

Acknowledgements

This book grew out of our enduring passion and shared interest for the subject of multilingualism. Both of us have made the study of multilingualism part of our academic careers. We represent two generations of researchers: Charlotte has been part of the 'first generation' and Anat the following generation of trilingualism researchers. We have been able to observe the diverse trajectories multilingualism studies have taken, the increased body of studies that have resulted from an ever-growing interest in the subject. Through our parallel and shared trajectory, we are fortunate to have been supported and motivated by many colleagues and students (invariably many of them multilingual themselves) to undertake this book project. We are grateful to a number of colleagues who have given feedback on early versions of parts of chapters and provided corrections and comments for improvement. We are indebted to the two anonymous readers who reviewed the manuscript and made a number of probing comments and valuable suggestions. Needless to say, any oversights and mistakes are ours.

Writing this volume would not have been possible without the support of several research institutions that awarded us grants to carry out collaborative research (a Basque government grant), sabbaticals (the Arts and Humanities Research Board and the Salford University Research Investment Fund) given to Charlotte Hoffmann, and the support and grant awarded by Beit Berl College and the Institute for Research and Innovation in Education at the Hebrew University issued to Anat Stavans. This support allowed both of us time during the early stages of the project. Above all, it has been the unfailing support, encouragement and understanding from our families that has enabled us to bring our project to a conclusion. We are especially indebted to Francisco Ariza for his engagement in reading and providing editorial support, and to Joel Stavans for his technological and artistic contribution to some of the figures. Last but not least, our gratitude goes to our children – Cristina and Pascual, as well as Eyal and Maayan, who have been the living evidence of simultaneous trilingualism from birth to maturity.

Introduction

I wish to place before the reader some of the usual descriptions
of the Taj, and ask him to take note of the impressions left in his
mind. These descriptions do really state the truth – as nearly as the
limitations of languages will allow. But language is a treacherous
thing, a most unsure vehicle, and it can seldom arrange descriptive
words in such a way that they will not inflate the facts – by help of
the reader's imagination, which is always ready to take a hand and
work for nothing, and do the bulk of it at that.

Mark Twain, Following the Equator, Ch. LIX

Our collaboration on this book began, fittingly, in the Basque country,
when we were invited to talk about trilingualism. It is probably not
accidental that this meeting should have encouraged us to embark on a
project about multilingualism: we found ourselves in a bilingual country, were giving our papers in a third language, English, and we were
drawing on our experiences of multilingual family environments.

For over half a century now, 'bilingualism' (the use of two languages) has become the subject of systematic scholarly investigation.
Bilingualism has been scientifically reported on as an alternative to
(sometimes as a divergence from) monolingualism. In this sense, the
study of bilingualism encompassed any language situation in individuals or societies that involved more than *one* language. Mostly it
covered contact situations between two languages but it also subsumed other contexts involving trilingualism or multilingualism. In
this book we propose to look at 'trilingualism' (the use of three languages) and multilingualism (the use of more than two languages)
as distinct from bilingualism because we feel that the subject merits
separate treatment, both when looking at individuals who acquire
and use three (or more) languages and when taking a wider sociolinguistic perspective. Naturally, it is not always possible to draw a clear
line between the number of languages present in certain contact situations, especially in sociolinguistic contexts, and our use of the term
multilingualism takes cognisance of that.

1

It is likely that many readers of this book are bilingual or multilingual themselves. It is for them, as well for those who have an incipient or established interest in the subject, that we put together our insights into this unique language condition, gained both from personal experience and in the course of our academic careers. It may therefore be relevant to introduce a personal note on each of the authors. Charlotte Hoffmann grew up with two mother tongues and later studied foreign languages as part of her education. When she moved to the UK to teach languages she added a third language to her repertoire and also gained a fourth one owing to family connections with speakers of yet another language. The use of her different languages has been dictated by social, professional and family considerations. Anat Stavans became multilingual because she was born to immigrant parents who spoke the same mother tongue but for ideological reasons raised their children in a different language. She had the opportunity to travel and live in several countries in different continents, acquiring various languages along the way. She had the privilege of a true multilingual to use and manipulate languages as needed. Eventually she made a home and social life with people who themselves are mostly multilingual, and she lives in a country where multilingualism is the rule rather than the exception. In similar ways, and yet in different geographical regions and temporal frames, both authors have had a comparable upbringing in and around multilingualism. In fact, be it in England or in Israel, our use of all languages throughout our daily routines is similar, and we share the experience of having raised our children with three languages and accommodating different cultures. This should explain why we have developed an enduring interest in all things multilingual and multicultural.

Our stories are replicated many times over all over the world, for it is factors relating to birth, upbringing and education, travel, marriage, personal contacts and occupation, and to the cultural and sociopolitical context in which one finds oneself, that clearly have a bearing on the development and maintenance of bilingualism and multilingualism. Multilingual issues are fascinating because, beyond their ubiquity and partial similarity, they always have an intimate personal dimension. We hope that what we say will reflect both our experience of researching and teaching the subject, as well as our own involvement with the reality of being multilingual – and will thus stimulate the reader's curiosity.

In this book, therefore, the term multilingualism is taken in its literal meaning: the presence of more than two languages either in individuals or in society. Our underlying thesis is that bilingualism is not the sum of two monolingualisms, and that trilingualism/multilingualism does not equal bilingualism with the addition of (an)other language(s). The difference is more substantial. Sometimes the term 'plurilingualism' is used in contrast to 'multilingualism' (for instance, by the Council of Europe) to emphasise the idea that learning and using other languages is not just additive but that individuals and communities are enriched both linguistically and culturally through the interaction of different languages. However, the 'multilingualism–plurilingualism' terminological distinction is not widely made, and it is not observed in this book. We tend to use 'multilingualism' to refer to both sociolinguistic and personal aspects, and 'trilingualism' when discussing individuals with three languages; most of the extant literature covers subjects using three languages, not more. To account for the multidimensionality of trilingualism/multilingualism a multidisciplinary approach needs to be taken, whether the focus is on individuals or groups and larger sociopolitical entities.

Multilingualism and multiculturalism have a long history. They are phenomena that change as political, economic, social, cultural and personal circumstances of speakers evolve. Some trends appear to be working against lesser-spoken languages and, therefore, linguistic diversity, but at the same time, other developments such as internationalisation, migration and revived interest in minority languages have the effect of stimulating multilingualism and challenging traditional attitudes that favour one-language-only constellations. In many societies, education is increasingly assigned a pivotal role in helping to promote or maintain multilingual language competence in pupils. It is clear that language plays an important role in the emergence of group identification and personal identity, and it is equally clear that new forms of multilingualism are emerging that include the presence of a lingua franca, predominantly English, in our increasingly interdependent world. We examine some of the many ways in which contemporary developments can have an impact on language-contact situations. Reference is made to different languages and locations, but the focus always remains on how societies as well as individuals react to, and are affected by, contact with and use of different languages. To this end, we approach our study of multilingualism not just as a language phenomenon but as a condition that involves culture, ethnicity and identity at the micro- and macro-levels of society (Lo 1999).

In recent years, the study of multilingualism – and more specifically trilingualism – has expanded in volume, disciplinary perspectives, methodology, theoretical scope and descriptive coverage. In addition to a number of journals that are solely devoted to the topic, other more general periodicals have also made room for this field of enquiry. Equally, a growing number of books and collections are providing a deeper understanding of contemporary trilingualism and multilingualism from different perspectives: for instance, publications focusing on psycholinguistic issues of multilingual competence and development (Herdina and Jessner 2002) and the educational system (Cenoz and Genesee 1998; in the Basque Country, Cenoz 2009); or books that provide insights on what people – embedded in different cultural practices – do when they read and write in different languages (Blackledge and Creese 2010; Martin-Jones and Jones 2000); or compilations that gather studies on trilingualism in the family and in the community as well as within the educational system, as family, community and schools are the main sources that enable the birth and growth of a multilingual individual (Hoffmann and Ytsma 2004). Other scholars have taken up a more psycho-sociolinguistic approach to multilingualism, and they see it through the impact of power relations (Pavlenko and Blackledge 2004) or through language use and attitudes towards three languages within the European bilingual context (Lasagabaster and Huguet 2007). There is also a recent comprehensive account of multilingual communication which maps different issues from different perspectives on the process of becoming, acting, staying and living multilingual(ly) (Auer and Li 2009).

In this book we try to present multilingualism as an evolving field of inquiry in its own right, and we highlight the multiple facets of trilingualism as a new 'lingualism order' in an era of globalisation. The choice of topics and the way they are developed were driven by the wish to bring together existing research as well as the need to analyse contemporary trends that promote multilingualism. These trends represent opposing forces and throw up issues that require special accommodation to the new multilingual realities worldwide and across the lifespan of multilingual individuals and societies.

The book is arranged into two main parts. The first four chapters focus on societal and global issues, and they provide a historical and theoretical backdrop to the discussion of contemporary developments. The second part describes individual trilingualism through an examination of what constitutes being, maintaining and developing into a multilingual individual in different contexts; it includes a review of the uses of – and attitudes to – the multilingual's languages, the way multilingualism is accommodated and, finally, the educational means that foster, preserve and encourage multilingualism.

Chapter 1 takes a broad sweep at multilingualism through history and introduces a number of multilingual contexts that have yielded early records of language contact; for instance, conquest and colonisation, both military and religious. Other topics covered concern intellectual revolutions such as the expanding role of reading, writing and education, migratory movements of populations and other geopolitical events leading to the emergence of multilingual territories.

A number of basic concepts relating to multilingual organisation are discussed and exemplified in Chapter 2. The aim of the chapter is to outline terms drawn from various disciplines that are used in the description of contemporary sociolinguistic trends leading to multilingualism. This entails looking at forces behind language spread and at the emergence of new patterns of multilingualism in society today. Certain contemporary developments (notably immigration) keep society and its sociolinguistic constellations in constant flux, as do the recognition of linguistic minorities and language spread that is accelerated by schooling and modern communication. Some multilingual states are guided by certain ideologies; others have elaborated language policies which they pursue consistently over a long period of time, while yet others respond to language issues if and when the need arises. A number of examples from diverse sociolinguistic settings and one longer case study are presented to illustrate the different patterns and developments.

The focus of Chapter 3 is linguistic minorities in multiple language-contact contexts. Sometimes the members of such speech communities are bilingual in their own language and the country's majority language; in other cases, linguistic-minority members are trilingual (or learn even more languages) because they need to use a regional or local minority language (or more than one) in addition to their own and the majority language. A number of issues specifically related to linguistic minorities such as questions of official legal status, language use and language survival are given prominence here, as well as some general factors that shape the particular character of linguistic minorities. The discussion of four case studies of minorities in two different multilingual contexts takes into account historical aspects, the territorial and social distribution of speakers, the sociopolitical status of the minority in relation to the majority language and the relationship of the three languages involved with each other.

Chapter 4 examines the linguistic repercussions of sociopolitical developments such as postcolonialism and globalisation, and also the general mechanisms involved in the spreading of a dominant colonial language, often accompanied by commercial exploitation and sometimes fuelled by religious or cultural motivations. A situation of competition and/or conflict between colonial and indigenous languages may continue even after political domination has ceased. Colonisation affected not only the political and economic structure of the colonised territories, but also their very cultural fabric. Postcolonialism brought a rearrangement of sociolinguistic patterns, and it left behind a linguistic legacy still visible today: three such new patterns of multilingualism are outlined in case studies from three continents. More recently, multilingualism has been discussed in the light of phenomena of internationalisation and globalisation that gathered momentum in the economic sphere; their linguistic concomitant, the spread of English, has touched the sociolinguistic situation of every continent. A consideration of three different types of multilingualism with English found in Asia, Africa and Europe ends this chapter.

The second part of the book surveys studies on multilingualism with a focus on trilingualism at the individual level, and it explores the main theme of how individuals acquire and negotiate their multilingualism as they go through their lives. We frame this part in relation to psycholinguistic topics such as competence, processing and language use, including code-switching. At the interface between individual multilinguals and their multilingual societies arise issues stemming from the influence of family and community, such as language choice and the negotiation of identities. To conclude, we look at certain educational issues involved in supporting, fostering and maintaining individual multilingualism.

Chapter 5 starts by looking at general concepts used in the study of child and adult bilingualism and multilingualism, and it then considers some of the similarities and differences between these two phenomena. An overview of case studies into individual multilingualism traces a number of different ways of becoming and staying multilingual. This leads to a discussion of factors that can have an impact on language development and subsequent use, such as the frequency and type of contact, the need to use the languages, and attitudes and emotional attachments towards them. A classification of multilinguals on the basis of age and manner of acquisition is attempted – and illustrated by reference to published case studies.

Individual multilingualism, as explored in Chapter 6, is driven by the need to use one's languages depending on why, where, how and with whom one is communicating. Seen from this perspective, multilingualism is all about making choices. Some are made by the language users and are based on knowledge and awareness; other choices seem to be made by cognitive mechanisms when processing the systems we have at our command. Children and adults differ in the way they develop multilingual competence, process multiple linguistic systems and put these to use. We argue that multilingualism is dynamic, not only at its inception but across the lifespan of multilinguals, depending on their linguistic needs and opportunities within social and personal circumstances. Considerable complexities are involved in the language behaviour of multilinguals, and their exploration requires broader, multidisciplinary analytical frameworks.

Chapter 7 deals with the question of how multilingualism is accommodated at different levels. The socioeconomic and geopolitical forces that are present in our lives and influence our interaction require that languages be accommodated at the micro- and macro-levels of human routines. This means that individuals, communities and nations must juggle a multitude of linguistic codes with social needs and economic and political changes. We try to look for answers to questions such as: How and where do multilinguals learn different strategies for organising the use of their languages and meeting the social, cultural and psychological requirements of the context in which they find themselves? What influences are brought to bear? What is the role of different beliefs, customs and cultural practices and how are multilinguals able to navigate such a plethora of considerations? Do they have multiple identities or one kaleidoscopic one?

Chapter 8 provides a further perspective to the formation of individual multilingualism, which is now looked at from the perspective of the established educational frameworks that provide tools, support and opportunities for its evolution and maintenance. As multilingualism all over the world becomes more widespread, institutionalised mechanisms and organisations have to respond so as to cater for the education needs emerging from new linguistic realities. Advances in technology and growing international mobility have led to the need to command more than one language. Literacy and communicative skills are changing as communication across geographic borders in real and virtual space generates more and more transnational multilingualism. This final chapter explores multilingual education in terms of contemporary perspectives on teaching and learning, and it discusses the consequences of multilingual education with regard to literacy. Depending on the specific context, multilingualism may characterise either underprivileged immigrant populations or privileged educated populations, i.e. it may be a necessity or an asset for different speakers. Multiliteracy, on the other hand, is not a natural concomitant of multilingualism, but it provides opportunities for those who have achieved it as it fosters the ability to communicate in multiple social spheres.

Throughout this book we bring together our own research on trilingualism and multilingualism as we weave our interests into a greater scheme of things related not just to language, individuals and societies, but also to the consequences and benefits of being multilingual. We try to make a clear case for the advantages of trilingualism and multilingualism as they offer opportunities to both individuals and societies that outweigh their inherent complexities or the alleged simplicity of monolingualism. Trilingualism and multilingualism build bridges between people, countries and cultures and, irrespective of whether these bridges are built top-down (global to individual) or bottom-up (individual to global), they contribute to the achievement of much-needed changes in polarised perceptions regarding the relative merits of uniformity and diversity within a society. We believe that cultural and linguistic pluralism are positive forces for social harmony, just as being able to handle several languages and operate in different cultural climates enriches the life of individuals.

Part I

Global and societal issues in multilingualism and trilingualism

1 Historical perspectives of language contact

By such innovations are languages enriched, when the words are adopted by the multitude, and naturalised by custom.

Miguel de Cervantes

1.1 INTRODUCTION

Multilingualism arises from contact between speakers of different languages. From earliest times people have moved around and had opportunities to come across groups with different linguistic features, whether in the pursuit of food or territory or trade, as regions that were fertile and accessible attracted peoples from different geographical and ethnic backgrounds and provided ample opportunities for cross-language communication. Whereas these may have been primary reasons for migration in the past, today we perceive such migration as ideologically motivated also by sociopolitical and ethnic identity. As such, ethnic groups have been defined according to real or perceived bonds such as race, religion or language (Edwards 1977, 1985) and, with regard to the latter, generally tend to be seen as being monolingual, although some have become users of two or more languages in the course of their history.

Their multilingualism eventually became a marker of their identity. From a present-day sociopolitical perspective, political units such as states very rarely are monolingual in the sense that all their citizens are speakers of one language only. The reason for this is simply that, in the case of old countries, the state boundaries have come about as a result of centuries of geopolitical changes and their emergence as independent polities. Younger states were seldom, if ever, drawn up according to ethnic considerations and therefore often cut across cultural and linguistic frontiers or encompass different linguistic groups. In this chapter we wish to address two major questions: What were the historical factors that brought about societal multilingualism?

And why has this multilingualism prevailed in some societies while in others it has not?

Historically, language contact has been facilitated by certain types of human organisation that go beyond single ethnic groups, and also by group behaviour such as migration of people either by desire or necessity. This can take the form of colonisation and immigration, or resettlement as a consequence of forced relocation in the aftermath of conquests or natural disasters. More recently, travel, education and communication over longer distances not only widen intellectual horizons but bring with them the necessity to acquire new linguistic and cultural knowledge, as do intermarriage and, in certain cases, conversion and acculturation, which, in the course of history, have occurred on both an individual level and one involving whole communities.

1.2   EARLY RECORDS OF LANGUAGE CONTACT

In the absence of written records, we can only make guesses about the type and extent of language contact and multilingualism that existed in prehistoric times, basing our assumptions on our knowledge of archaeologically testified expansion and migration of peoples in certain parts of the world.

But once we move into historical times, when attested records and dates become available, there is evidence of language contact in areas of early and rich civilisations, most notably in the Near and Middle East. The information contained in these early records, often in the form of inscriptions, refers to such things as names of languages or their speakers and their status, whether the languages existed in a written form and what they were used for. They may contain references to inventories or documents written in particular languages, about translations that were made, and they can provide clues as to language spread and language shift. For instance, one of the earliest records is that of a Babylonian epic poem called the Gilgamesh Cycle dating back to the second millennium BC. As the story spread, it became translated into an ancient Semitic language used in Babylon and later rendered into other Near Eastern languages. The main story is similar to the later Greek epic of Orpheus. There are other themes that reappear in the writings of later civilisations.

All the great empires of antiquity were multiethnic and multicultural, from the Babylonian to the Persian, Greek and Egyptian, as were the Roman and the Ottoman Empires that followed later and encompassed parts of Europe. The factors that led to language contact in the first place followed a similar pattern, namely conquest and occupation, as did the manner in which the imperial language then spread. With the rise of the dominant power, peoples from different language backgrounds came under its military command and political influence. The language of administration was one for which a written script had been developed, such as Aramaic, Arabic, Greek, Egyptian and Latin. Spoken languages were initially used, with the aid of translators, for dealings between the conquerors and the conquered. With increased usage, the language of the empire gradually became a lingua franca for different communicative purposes for both native and non-native speakers. As local and regional languages continued to be used, multilingualism was a common feature, at least among the indigenous educated upper and middle classes.

The development of the Semitic language Aramaic into a lingua franca provides a good example of language contact and subsequent multilingualism. Aramaic was one of the languages spoken in Mesopotamia and became the imperial language in the course of the long dominance of the Babylonian Empire, which lasted from the eighteenth to the sixth century BC, when it fell to the Persians. It continued to be used during the great Persian Empire and spread to many areas outside Mesopotamia, among them Egypt and Palestine. Whereas at first only high-level officials were competent in it and the majority of the population in the Kingdom of Judah was largely monolingual Hebrew-speaking (Spolsky and Shohamy 1999: 7), Aramaic later became widely used in both its spoken and written form and turned into a language of everyday use. By the time of the first century, its role had changed from that of an imperial language of wider communication used between different groups of speakers to one of a local vernacular used by the non-Jewish inhabitants of Palestine as well as by Jews for in-group communication. With the destruction of the Persian Empire by Alexander the Great and his successors, Greek became the imperial language while Aramaic remained in widespread use in the Greek and other kingdoms, but it gradually split into diverse dialect groups.

Spolsky and Shohamy (1999: 9) report that by the beginning of the Common Era, Jewish people used three to four languages, each language fulfilling different functions: Aramaic was used for communication with non-Jews; Greek (or occasionally Latin) was the language of government as well as that of the inhabitants of the Greek colonies; and Hebrew was the language of religious life for all Jews and the first spoken language of the Jews in Judea. They quote a passage from the Jerusalem Talmud (written, incidentally, in Aramaic) that illustrates the relative status attributed to each of the languages. Four languages are of value: Greek for song, Latin for war, Aramaic for dirges, and Hebrew for speaking (Megillah 1, 71b). One may assume that the passage reflects the linguistic preferences of the clerics who wrote it, or perhaps expresses how they wanted to see the languages being used.

There are many written references to language in Jewish religious texts such as the Old Testament and Talmudic writing. Some of them contain value judgements on particular languages or the way they are being used by certain speakers; others deal with the status of Hebrew vis-à-vis other languages or they urge Jews to maintain Hebrew and pass it on to their children. One becomes aware of competition between the languages of Palestine, and of the fact that Jewish multilingualism was not without conflict. According to Spolsky and Shohamy (1999), language shift towards Aramaic was attested in the second century BC when, worried about the erosion of Hebrew, the rabbis proclaimed it a religious duty to teach Hebrew and urged fathers to speak to their sons in Hebrew. One rabbi is quoted to have promised that a man who speaks with his son in the Holy Tongue is guaranteed a place in the world to come. This, from today's perspective, surely is an unusual incentive for language maintenance, although a similar celestial link between language and religion was established by Islam as soon as that faith became established in the seventh century BC.

Like Palestine, Egypt is in a geographical position where three continents, and thus different peoples and cultures, meet. In ancient times it developed empires that reached well beyond its modern borders. It has, in turn, also been conquered by others and been part of powerful empires, such as the Babylonian, Greek and Roman. The Rosetta Stone, named after the place where it was found (the village of Rashid in the Nile delta region), provides historical evidence of the existence of bilingualism, if not multilingualism, at the time when it was erected in 196 BC, some time after Alexander the Great had invaded Egypt. On the stone was carved a decree published by a general council of priests that had met to commemorate the coronation of Ptolemy V Epiphanes, King of all Egypt. The text concerns honours bestowed on the king for services rendered and it also contains details of priestly privileges. The significance of the 144 cm high black stone is the fact that it is a very early example of a bilingual text (Egyptian–Greek). In fact, the text displays three parallel inscriptions, each carved in a different script: Greek, hieroglyphic and demotic. The Egyptian text written in hieroglyphic script was the one most suitable for a priestly decree. Greek was appropriate as it was the language of the rulers and their administration. Demotic was a more accessible variety of Egyptian that evolved from the classical form. A cursive demotic script was developed late in Egyptian history and was used by government officials, in most cases only for secular documents. The Rosetta Stone provided an invaluable key, in the form of the Greek translation, to nineteenth-century Egyptologists in their quest to decipher hieroglyphic and demotic writing. In the context of our discussion here, it testifies to Egypt's multicultural and multilingual past.

During the times of subsequent empires, similar linguistic developments took place: quests for political dominance and economic influence were followed by the territorial expansion of the victor's language as it became the language of administration. During the time of the Greek Empire, knowledge of Greek brought with it the advantages of participation in the business and cultural life to be found in the Greek colonies, while in Roman times the use of Latin could bring material rewards or full citizenship with rights and privileges. In contrast, the Vikings – after their invasions in Europe in the eighth and ninth centuries and once they had consolidated their position and extracted the material gains they were after – adopted the language of the conquered lands and assimilated with the local communities, thereby preserving linguistic continuity in administration and cultural life so as to exercise political and social control.

It must be remembered, however, that the same factors that give rise to the spread of one language can also lead to its decline as the political, economic and cultural life of a community evolves and its fortunes are reversed. The popularity of Greek extended far beyond the time of the Greek Empire of Alexander the Great and his successors. It was preserved in the Roman Empire well into the fourth century, but then it diminished with the general decline in Roman cultural life and coincided with the rise of the influence of the Christian Church and its use of Latin for religious as well as administrative purposes and, notably, education and learned discourse.

1.3 RELIGION, MILITARY CONQUEST AND COLONISATION AS DETERMINANTS OF LANGUAGE CONTACT

Religion has been a consistent and powerful determinant of language contact and language spread. It is as well to remind oneself that it was not the faiths as such that led to language contact and competition,

but rather the way in which the believers chose to interpret their
beliefs and the missionary zeal they inspired in them. The spread
of a religion and the language with which it was linked was usually
spearheaded by military action and followed by political and economic domination that accompanied the imposition of cultural and
religious customs and the expansion of major trade routes.

The intimate relationship between Arabic and Islam and a traditional link between Christianity and Latin are examples. Nowadays,
the classical varieties of these languages used for religious practices
and rituals do not form part of the believers' communicative linguistic repertoire and are therefore not considered constituents of multilingualism. However, in times past when these religions were being
spread across wide parts of the world, they brought in their wake
new constellations of multilingualism. In some cases, this turned out
to be of a transitional nature, while in others it was more permanent,
such as the Spanish colonisation and Christianisation that led to the
dominance of Spanish in Central and South America. Map 1.1 illustrates how trade brought people of different religious and linguistic
backgrounds into contact with each other.

Classical Arabic originated in the seventh century BC when the
masterpieces of pre-Qur'anic poetry were composed (although they
were not written down until later) and the Qur'an itself was compiled,
as were the Prophet Muhammad's sayings. The Qur'an immediately
became the sacred text of the new religion of Islam, supplemented
by subsequent Qur'anic writing, and to date it is still a requirement
to recite it in that language. So from the beginning, when it became
a *sine qua non* for the Islamic faith, Classical Arabic was a literary and
religious language. After Islam had taken root in the Arabic Peninsula
it was taken to many parts of the world during the course of Islamic
conquests, for it was a militant religion. In the rapidly spreading new
Islamic states of medieval Asia and North Africa, and also parts of
Spain and Southern France, the Arabs spread their spoken language,
which became increasingly diversified in time, along with their religion and Classical Arabic. However, Arabisation that included cultural and linguistic conversion alongside the adoption of Islam was
never completed. In large parts of North Africa, Berber continued to
be spoken alongside Arabic, as did other languages in Saharan Africa
(Wardhaugh 1987). Wherever the Arabs went during their crusades
they left the same religion behind – one that encompasses spiritual as
well as temporal aspects of life – but different legacies in sociolinguistic terms, ranging from Arabic monolingualism to different forms
of multilingualism that included Arabic. Naturally, as is normal in

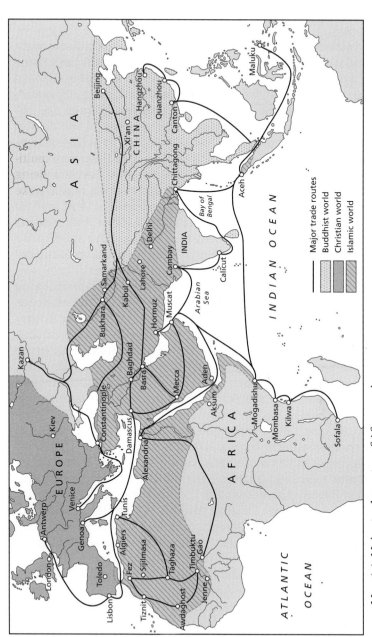

Map 1.1 Major trade routes of Afroeurasia

(Reproduced with permission from World History for Us All, National Center for History in the Schools, University of California, Los Angeles. http://worldhistoryforusall.sdsu.edu/images/bigeras/era5/Major_Trade_Routes_of_Afroeurasia_c1300_CE. Accessed 28 April 2014.)

language-contact situations, the linguistic legacy also includes cross-linguistic influences on the indigenous languages that Arabic was in contact with.

The colonisation of Latin America by Spain and Portugal also brought a new religion and language to the conquered lands. Although ultimately the Spanish language and Catholicism did not lead to the kind of strong feeling of unity among its people that exists among Arabs – of being bound together by a common language, religion and history – both have nevertheless proved to be of powerful and durable influence. In pre-conquest times, many hundreds of indigenous languages were spoken in the Americas with some of them performing the role of lingua franca within their vast empires. Quechua played such a role in the Inca Empire in the Andean region, and Nahuatl in the Aztec Empire. There were other languages that were used for wider communication, such as Mayan in the Yucatan Peninsula and Guaraní in the region of present-day Paraguay. Quechua and Guaraní have continued to be major players in Latin American multilingualism to this day (von Gleich 1994).

The conquest and subsequent colonisation of Latin America were driven by the twin motives of extending the political and economic power of the Spanish state at a time when other European powers were also engaged in empire building, and of spreading the Catholic faith. The former served to expand Spain's political influence in the world and brought with it an immense increase in economic power with the exploitation of the colonies' raw materials and the establishment of lucrative trade routes. The latter motive, Christianisation of indigenous peoples, has often been seen as the ideological justification for conquest and colonisation. There were, consequently, two bodies charged with the colonisation of the American continent, the Spanish Crown and its administrators, and the Church and its clergy. Both can be seen to have affected the Latin American linguistic configuration (Mar-Molinero 2000: 28).

From the beginning, Castilian Spanish became the language of those areas of public life where the colonisers wanted to exert their power: administration, trade and commercial and legal transactions. In the early colonial period, the Spanish encouraged the use of native languages, especially Quechua, which was already used widely as a lingua franca (referred to as *lengua general* or *lengua general del inca*) by early Spanish authors. The reasons behind this were probably more pragmatic than ideological as there were not enough Spanish-speaking local people who could be entrusted with the political and administrative control of the conquered territories. This practice meant that Spanish members of the administration and clergy had to be bilingual, making Spanish a contributor to the colonies' multilingual repertoire. Members of the clergy started to study native languages, wrote grammars and vocabularies of them and produced material to be used for missionary work. The Church controlled printed material very carefully, and all language material and translations also had to be checked by the heads of the four regional colonial administrations. A wholly unintentional upshot of this was that Quechua, previously used as an oral language only, became standardised and codified in this process which, in turn, contributed considerably to its further spread and prestige vis-à-vis other native Indian languages. Right from the beginning there was friction between different factions within the Church and administration favouring or opposing the use of native languages on theological, ideological and political grounds (Cerrón-Palomino 1989). The final shift to compulsory Castilianisation was decreed by Charles III (1770) at a time when language policies in Spain were geared towards centralisation, which resulted in severe repression of linguistic minorities. With regard to Latin America, the decree reflected 'Eurocentric colonial thinking' (von Gleich 1994: 86) and was followed by cultural and linguistic repression of the indigenous population designed to quash any aspirations of independence. Quechua was no longer used in education and in missionary work, and with its loss of formal functions it began to lose users and prestige. With respect to furthering the spread of Castilian Spanish, these policies were less effective because schooling, especially in rural areas where native languages were much more predominant, was extremely slow to be formally established. Thus, popular multilingualism on an informal level continued to exist, although a lack of formal support led to the slow erosion of many indigenous languages, while increasing social and economic need provided the motivation to acquire and use Spanish. To this day, multilingualism in Latin America reflects the uneven power relations between the different languages and their speakers as it tends to be a feature of the poorer, less educated rural members of society.

1.4 THE ROLE OF READING, WRITING AND EDUCATION

A further reason why Aramaic, Greek, Latin, Arabic and Spanish, among others, were able to have such a profound impact was that written systems had been developed for these languages. Written communication brings advantages in terms of economy of time, scale and effort. A language that also has a written form can count on higher prestige both for the language itself and for its users. Written documents such as decrees, regulations and administrative communications to and from local and state government officials could be spread across a wide region relatively quickly and thereby helped consolidate and centralise colonial administrations. Written diaries, letters and reports could be sent in either direction to provide information and maintain linguistic contact between the colonies and the home country. With the advent of the printing press, this process received further impetus as not only greater quantities of written material could be produced and dispersed among a wider audience, but also many different types of printed products were published. Thus the power of the written language is exploited for the preservation of colonisation both of time and distance.

The historical documentary evidence we use today in the investigation of early language-contact situations enables us to reconstruct certain sociolinguistic constellations of times gone by. There have always been societies with purely oral traditions. Although they found their own ways of recording their past, passing on knowledge to the outside world about such things as what and how many languages they spoke depended on literate outsiders, such as visitors and travellers, reporting on them. It was not until the advent of modern anthropology that more reliable information about societies with no written tradition became available. Thomason (2001: 7) warns that they 'are seen primarily through the eyes of majority cultures, and this circumstance limits our understanding of language contacts among other peoples, especially before the twentieth century'. This is obviously an important consideration in an overall assessment of language contact, although it does not change the facts that the possession of a written form can play a very effective role in language-spread situations and that languages with a written system became primary candidates for language spread.

Naturally, in order to be able to read and write the superposed language it was necessary to learn it in the first place. Thus, while the existence of a written language can be seen to facilitate language spread, education and its concomitant, the acquisition of literacy, are important factors contributing towards the establishment and maintenance of multilingualism. In the days before access to education became available to wider sections of the population, education, including the acquisition of additional languages, was the privilege of the upper classes. In Ancient Rome, boys had Greek tutors, and during the Middle Ages, learned activity in most parts of Europe required an active knowledge of Latin. Consequently, children were sent to school first to learn Latin and subsequently to be taught in it. Educated elites were expected to be fluent in other languages, and in those territories that were under foreign rule it was necessary for reasons of personal gain and social advancement to know the language of the ruling classes. For instance, in fourteenth-century Granada or Cordoba Jewish merchants would have needed to speak both Arabic and Spanish and possibly also be able to read and write in these languages. But at home and within their own community they would have spoken Ladino, also known as Judezmo, the language of the Sephardic Jews, for which a written version did not exist, in addition to using Hebrew, which they either read out or recited for religious practices. During part of the time of the Habsburg Empire, members of the state administration needed to be able to function in three languages, too. Latin was the official language of the government, used primarily in written state documents. German was the vehicle for trade, education and science. And many people spoke a different tongue as their first language, such as Hungarian, Romanian, Croatian, Slovakian, Slovene or Ruthenian. In the Hungarian part of the Empire, Latin was officially abandoned and replaced by Hungarian as late as 1844.

Thus, education and the languages required or available for reading and writing were contributing towards the establishment of a particular type of multilingualism, one where these languages were used for limited but prestigious functions in the public space. Often only affordable by the wealthy, schooling imparted the knowledge of additional languages, or that linguistic knowledge was a prerequisite to accessing the education system in the first place. In order to take part in a country's administration, for instance as scribes, clerks and court officials, literacy in the official language(s) designated for that role was necessary. Particularly in earlier times, when only relatively few languages had been codified, the choice of this official language did not necessarily reflect the extent to which it was known among the population. In these contexts, access to literacy and multilingualism afforded power to those who possessed it while excluding those who did not from having influence in society.

1.5 THE CREATION OF MULTILINGUAL STATES AS A RESULT OF DYNASTIC POLITICS

Political practices other than conquests and colonisation have shaped Europe's multilingualism in its more recent history. As

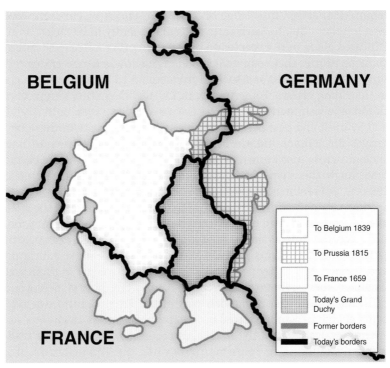

Map 1.2 Partition of Luxembourg

a result of political marriages, i.e. royal marriages arranged for political expediency, or other acquisition and succession agreements, territories of different linguistic backgrounds came together under one ruler and with it one language of administration. Border changes resulting from peace treaties following armed conflict had the same effect, as did the creation of new states following the reorganisation of Europe after the Napoleonic Wars. The histories of Luxembourg and Malta provide illustrative cases of all of these factors, which, combined with their geographical position, have shaped their multilingual status. The two historical powers most frequently involved in all manners of dynastic arrangements in Europe were the Holy Roman Empire of the German Nation and the Habsburg Empire (both its German and Spanish branches). As political entities of vast expansion, they acquired and lost territories in diverse parts of Europe in a most inorganic fashion as far as linguistic, cultural and ethnic homogeneity were concerned. Thus, many of the multilingual regions and states that emerged after the demise of these empires, such as Belgium, Luxembourg, Tyrol and Alsace, have German as one of their languages. The varieties of German in some of these areas are now considered languages in their own right, such as Alsatian and Luxembourgish. On the other hand, Germany and Austria, successors of once multilingual states, are today largely monolingual insofar as they have only a few small indigenous linguistic minorities.

The dukedom of Luxembourg goes back to the tenth century, when a number of French- and German-speaking territories came together through accession by marriage and inheritance.

Although the shape and extension of the duchy changed over time under French, Austrian, Spanish and Dutch rule, (as illustrated in Map 1.2) the Germanic–Romance linguistic border remained. The French- and German-speaking communities were considered separately by the administration according to a decree passed in 1340 by John the Blind. In contrast to the 'old' Luxembourg, the 'new' Luxembourg, which goes back to 1839, no longer has a monolingual French-speaking section of the population (Newmark 1996). Whereas French and German are official languages, each used in particular domains and for specific purposes in administration and education, the national language, enshrined in the revised Constitution of 1984 and spoken by everybody, is Lëtzebuergesch. Over the centuries, political developments in Luxembourg have preserved its bilingualism overlaid by the country's own and distinct linguistic variety, thus making the state officially trilingual.

Slightly different is Malta's sociolinguistic history. It provides an interesting example of a trilingual European country on the linguistic frontier between European and Semitic languages.

Positioned like stepping-stones between Europe and North Africa, the Maltese Islands have been of strategic significance to whoever wanted control of the Mediterranean Sea. Evidence of human habitation goes back to prehistoric times and the first bilingual evidence is from the time of Carthaginian colonisation of Malta, in the form of a pair of marble columns with a Greek and Punic inscription from the sixth century BC (just as in the case of the Rosetta Stone, the Greek version of the inscriptions provided a key to deciphering Punic). From 218 BC to 870 CE, the islands came under Roman rule and were among the first territories where Christianity was successfully established. Latin became superposed as the language of secular administration and of the Church.

In 870 CE the Maltese islands were conquered and settled by Arabs who imposed Arabic for official and literary purposes. Arab rule lasted until the Norman conquest of 1090, which was launched from Sicily and again brought a Romance language to the islands in addition to restoring the Christian faith. The islands became Romanised but complete language shift did not follow owing to the continued presence of spoken Arabic until the expulsion of the Muslims in the second part of the thirteenth century. Latin, the language of the Church, and Sicilian – eventually, Tuscan Italian – became the languages used for administration and by the educated members of society. The peasantry remained Maltese-speaking only. While some believe that the origin of Maltese goes back to the ancient Punic language, a more widely held view by scholars today is that it originates from the Arabic brought by the conquerors (Brincat 1991). Of interest here is not so much the exact origin of the Semitic component of Maltese but the fact that the Semitic language spoken in Malta has a long history of contact with Romance languages, first Latin, later Sicilian, Italian and Spanish. Legal documents from the fifteenth century in which reference is made to *lingua maltensi* as opposed to the previously used *lingua arabica*, serve as evidence of 'contemporary local consciousness about the language spoken on the islands' (Cremona 1994: 284).

In 1530, Emperor Charles V gave the Maltese islands to the Order of St John, a multilingual institution whose members came from a variety of European aristocratic backgrounds, the majority of them Romance-speaking. Their rule came to an end when Napoleon invaded the islands, but the French influence was short-lived and Malta was liberated in 1800 and in 1814 became part of the British Empire. It gained independence in 1964. It was during that time that Malta became officially trilingual, even though English did not enjoy then the same popularity as it does now. English was the language of the administrators; Italian continued to be used by the educated sections of society, and Maltese was the popular vernacular used for spoken communication. Today, these three languages still account for Malta's trilingualism, although their status and use have changed: English is far more widely used than Italian and it is co-official with Maltese, the nation's national language and the only Semitic language that is written in the Latin script. Maltesers typically have an English first name and an Italian family name, and they use Maltese for most of their communicative needs. Their multilingualism is established primarily through education, but English and Italian are not only required for international trade and commerce, they are prominently seen and heard all over the islands.

1.6 THE CREATION OF MULTILINGUAL STATES AS A RESULT OF FEDERATION

According to Fasold (1984: 11) a federation is 'the union of diverse ethnic groups or nationalities under the political control of one state'. In view of the inherent difficulties that seem to mar attempts to join people of diverse backgrounds and persuade them to accept the authority of a body that may be composed mostly of members of other groups, it is not surprising that many existing federations were imposed rather than formed voluntarily. In what follows, we illustrate the formation of federations as instances of power struggles leading to multilingualism. We mention two examples of consensual federations (Switzerland and Belgium) and two of imposed federations (India and Cameroon) where their creation and continued existence were not free from conflict.

Switzerland's history is not entirely free of strife and coercion, but the Helvetian Confederation can nevertheless be held up as a state that has evolved fairly peacefully and, more importantly, in a more pluralist way than its neighbours, perhaps not so much by design but because of its lack of effective central institutions. The original defensive alliance of 1291 comprised only three cantons which, over the next couple of centuries, were joined by more and more cantons. By 1513, thirteen cantons had joined the federation. All but one of them, bilingual Fribourg, were monolingual German-speaking. Linguistic diversity was not an issue at the time, and German remained the only official language until 1798. From the sixteenth century onwards the Old Confederation extended its influence over neighbouring French-, Italian- and Romansh-speaking areas, which were eventually joined with the Confederates, although initially they were not granted equal status. The original cantons adhered to their own traditions of cantonal self-government, and they respected local autonomy and linguistic diversity in all their territories. The Old Confederation was essentially a system of alliances: as a state it lacked cohesion and was wholly undemocratic in the way its constituent cantons were ruled over by assorted secular and ecclesiastical aristocratic rulers.

In 1798 the Old Confederation collapsed when it was invaded by Napoleon's army. A new centralised Helvetic Republic was imposed where all cantons had equal rights and all three languages (Romansh was not included at the time) were given equality before the law. McRae (1983) comments on the irony that the birth of official Swiss plurilingualism and linguistic equality somehow incongruously originated in a form of government imposed by foreign occupation and was sharply at variance with earlier Swiss traditions. And he adds that 'the fact that linguistic equality never had to be fought for but rather was thrust upon Switzerland from the outside, almost prematurely, may be more significant for linguistic peace than most Swiss historians have been prepared to admit' (1983: 40–41). After the Napoleonic era, in 1848 a new constitution laid the foundation for a democratic federal state in which the three principal languages, German, French and Italian, were proclaimed the national languages of the Confederation. In 1938 a constitutional amendment added Romansh as a fourth national language but declared the other three also to be official, in addition to national, languages. Official recognition of Switzerland's linguistic pluralism and its concomitant linguistic equality was obviously something the Swiss had come to value and the fact that it was never fought for, i.e. there were neither winners nor losers, meant that it could be embraced equally by everyone. Relative linguistic harmony is helped by the fact that there is a large degree of economic prosperity throughout the country.

The development of modern Belgium has been less fortunate although, like Switzerland, it is a state whose constituent French-, Flemish- and German-speaking parts initially came together in voluntary federation in 1830. Throughout the history of this relatively young state, linguistic peace and political unity have been more elusive. In part, this is because of the sharply defined linguistic frontier that runs roughly across the middle of the country, separating Flemish speakers in the north from the French-speaking Walloons in the south. Another contentious issue concerns the linguistic status of the capital: although it lies within the Flemish part and was once predominantly Flemish-speaking, over the past century French has become the dominant language in Brussels. Much of Belgium's earlier history has been dictated by outsiders. The country was under the rule of the Spanish branch of the Habsburg Empire, then it was annexed by France under Napoleon, and later (after the Congress of Vienna in 1815) it was forced into a federation with the Netherlands. Internally, too, there has been a long history of conflict between the Flemish and the French, the former resenting the hegemony of French and the latter the injustice endured during their union with the Netherlands when Dutch became imposed as the language of government and administration. The Constitution of 1831 confirmed the Belgians' linguistic freedom, as it stated that the choice of spoken language should be free and left further regulation to legislation. However, the language issue continued to divide the country, not least because of unstable administrative language boundaries and the unequal distribution of wealth between the two halves of the country. In the 1960s constitutional reform aimed at decentralising the state and new language legislation provided a firmer basis for peaceful coexistence. Linguistic boundaries were fixed, and political power with clearly defined authority became segregated on three levels: the national, that of the language communities (French, Flemish and a much smaller German) and the regional, which comprised the Flemish and Walloon region and the bilingual capital, Brussels. Yet since then, and in spite of subsequent constitutional changes, Belgium's political situation has remained volatile. All too frequently, elected parliaments have failed to establish stable governments, leading to premature resignations and the leadership of the country being given over to caretaker governments. Clearly, the political impasse is not only due to disagreement on questions of language alone, for these factors have always been entwined with social, economic and political issues. So, although originally there was the political will to form a multilingual federation, the country has not really been able to overcome deep-seated tensions between the two main linguistic communities.

Colonialism, forced federation of multilingual territories and fraught attempts at nation building often go hand in hand. Nevertheless, many former colonies have formed federations that stayed together after independence and have been able, with varying degrees of success, to weather subsequent ethnic and national conflicts. This is exemplified by the following two examples, one from Asia and one from Africa.

Colonisation of India is usually thought of as an entirely British enterprise, but Portugal, France, the Netherlands and Denmark have all had outposts in South Asia. During the times of the British Empire, a large number of territories containing peoples of different ethnicities were forced to come together under British rule. They were governed either directly by the British or indirectly by princes and rulers who had varying degrees of autonomy. When the British Empire came to an end, they had to relinquish their rights, as, for example, in the case of India: upon independence in 1947, it became necessary for the territories to accept incorporation into the new Indian state with the official title of 'Union of India'. The new federation could not be kept together as issues of religion, language and ethnic group differences proved to be far too divisive. First Pakistan split from India to become an Islamic Republic, and later, in 1971, East Pakistan seceded to become the independent state of Bangladesh. Both Pakistan and

Bangladesh are predominantly Muslim countries and, although they differ in their ethnic and linguistic composition, they are relatively stable geopolitical entities. India's linguistic, religious and ethnic mix is on quite a different magnitude, with major divisions between north and south and a myriad of subdivisions. With regard to linguistic peace, Indian language planning appeared to promise a relatively well-balanced formula for public language use with its proposed three language policy. But this planning has not materialised, mostly because northern Hindi speakers refused to learn southern Dravidian languages. This is, then, a case where the gap between planning and implementation has been hampered by injustices and recriminations along ethnic and – particularly – religious and social-class lines, which continue to spark conflicts with bloody outcomes.

Cameroon's multilingualism is also a result of federation, but it is somewhat unusual in that it represents a double act of both forced and voluntary federation. Cameroon was a German protectorate from the 1880s to the First World War when, under a League of Nations Mandate, the more extensive part came under French and another area under British rule. French Cameroon became independent in 1960 and the southern part of British Cameroon joined it a year later to form the Federal Republic of Cameroon. This fact explains why both French and English are the official languages of a country whose population of approximately 20 million (according to a 2009 UN estimate) is divided into more than 250 different ethnic groups. French is widely used, while Cameroonian Pidgin English is the lingua franca spoken in the former British-administered territories. Since 1984, the official title of the state is simply the Republic of Cameroon, and although the country is held together by relative political and social stability, there are significant political divisions between the English- and French-speaking territories, with the primary political opposition to the French-speaking ruling power coming from the anglophone regions.

The four examples discussed in this section show how official societal multilingualism can become established by means of federation of different monolingual speech communities, as in the case of Switzerland and Belgium. India and Cameroon represent examples of multilingual regions coming together to form states with an even larger degree of linguistic diversity that is further augmented by the addition of one or two former colonial languages. (This particular kind of multilingualism will be discussed in more detail in Chapter 4.) While both voluntary and involuntary federation may lead to the formation of multilingual states, there are a large number of other determinants that influence political unity and linguistic harmony: for instance, the degree of consent and imposition of the original federal arrangement, the socioeconomic status of the constituent language groups and the degree to which historical antecedents can be made to work in favour of the new state or prove too controversial to overcome.

1.7   MIGRATION AND RESETTLEMENT OF PEOPLE

Throughout history, migration has played a role in both language contact and language spread. The movement of significant numbers of speakers is not something that happens spontaneously; rather, it is triggered by political events and their socioeconomic consequences. The term migration covers different types of movement in one direction such as emigration (out of a country) and immigration (into a new host country) and also remigration (a return to the country of origin). Thus, as we have seen in the examples above from the ancient world, colonisers were encouraged to settle in conquered territories as, for instance, Greeks in Palestine and Egypt, and the conquered Jews were forced to migrate to Babylon.

The history of the Russian Germans offers a good example of settlement, immigration, forced resettlement and remigration. In both older and more recent times, governments interested in the economic development of scarcely populated parts of their territories have encouraged people from outside, sometimes whole communities, to settle there. Thus, in the eighteenth century, the Russian Empress Catherine the Great, who was of German descent herself, encouraged German immigration into Russia. It had been started under her predecessor Peter I, and it was to be followed by subsequent waves of immigrants right up to the twentieth century. The promise of land and relative freedom, including religious freedom, was an attractive proposition to many German settlers, who initially colonised the region around St. Petersburg and the steppes of the Volga basin. In the late eighteenth and nineteenth century, as the Russian Empire expanded, new German colonies were started in the Ukraine and Bess Arabia, Georgia, Moldavia and the Crimea, and later beyond the European part of Russia, in Azerbaijan and the Altai Mountains. The resulting multilingualism entailed primarily Russian and varieties of very diverse German dialects reflecting the immigrants' linguistic origins in Germany, Austria and Switzerland. With time, the various German dialects merged into a more homogeneous Russian-German dialect variety. As many regions enjoyed a considerable degree of autonomy, German was widely used also for official purposes among the German minorities, many of whom also used the local language of the region where they lived besides Russian.

The end of World War II and the ensuing period brought tremendous population changes in the Soviet Union caused by mass expulsion, displacement and resettlement. The majority of the German minorities who had not fled to the west and had survived dispersal found themselves in Siberia and other Asian republics such as Kazakhstan, Uzbekistan and Kyrgyzstan, where Russian Germans resettled. Following the Soviet language policies of the time, non-Russian citizens had to be able to use Russian as a second language in addition to the official local language (Haarmann 1992; Kreindler 1982). Intermarriage, mobility and a host of other factors worked against the maintenance of German, which for many came to hold symbolic rather than real communicative value. In the late 1980s came the demise of the old communist regime and with it more liberal policies allowing people to leave the Soviet Union. The Federal Republic of Germany offered attractive measures facilitating remigration for those who could prove ethnic German descent, and this option was taken up by a substantial number of Russian Germans. Since 1960, some two million ethnic Germans have remigrated to Germany from Eastern Europe and the Soviet Union. Of these, approximately 400,000 came from the former Soviet Union (Hoffmann 1994). The example of the Russian Germans shows that, over a period of almost 300 years, different types of population movements experienced by this group have required them to learn and use several languages. As a linguistic minority, they were characterised by multilingualism of a type where two languages of their linguistic repertoire, German and Russian, remained constant whereas the third language changed depending on which speech community of Russia, and later the Soviet Union, they found themselves in. But now, in Germany, they have ceased being a linguistic minority and their multilingualism is becoming recessive as their need to use languages other than German decreases.

The slave trade brought about the biggest forced movement between continents of people of diverse linguistic backgrounds, as can be seen in Map 1.3, yet the particular practices that were followed by traders and plantation owners, such as dispersing members of different linguistic groups and forbidding the use of native languages, prevented the maintenance of the different African languages and the establishment of multilingualism.

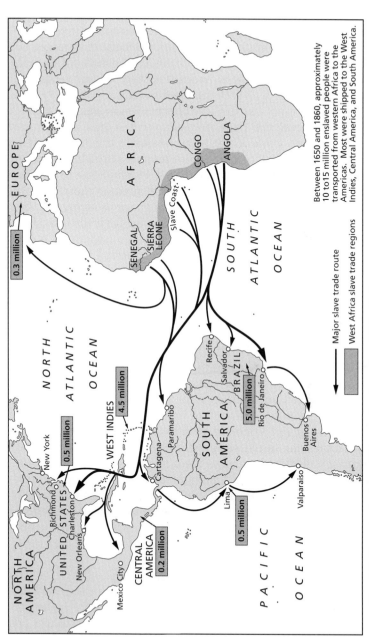

Map 1.3 Slave trade from Africa to the Americas 1650–1860
(Adapted from www.slaverysite.com/slave%20trade.htm. Accessed 28 April 2014.)

After the abolition of slavery, the colonial powers continued to be the instigators of movements of people. Both Britain and France encouraged their own countrymen and women to settle in the colonies, which helped consolidate the position and use of European languages there. Thus, French became firmly established, for instance, in Tunisia and Algeria in the nineteenth century, adding yet another language to North Africa's sociolinguistic mosaic.

The colonial powers also furthered population movement between their colonies. From the 1860s, for example, the British indentured Indian workers to work on their plantations in the Fiji Islands, an island group in the Pacific Ocean, which became a British Protectorate in 1870. Originally two pidgin varieties, Pidgin Fijian and Pidgin Hindustani, developed as contact languages used on the plantations between Fijians and Indians of different language backgrounds. Since independence in 1970, Fijian and English have been the official languages but, as the inhabitants of Indian background are so numerous – they account for around half of the population – Hindi and Urdu are also used in the media and in education; many Indians also know Fijian. Yet division along ethnic rather than linguistic lines is still an issue as political events in Fiji around the turn of the twenty-first century demonstrated when a political coup was carried out by Fijians who resented a newly elected government led, for the first time, by a Fijian-speaking prime minister of Indian descent.

The conquest and subsequent colonisation of Latin America by European colonisers, in particular the Portuguese and Spanish, entailed prolonged immigration from Portugal and Spain (Map 1.4). This colonisation was of substantial scale and intensity, especially in times of political and economic crises in Europe.

Emigration from the old world to the new lasted well into the twentieth century until, at the end of the century, it turned into reverse, with more Latin Americans immigrating to Spain than Spaniards leaving for America. Apart from some members of the early generations of colonisers who had to learn indigenous languages in order to communicate with the local population, there was generally no need for these immigrants to become multilingual. As we have seen above, by bringing Spanish and Portuguese to the colonies, the Europeans contributed to multilingualism among the local population in Latin America. However, this multilingualism was one-sided in the sense that it was a feature of those native Indians who spoke Indian languages and had contact with Spanish (or Portuguese) speakers and therefore needed to acquire this language. The urban population, above all the members of the ruling classes, and those who aspired to

Map 1.4 European colonisation of Latin America

join their ranks, needed just one language. The steady influx of Iberian native speakers over the centuries helped to maintain a remarkable degree of linguistic uniformity between the two continents.

Voluntary migration by some can lead to involuntary displacement for others. Immigration to what Europeans referred to as the 'newly discovered' territories in North America took on a different shape and had different political and linguistic outcomes than in the southern subcontinent. Early contact between colonisers and the native-American population was relatively unproblematic as there was plenty of land for all and the European concept of ownership of land was not one the local peoples shared. The situation changed when ever larger numbers of European immigrants wanted American land. The outcome of the ensuing conflict for the Indians who were pushed further and further to the west is well known. The demise of the indigenous population meant a drastic reduction in linguistic diversity, too. In the Americas, colonisation and subsequent immigration have turned the erstwhile indigenous majorities into linguistic minorities and everywhere large numbers of indigenous languages were wiped out in the process.

Language death was quicker and more radical in the north of the American continent than in the south, where a few of the major indigenous languages that have survived are today contributors to both societal and individual multilingualism, for example Quechua in Ecuador, Bolivia and Peru. A discussion of postcolonialism and its impact on language spread and linguistic minorities in a variety of states forms part of Chapter 4.

Unlike immigration to South America, which was predominantly from the Iberian Peninsula and brought just one language to each part of the South American subcontinent, North American immigrants came from a large number of linguistic backgrounds. The early colonisation of the east coast was undertaken by English speakers and was ruled by the British Crown, which determined the language of administration of the colonies, especially after the French had been pushed back into an inferior position. In a study on multilingualism in New York (which was originally a Dutch settlement and called New Amsterdam), García (1997: 20–21) offers quotations from several seventeenth-century chroniclers who have commented on the linguistic situation. According to one such source, Manhattan had a population of 400 to 500 people who spoke eighteen different languages, while another writer referred to New Yorkers as being racially of a great variety, listing Dutch, Walloons, French, English, Portuguese, Swedes and Finns, and also a few Jews and many black people from Brazil and elsewhere. Others have pointed to a great mixture of nations and commented that the English were in the minority. In the eighteenth and nineteenth centuries, large-scale immigration from a number of European countries made it possible for Russian, Polish, Italian, Norwegian, German and many other immigrants to establish communities who could use their own community language for a variety of functions, including educational and administrative, with

English serving as the contact language to be used with everybody else. However, this kind of societal multilingualism and individual bilingualism was usually of a transitory nature, lasting two or three generations until those concerned had become assimilated to mainstream English-speaking society. Increasingly, the official approach at both federal and state level was to use English as the sole language for all official purposes, to the exclusion of all others. Whereas originally it was possible to speak of the 'great American melting pot', it would be more precise to refer to the expected outcome of immigration as 'assimilation'.

In the more recent past, immigration to North America has again changed its shape and trajectory. Currently the largest groups of immigrants have come from Asia and, above all, from Central and South America. Linguistic assimilation to English among these groups may not occur quite so quickly, if at all. The reasons behind this phenomenon will be examined in the context of contemporary sociopolitical developments and trends in the next chapter.

1.8 CONCLUSION

We have taken a broad historical perspective on contributory factors to multilingualism and illustrated these by reference to a number of multilingual settings in different parts of the world. Early historical records rarely deal specifically with matters of language, and history tends to be written by the winners rather than the vanquished. Therefore, a certain amount of deduction and interpretation of existing sociocultural knowledge of the time is inevitable. The factors we discuss should be seen as causes and events that have come together either in succession or simultaneously and have affected the linguistic behaviour of communities, especially those who were at the receiving end of power politics meted out by conquerors, colonisers, political rulers and influential economic, social and cultural elites. Here is a list some of the most salient multilingual outcomes:

- Military conquests were frequently followed by colonisation and the spread of a new language; indigenous populations were either driven from their land or forced to adapt to new linguistic and cultural customs.
- The invention of printing and a general rise in education and literacy among wider sections of the population facilitated the spread of the new colonial languages.

- The enforced change of power relations meant that erstwhile native linguistic majorities became marginalised, oppressed sections of society lacking the material, educational or spiritual means to support their language.
- Colonial powers set up new hierarchies that allowed long-distance control of the colonies and created socioeconomic as well as linguistic dependency on the colonising powers.
- Multilingualism can be the outcome of increased access to literacy and education on the part of the more advantaged members of society. Conversely, it can also reflect uneven power relations and be a feature of the disadvantaged native population, who needed to acquire the language of the monolingual ruling elite in order to advance in society.
- The creation of new multilingual states brings together people from diverse speech communities. Political unity may not bring about national unity as ethnic and linguistic differences can pose insurmountable difficulties when they are accompanied by economic inequality and real or perceived social injustice.
- The assimilationist North American model requires multilingual individuals and groups to conform to one language, i.e. English only. It may not remain sustainable in future in the face of the demographic developments among the country's largest group of immigrants.

2 Patterns of societal multilingualism

If you talk to a man in a language he understands, that goes to his head. If you talk to him in his own language, that goes to his heart.

Nelson Mandela

2.1 INTRODUCTION

This chapter sets the stage for the discussion in the rest of the book, and the perspective adopted changes from the historical to the contemporary. First, clarification is offered for a number of terms and concepts used for the description of languages and their speakers in multilingual contexts. A brief overview of some of the most salient present-day social developments that encompass language contact in intra-national as well as international situations then leads to the discussion of the following questions: What are the basic patterns of societal multilingualism in terms of languages and speakers? What criteria determine these different patterns? What ideologies and legal principles guide multilingual organisation? The summary case study of Peru in the final part of the chapter exemplifies a number of the theoretical issues introduced in the earlier sections.

2.2 COMMONLY USED TERMS TO DENOTE TYPES OF LANGUAGES AND GROUPS OF SPEAKERS

2.2.1 Terms relating to languages

Most people have a clear notion of what a language is and an understanding of concepts such as dialect and standard, although the proposition that the standard version of Language A is just another dialect of A may seem less obvious. Even less straightforward is the task of defining and distinguishing between these terms, especially when faced with varieties that appear to be similar yet are perceived to be different linguistic entities by those who own the language. In sociolinguistics the question of whether one is dealing with a dialect or a language, or what exactly delimits one language from another, always involves considering social criteria in addition to linguistic ones. For instance, 'mutual intelligibility' is one of the linguistic criteria used to decide whether the respective varieties one is dealing with are dialects or languages. In traditional dialectology, different dialects are supposed to be intelligible to other dialect speakers of the same language, especially if they are not too distant from each other on the dialect continuum. However, mutual intelligibility alone does not have enough explanatory value, as can be seen from the following two examples.

Chinese is said (by the Chinese themselves) to comprise a number of dialects although they are mutually unintelligible to its speakers (Wardhaugh 2002). However, the Chinese people feel that they are united linguistically through a common writing system. This is an iconic system based on concepts, i.e. it does not have direct spoken–written (sound–symbol) relations for coding meaning, as do alphabets. Because iconicity is symbolic, the same system can serve several dialects or languages and play a role in symbolising a tradition of political, social and cultural unity that is shared by all Chinese speakers.

The two Indo-Aryan languages Hindi and Urdu, on the other hand, are said to be almost identical at the level of grammar (Gumperz 1982: 20) and intelligible to each other's speakers. With regard to its everyday use, Wardhaugh describes the boundary between the spoken varieties of Hindi and Urdu as somewhat flexible and one that changes with circumstances (2002: 29). The explanation for their perceived difference on the part of their speakers must be sought in socio-historical factors. In fact, in Dalby's *Dictionary of Languages* they are referred to as twins who are a world apart culturally (1998: 663). Hindi uses the Devanagari script, written from left to right; it has Sanskrit borrowings, is associated with Hindu culture and religion and is a national language for India. Urdu, written from right to left in the Arabic-Persian script, draws on Arabic and Persian sources for its lexical borrowings. It is the national language of Pakistan and a scheduled, i.e. official, language in some regional states of India. It is used by many of India's Muslims either as a first or second language and also functions as the literary language of the Panjabi and Lahnda speakers of Pakistan. Urdu has a long history of being used as a lingua franca among traders in big cities such as Kolkata and Mumbai. In the nineteenth century, spoken Urdu, one of the major languages of British India, was called 'Hindustani' after the subcontinent whose Persian name is Hindustan. Both Hindi and Urdu have great literary traditions and ideal standard versions that reinforce their speakers' belief in their separateness, even if in their spoken versions there may be close resemblances.

In the following we clarify a number of terms as they are used in our sociolinguistic discussion of multilingual contexts. Thus, *language* is described and explained by taking recourse to sociopolitical or sociocultural indicators, notably those that refer to its uses, functions and status, as perceived by its users as well as the wider sociopolitical context. A *vernacular* is a spoken variety used in popular or common speech associated with a particular region and, typically, the one a child first encounters as it acquires language. It is often contrasted with an educated, written variety of the language. Owing to their lack of formalised grammars and lexicons, vernaculars are usually considered less prestigious than standard languages. This can change when a vernacular becomes standardised or when a vernacular previously used as a regional language becomes promoted as a common national language, as has been the case of Tagalog in the Philippines. A *standard language* is one for which usually a written system has been developed as part of its standardisation process. Sign languages, for instance British Sign Language, also have a standard signed version. *Standardisation* includes the codification of grammar, vocabulary, pronunciation and orthography. Regular revisions are undertaken by the appointed authorities such as academies or dictionary producers, for instance, in the form of revised grammars and dictionaries that list new forms and meanings. The role and functions of the standard variety will have been established in its use in administration, education and the media, and there is normally general agreement among its speech community as to its prestigious status.

Official and national languages are standard languages, and both terms reflect the legal status a state has afforded them. Whereas the term 'official language' denotes a variety that has been chosen for public communication, a national language is one that over and above official uses plays the role of symbolising the country's nationhood. Some states include in their constitution a declaration of their linguistic choice of national language, others do so by way of other legislation; again others make no legal provision at all. In many cases the national and official language chosen by a state are one and the same, for instance, French in France or Turkish in Turkey. The Republic of Ireland chose Irish Gaelic as its national language although it is used by only a minority of Irish citizens – most use English, which serves as an official language. Multilingual countries may have one national language and more than one official one, such as Spain, where Spanish is the national language and Catalan, Basque and Galician are official in the constitutionally designated autonomous regions. Alternatively, more than one language may be assigned the role of national language, such as Hindi and English in India.

When we speak about an *international language*, more often than not we tend to think of English, although there is, of course, no inherent reason to do so. The term denotes a language, usually a standard, that is used for communication between different countries. Varieties referred to as a lingua franca or *languages of wider communication* are similar, though they may be either written or oral languages, standardised or non-standardised. They may function as a medium of communication across language boundaries within a nation or across national frontiers. For instance, Swahili is a Bantu language strongly influenced by Arabic. Used in its spoken form as a lingua franca by traders and settlers along the East African coast for many centuries, Swahili underwent a good deal of corpus planning when it became official in Kenya and Tanzania, followed by Uganda and the Democratic Republic of Congo. For some, it is the first language acquired, but for some hundred million speakers it is a second language; it is a language of wider communication both within and across nations in much of East Africa.

When we want to paint a profile of the sociolinguistic situation of a multilingual country we try to identify the number and type of languages used and also establish what *uses and functions* they fulfil. In the 1960s, the American linguist William Stewart worked on refining models of sociolinguistic typologies, proposing a number of features that linguistic systems such as dialects, pidgins, vernaculars, classical languages and others either display or lack – for instance, whether they have been standardised, whether they are living languages and whether they are autonomous. He puts forward a comparative framework for describing national multilingualism and suggests a technique for describing sociolinguistic situations in multilingual states that emphasise the 'kinds of social, functional, and distributional relationships which different linguistic systems may have within (and to some extent across) national boundaries' (1968: 533). He outlines ten different functions which he considers to be sufficient for an adequate description. The categories he lists comprise official, provincial (i.e. in a designated region), wider communication, international, capital (i.e. a primary language in the national capital and its vicinity – especially important in contexts where political power, economic activity and with them social prestige are centred in the capital), group, educational, school subject, literary and religious.

These functional categories are by no means mutually exclusive, for the same linguistic system may occupy more than one functional slot. For instance, in Quebec French can be used for all these functions, whereas in Vancouver it may be limited to three or four. The reverse can also be true, so that within a multilingual state more than one language is used for the same functions. Functional use of language in a multilingual state must be examined in terms of degree of use. Certain functions represent a much higher degree of use, such as in public communication, including media and administration, while there is more limited use of languages reserved for religious worship, literary or scholarly purposes. However, measuring the degree of use according to functions is complex because the only measurable unit is the percentage of users a particular language has within a speech community, and even that is only one way of judging relative significance as one does not know how much use speakers make of their language(s). As we have seen, Irish Gaelic is not widely spoken in Ireland and its use is for restricted purposes only, yet it is considered prestigious enough to serve as the nation's national language.

Mother tongue is a term that denotes neither type nor function but refers to someone's 'native', 'home' or 'primary' language. The notion of 'mother tongue' is often associated with the first language acquired, possibly the one that one knows best and quite likely the language that defines our group identity. However, there can be ambiguities when the term is used in multilingual contexts. Many children acquire two languages from birth: do they have two mother tongues? In subsequent bilinguals, the second language may develop into their dominant one, which of the two is their mother tongue? Some linguists (e.g. Skutnabb-Kangas and Phillipson 1989) argue that the term often denotes bias and prejudice when it is applied to different minority groups who are seen by the majority to have a lower social status within society, notably countries with large immigrant populations. For instance, in the context of education, 'mother tongue teaching' can refer to language provision for the children of minorities.

However, there are other situations where the term 'mother tongue' can convey a more specific meaning. In the translation and interpreting business, 'mother tongue speakers' are required for certain language tasks; here the mother tongue is taken to be a person's strongest language. Census and language survey questions often ask for 'mother tongue', and sometimes an explanation is offered. For many years, Swiss census instructions have defined mother tongue, with slight variations, as 'language in which one thinks' or 'language which one understands best', and insisted that only one language should be entered. Increasingly, as the term has become associated with social and power positioning, it is falling out of use and the notion of *home language* is applied as a more neutral alternative in research studies and official surveys.

2.2.2   Terms relating to language users

The remainder of this section discusses some terms and concepts relating to different groups of speakers' multilingual contexts. *Majority* and *minority* are very common terms. The primary meaning of this pair relates to their relative size vis-à-vis each other, but in a sociological context, further associations are often made involving elements of difference or even superiority and inferiority. Thus, minorities are those groups in society who are seen to be racially, politically or otherwise different from a larger group within the same overall unit. Unless the term is preceded by the words 'elite' or 'ruling', a minority is usually regarded as inferior by the majority. 'The label "minority" is simply a euphemism for non-elite or dominated', Romaine writes (1995a: 323). Hamers and Blanc take this interpretation even further when they state: 'A minority group is characterised by its powerlessness to define the nature of its relationship with the majority and therefore its own identity' (1989: 59). Frequently, a minority is referred to as an 'ethnic group', a kind of neutral term that focuses on the element of otherness; this practice is adopted in this book. However, *ethnicity* is quite a complex concept and not easy to define. Members of *ethnic groups* are characterised by common traits such as their religion, language, racial origin, shared history and/or traditions. In themselves, these are all elusive notions when it comes to delimiting them, but there is no doubt that they play a role in arousing feelings of shared identity among group members and as markers that set them apart from others. The problem is that not all groups that display some or all of these markers are labelled as ethnic groups. Race appears to play a bigger role than the other features that indicate otherness, and this can be confusing. For instance, the Polish or the Irish communities in New York are not seen as 'ethnics' in the same way as the Chinese or Haitians are. The second problem is the question of when one stops being a member of an ethnic group. Are the second- or third-generation bilingual descendants of immigrants from Vietnam, Russia or Costa Rica in the United States still members of distinct ethnic groups? Does someone of mixed parentage belong to two or one ethnic groups, and if the latter, which one? In spite of the problems and ambiguities, the terms 'ethnic group' and 'ethnic language' are widely used, including in this book, for lack of any better denomination.

We are on safer ground with the term *linguistic minority*, as language is the highlighted feature that marks members of this group. Linguistic minorities may be further qualified, for instance with reference to their origin. *Autochthonous* or *indigenous linguistic minorities* are people who share a common language (and possibly other traits) and who perceive themselves to be different from the majority group. Normally (i.e. unless they have been displaced) they are settled in a given area where they have lived for a considerable length of time. Frequently they are found on the fringe of larger linguistic areas – as, for example, Basque speakers in France straddling the French–Spanish border. In American, Australian and New Zealand usage terms such as 'ancestral language' and 'aboriginal language' are used instead.

Non-indigenous linguistic minorities, on the other hand, are composed of those groups that are not long-established members of a state. They comprise the people who are first- or subsequent-generation immigrants and have formed recognisable communities, typically in larger urban centres. Another term is *new minorities*, which can be contrasted with *old*, or *historic* (i.e. in the sense of indigenous). For instance, we could describe Australia's sociolinguistic composition as consisting of indigenous aboriginals, descendants of British settlers, older linguistic minorities from Europe and South America and new linguistic minorities from South East Asia. In public use the terms 'immigrant language' and 'minority language' have been replaced by alternatives such as 'heritage language' in America or 'community language' in Australia and Britain. However, it appears to be impossible to find neutral terms that stay neutral. What is politically correct in one decade may be considered pejorative in the next.

2.3   SOME CONTEMPORARY SOCIAL TRENDS CONTRIBUTING TO MULTILINGUALISM

2.3.1   Immigration

A number of the determinants of language contact discussed in the previous chapter can be seen to be at work in contemporary society as well, notably migration/immigration. As a consequence, countries that traditionally have seen themselves as being of the 'one language, one nation' type have experienced a continuous influx of people from other parts of the world, who by maintaining their

language and cultural heritage, have turned the country into a de
facto multilingual and multicultural one. Since the 1960s, most big
urban centres in Europe have attracted migrants and immigrants
from Africa, Asia and Southern and Eastern Europe. Immigrants have
formed established communities with their own commercial and
cultural centres that facilitate the continued use of their native language. London's East End has turned into a diverse multilingual and
multicultural environment; Berlin is the city which has the highest
number of Turks living together outside Istanbul, and it also has sizeable Russian- and Polish-speaking communities. Paris and Marseille
have attracted the lion's share of France's approximately 1½ million
immigrants of Maghrebine origin. In the United States, a traditional
immigration country where the assumption and actively pursued
policy was that immigrants should quickly assimilate linguistically,
contemporary immigration now yields multilingualism rather than
assimilation to English. For instance, Hispanics (over 50 million,
representing 16.3 per cent of the population according to the 2010
census) are the fastest-growing section of society: predominantly,
they are bilinguals who continue, across generations, to use Spanish
even though the majority of federal states offer little help for their
language maintenance. The paradox is that, when given the opportunity, a surprisingly high number of Hispanics themselves have
shown support for English-only policies.

Increasingly, as the twentieth century progressed into the twenty-
first, more of the world's population settled in areas further and
further away from their place of origin, with the result that the linguistic map of many countries has become more diverse and many
people have become multilingual through immigration. For example,
Canada passed legislation (the 1969 Languages Act and subsequent
legislation) recognising French as an official language alongside
English. Further legislative measures were approved granting certain rights to Canada's so-called heritage languages (i.e. those of its
indigenous minorities of Indian and Inuit origin, as well as newer
immigrant ones) and proclaiming multicultural policies. In consequence, the balance of different speech communities has changed
markedly. Vancouver is said to have the biggest Chinese community outside China. At the turn of the century, the allophone population (speakers of non-indigenous languages) was said to amount to
approximately 30 per cent of the overall Canadian population and be
roughly equivalent to that of francophone Canadians (Edwards 2001:
324). Many young people from immigrant communities are growing
up multilingual, live in multilingual landscapes and acquire one or

two languages at home and one or two through schooling (Edwards 2001; Lamarre and Dagenais 2004).

2.3.2 Language policies, globalisation and internationalisation

State building and language policies can be seen as more recent determinants of both societal and individual multilingualism. In the latter half of the twentieth century many new and developing nations found themselves in a position where they had to decide which language, or languages, to choose for official purposes such as administration, education and use in the media. Linguistic patterns that had emerged under colonial rule became altered, or adopted formally, as these states engaged in language planning designed to promote one or several of their indigenous languages and find a role for the old colonial language in the new state, for none of them found it opportune to abandon it outright. Often the colonial language represents a neutral alternative to competing native languages. Both developing nations and the countries of the old world have been caught up in globalisation and internationalisation. A revolution in communications and the phenomenal acceleration in the rate and extent of mobility of people, goods and services have greatly increased the potential of interlingual contact. These all-embracing trends bring in their wake a constant presence of English and the need to equip citizens to acquire this language. In response to this demand, many states now lay more emphasis than ever before on the teaching and use of English, whereas others have decided to afford it official status within their state. The net outcome of these decisions has been an increase in the incidence of both societal and individual multilingualism. Chapter 4 offers a detailed discussion of these developments and some of the issues raised by them.

2.3.3 Recognition of indigenous linguistic minorities

Another social trend that has an effect on a country's sociolinguistic profile is the change of attitudes and subsequent policies that have led to the recognition of linguistic minorities. This development differs from the above two: it is not a case of an exogenous language, i.e. one that is not indigenous to the country, being added to a society's linguistic repertoire, but rather a situation where one (or sometimes several) of its indigenous languages becomes legally recognised, its status and functions are determined and, perhaps, a programme for its promotion set in motion. Such measures are in stark contrast with the practices of centralist governments, especially in eighteenth- and nineteenth-century Europe and, by extension, their colonies in the

Americas. For example, in Spain the Bourbon dynasty systematically suppressed the use of Catalan, Basque and Galician – a practice repeated by the Franco dictatorship in the twentieth century. The supremacy of French over the other regional languages of France was already advocated under the *ancien régime*, and by the time of the French Revolution (1780–99) the Jacobins adopted a rigorous approach to linguistic unity. After proclaiming the ideal of '*une language, une nation*', they came to believe that national unity under a new democratic system could only be achieved by abandoning the use of regional languages and creating a 'community of communication' (Wright 2004). At the time, French was actually spoken by a minority of the French population, predominantly by the upper social groups. It had become a practical necessity to have a common means of communication if a total reform of the political system was to be carried through.

The philosophical underpinning of this view was provided by eighteenth- and nineteenth-century philosophers such as Gottfried Herder, Johann Gottlieb Fichte and Wilhelm von Humboldt, who had speculated over the origins of language, its role for the individual and for society and its significance for national identity. In their philosophical constructs, which idealised the relationship between language, its speakers and their state, there was room only for one language. It was a view favoured by statesmen, as administering and keeping control of peoples with different cultures and languages, and possibly loyalties, has always been more complicated than governing a more homogeneous body of citizens. Thus, in the course of the nineteenth and a good part of the twentieth centuries in many parts of Europe, America and Australia, minority languages were ignored and bilingualism tolerated but not supported until, gradually, a change in social attitudes and more nuanced ways of thinking about the role of language in society led to more relaxed practices and the formulation of different language ideologies. Increasingly, rather than simply equating languages with particular groups of speakers, studies of linguistic behaviour began to consider how power relations, social justice and different interpretations of cultural conceptions of language have an impact on language use and beliefs (Blackledge 2000).

From the 1960s onwards, many countries saw the emergence of national movements that demanded civil rights, including linguistic rights, for minorities. Political pressure from within and from supranational bodies such as the United Nations and the Council of Europe, coupled with a generally more liberal intellectual climate that helped change ideas about political and cultural pluralism, led a number of states to reassess the position of their linguistic minorities. To cite some examples of new language legislation, the first bilingual education programmes were set up in a number of South American countries as well as in the United States and Canada; Wales got its Welsh Language Act in 1967 (and a more comprehensive one in 1993); and in the Netherlands, Frisian–Dutch bilingual education started to be put into practice in the late 1950s and a long and bitter language conflict was finally solved in 1972. Towards the end of the 1970s and following the demise of the Francoist dictatorship, Spain underwent fundamental constitutional reform, as a result of which a highly centralised system of government was turned into a decentralised one that afforded linguistic autonomy to Catalonia, the Basque Country and Galicia. In South Africa, too, the new constitution passed by the post-apartheid democratic government meant official recognition of a number of African languages as official languages, whereas previously only Afrikaans and English had the status of official national languages. Chapter 3 offers a more detailed discussion of several issues related to old and new minorities.

2.3.4 Education

The emergence of new linguistic minorities created through immigration, language policies involving the promotion of several languages in newly dependent states and of minority languages in old ones, and the spread of English worldwide are developments that have affected societies and individuals and frequently increased the linguistic repertoire of states and sections of their citizens. A pivotal role in these developments was played by education, in its broader meaning of increased access to literacy and knowledge as well as in the more specific sense of language education. Informal language contact becomes consolidated when the languages concerned are taught as subjects or used as vehicles of instruction. At the same time, the status of minority languages, and with it that of their speakers, can become enhanced. Ultimately, the use of minority languages in the education system can be seen as an effective contribution to language maintenance. Chapter 8 presents an extensive consideration of both applied and theoretical aspects pertaining to education and multilingualism; however, given its significance for the individual and society, education forms part of the discussion of most other chapters as well.

While these contemporary trends offer opportunities for multilingualism to spread, the linguistic outcomes may also be quite different. Language contact and language competition are never very far apart.

Speakers of majorities as well as those of minorities are influenced by a host of intervening factors and conflicting language ideologies – not least those relating to the power relations between different speech communities and those entrenched at an institutional level. Left to their own devices, weaker languages (i.e. their speakers) invariably lose out to the hegemonic pressures of the stronger ones. Even when a state does support a multilingual language ideology and attempts to enhance the status of a minority language by assigning new functions to it, there is no guarantee that such measures will actually lead to a growing number of minority language users.

2.4 MULTILINGUAL ORGANISATION

2.4.1 Some basic patterns

No two multilingual states are identical in their sociolinguistic makeup. However, there are certain features that are shared by some while they are absent in others, so it is possible to depict some basic types of multilingual organisation. It is proposed here to outline five general patterns that can serve, in a suitably adapted form, for the description of individual countries.

The criteria used to distinguish these patterns are the relation between the number of languages used by a country's population and the incidence of individual multiple language use. The degree of multilingual use will vary depending on the prevailing conditions that determine the function and acquisition of the different codes.

Table 2.1 summarises the five patterns of multilingual organisation described below.

First, there are those countries where several languages are spoken throughout the territory and most of the inhabitants speak several linguistic varieties because these have different communicative functions. The example of a highly developed state such as Luxembourg mentioned earlier represents one end of the scale. Virtually all native-born citizens acquire Lëtzebuergesch (Luxembourgish) as a first language and German and French as second and third languages, and they habitually make use of all three. Similarly, in many African states one language is acquired in the family and the village and a second language, perhaps a pidgin or a language of wider communication, is picked up subsequently in the market and similar places where people from different tribal backgrounds converge. A third language, perhaps a standardised African language, is used for most official transactions and also in education; besides this, in many African

Table 2.1 *Summary of five patterns of multilingual organisation*

Pattern	Features	Examples used from	References
I. Territorial multilingualism Type A	Functional distribution between languages; high incidence of individual multilingualism.	Luxembourg, Guinea-Bissau	Newton 1996, Benson 2003
II. Territorial multilingualism Type B	All languages used for formal functions; some separation for informal functions; high incidence of bilingualism or multilingualism among different ethnic groups.	Singapore	Romaine 2004
III. Territorial monolingualism	One official language for each region; access to other languages seen as desirable but not essential.	Canada, Belgium	Edwards 2001
IV. Predominantly territorial monolingualism with urban multilingualism	One official language in predominantly monolingual country; concentration of linguistic minorities mainly in urban centres; varying degrees of individual multilingualism among minority members.	Barcelona, London	Turell 2001, Edwards 2001
V. Diglossia	(i) Two varieties of same language used for different functions; or (ii) two different languages used for different functions; widespread individual multilingualism.	German-speaking Switzerland, Paraguay	McRae 1983, Barbour and Stevenson 1990, Rubín 1968

states the old colonial language plays a role in education and administration. Whereas the first two languages are likely to be acquired by exposure and use, access to the third (and fourth) depends on people's social circumstances, and also on the economic and political situation of the state, as the following example illustrates.

The Republic of Guinea-Bissau, on the west coast of Africa, has a population of an estimated 1.6 million people. Guinea-Bissau has seen years of civil war, and it is one of the poorest countries of the world. It has an extremely low adult literacy rate; school enrolment is low and dropout rates are high. At least thirty different languages are spoken by distinct ethnolinguistic groups which are usually distinguishable by region. A study by Benson (2003) on trilingualism and education in Guinea-Bissau identifies two further linguistic layers: Kiriol, a Portuguese-based creole, used as a lingua franca for trade and contact with speakers from different linguistic groups, is spoken by close to half of all Guineans and usually acquired naturally as a second language. The official language, Portuguese, is only learnt by those who have enjoyed formal schooling; in 2011 only 14 per cent of the population were reported to speak it. Yet apparently there is 'a widespread, unquestioning belief in its value for future employment and other opportunities' (Benson 2003: 171). A previous census (1981) showed 12 per cent of the population to be trilingual, 30 per cent bilingual and 54 per cent monolingual. It is unlikely that these figures will have changed significantly in the intervening years.

Second, a variant of this pattern of multilingualism is found in those states where several languages are recognised as official languages that can be used anywhere in the state, although its citizens need to be proficient in only two. Singapore is comprised of three main ethnic groups, and their languages, Mandarin Chinese, Malay and Tamil, are official, as is English. The ethnic languages function as family and community languages; schooling is in the home language and in English. English is mainly acquired through education, although increasingly it is also becoming a home language for younger Singaporeans. All four languages can be used in parliament and in the courts and the media. English has become the language of choice for business and politics, and a particular variety of Singaporean English functions as a vehicle for interethnic communication. Among the whole population there is, generally, a noticeable shift towards wider use of English, and the increasing incidence of individual multilingualism has been observed.

The third pattern is found in states where different languages are spoken, and accepted as official, in the component regions.

Any one region uses just one language for all purposes. Day-to-day communication is monolingual and only those working in specific areas of administration or business are required to be bilingual or multilingual. This pattern of territorial monolingualism can only work well in polities which grant their regions a high degree of autonomy and where all languages enjoy equal status. Such a degree of linguistic pluralism is rare and the inhabitants of such states, especially those who do not constitute the majority group, are often proficient users of the other national languages. Modern lifestyles, certainly in the developed world, involve mobility and communication across language boundaries. French-speaking citizens, for instance in Belgium, Switzerland or Quebec, have access to the other national languages of their country through education and the media, but their daily communication needs within their region is in French only. Theoretically, language learning and the fostering of positive attitudes are considered highly desirable for employment prospects and for maintaining national harmony, but these ideals are not always achieved in practice.

The fourth pattern is exemplified by countries with partial multilingualism, i.e. countries that are predominantly monolingual but have some areas where other languages are used by linguistic-minority speakers in addition to the dominant one. Often the population of such areas is bilingual, but there may be communities that are trilingual. This can occur when indigenous and new immigrant minorities converge in the big urban centres of regions with two official languages. In Barcelona, for instance, Catalan, Spanish and Moroccan Arabic will form part of the linguistic repertoire of those Moroccan immigrants who have been exposed to Catalan education in Catalonia and who have picked up Spanish from their surroundings and at work. Administration and education is largely monolingual in Catalan, but there are many Spanish speakers, especially in the working-class areas of industrial cities that have a concentration of migrants from other parts of Spain.

A fifth type of multilingual pattern can be found in bilingual countries where there is also diglossia in the sense first described in a seminal article by Charles Ferguson (1959). Ferguson discusses situations where, in addition to the primary dialects of a language, which may include a standard language or a regional standard, there exists a highly codified superimposed variety that has a respected literary tradition and is learnt largely through formal education and used mainly for written purposes; but this variety is not used by any part of the community for ordinary conversation (1959: 336). He labels this variety the High variety (H), whereas the other(s) is/are the Low variety or varieties (L) – normally used as the medium for less formal, usually oral communication. The most important feature of diglossia is the functional specialisation of two varieties of the same language. Any educated speaker will be able to use them appropriately according to the conventions established by the speech community. Among the examples of linguistic contexts Ferguson discusses that display such a complementary relationship is written standard German (H) and the various Swiss dialects known as Schwyzerdütsch (L). A German national is often unable to follow a conversation between Swiss-dialect speakers, but because of the latter's familiarity with written and oral Standard German they have usually no problem understanding Germans. On account of the marked linguistic difference between Schwyzerdütsch and Standard German, Swiss diglossia can be seen as a form of bilingualism and within the context of the whole Swiss Confederation with its four languages, diglossia adds a further dimension to the country's multilingualism.

The concept of diglossia has been further developed to allow for the sociolinguistic description of situations where two distinct languages are used for different functions, as opposed to two varieties of the same language (Fishman 1967). The standard example quoted is usually Paraguay, where a large part of the population is said to be bilingual in the two official languages, Spanish and Guaraní, an Amerindian language. Spanish is the language used for formal communication, in the media and in higher-level education, whereas Guaraní is the choice for informal, largely oral communication, especially in rural areas. Joan Rubín (1968) was the first to present a detailed description of language choice in Paraguay, identifying categories such as location, degree of intimacy and seriousness of discourse as criteria governing choice of language. Unlike the German Swiss situation, not everybody knows the two languages. Of the country's estimated 5 million inhabitants, 90 per cent speak Guaraní, but not all as their first language; and some 1.6 million of them are monolingual. There are approximately a quarter of a million monolingual Spanish speakers, mainly in the bigger cities. In the Chaco region in the west of the country, there are sizeable numbers of speakers (over 20,000) of other Amazonian languages, and also varieties of German spoken by Mennonite communities (some 20,000–40,000; all figures from Baker and Jones 1998). Thus, Paraguay's multilingualism can be said to be made up of a variety of overlapping patterns: most of its inhabitants speak two or more of the country's range of languages, but there are also those who are monolingual.

The term diglossia has also been used in a much broader sense with the emphasis on the linguistic inequality felt to exist between two languages, or rather, resulting from the social inequality of the speakers of a dominant majority and a dominated and 'minoritised' group. Thus, for instance, in traditional Spanish sociolinguistics, Galician and Catalan were sometimes described as being in a diglossic relationship with Castilian Spanish. That was before the new Spanish Constitution of 1978 and an extensive process of linguistic normalisation, i.e. standardisation and elaboration of the functions of Galician and Catalan, was undertaken. Cerrón-Palomino (1989: 27) writes about the diglossic nature of Peruvian society, where Quechua and Aymara, confined to domestic and local functions, are becoming impoverished languages in a context where Spanish can fulfil all communicative functions. This is further illustrated in the Peruvian case study at the end of this chapter.

2.4.2 Determinants of multilingual patterns: languages, speakers and their political status

The second objective of this section is to explore the factors that determine multilingual language use and thereby pave the path for the formation of a pattern of multilingualism. Broadly speaking, the answers are to be found in those individual, sociopolitical and sociocultural determinants that relate to the language, its speakers and the wider political context. Naturally, these factors are interrelated as living languages only exist through their speakers who, in turn, shape their state, even if not all sections of society are involved in political decision-making.

With regard to language, one can mention factors such as the distinctiveness of the linguistic systems in terms of origin, whether they are oral or written languages and whether dialect or standard forms are involved. Furthermore, the fact that a language may also be used in another state, either as a minority or a majority language, can be relevant.

Speakers' language use is subject to many different influences. Demographic factors such as group size and social composition and status in relation to other language groups are relevant, as is their geographical distribution. If such groups are isolated at the fringes of a country, cut off from the mainstream communication network, language contact and therefore multilingualism is less extensive. If the speakers of a minority language are isolated from each other, the danger exists that a viable language community may cease to exist and the majority language will prevail. A similarly precarious situation for minority languages may arise when speakers of different ethnic languages are in close contact and the need to use a lingua franca becomes paramount. If the choice for such a language then falls on an 'outsider language', that could eventually weaken the position of the ethnic languages as their use may become more restricted. The social status of speakers of different languages is important, as it becomes attached to the language itself and may influence attitudes. This determinant may be of such significance that it overrides group size. The question of language choice, i.e. when and why a multilingual speaker chooses to use a particular code, is rarely a free choice. Rather, it is a matter of following conventions established by society according to standards determined, in the main, by those in a position to fashion social norms and influence the legal and political position of the wider population, including specific subgroups and their languages.

The position of individual languages within a state is affected by legislation aimed at determining their status and ambit of use, often within the framework of a specific language policy. Questions of power and status of the stakeholders, their politics and ideology, and beliefs about the relationship between language and identity may play a far greater role in this process than issues of communication (Blackledge 2000). Thus, a language may be recognised as the sole *national and official language* of a state, such as Japanese in Japan and German in Austria. Alternatively, it may be a *joint official language* such as Xhosa and Zulu alongside Afrikaans and English and a further seven languages in South Africa, or Finnish and Swedish in Finland. A *regional official language* is one that has official status in a designated region, for instance Welsh in Wales or Guajarati in India. Finally, a language may be a *proscribed language* when official restrictions of its use and sanctions against its users are imposed. The history of many linguistic minorities is full of appalling stories of repressive measures taken against such languages and their speakers at various times in history. The Inuits in Canada, native Indians in both North and South America, Aborigines in Japan and New Zealand, Welsh speakers in Wales and Basque speakers in Spain are just a few examples of those who have suffered such treatment.

Apart from these four legally recognised types of status, there are various intermediate positions that languages may occupy. Often there exists no particular legislation at all with regard to official use and status of a minority language. Thus, a *tolerated language* is used by its speakers as a home or community language but is not officially recognised. Typically, this is the position of the languages of most immigrant communities and many indigenous linguistic minorities. The extent to which a minority language is used and maintained depends on the amount of pressure – political, economic and social – put on its speakers. Without explicitly prohibiting the use of a particular language, official regulations concerning language requirements for access to citizenship and nationality, public service, employment, higher education and other areas can have the effect of drastically curbing the range of functions for which a minority language is used. On the other hand, if state authorities use minority languages for certain purposes, or support their use – for instance, in education – then one can talk of *promoted languages*. For example, in Cameroon, a country that is linguistically complex and multilayered with over a hundred first languages, several second languages and two official languages (French and English), Cameroonian Pidgin English widely serves as a lingua franca.

2.4.3 Formative principles of multilingual organisation

The third issue that concerns this section is to understand what general principles guide states in language legislation in general, and more specifically what ideology impacts on their language policies. Decisions of a general nature such as the degree of recognition of languages in multilingual states, their use and the rights granted to their speakers follow two basic principles: either a language is tied to a particular region or it is an attribute of the individual who has the right to use it anywhere. Thus, the *territorial* or *territoriality principle* takes geography as a marker of linguistic boundaries. It sees language as belonging to a particular region and determines which language, or languages, have official status there and are used in public contexts. The principle is applied in different multilingual situations, leading to either *territorial multilingualism* or *territorial monolingualism*. For instance, in bilingual Canada, Quebec is a declared monolingual French region. In Belgium two regions are marked out as monolingual, Flanders (Flemish) and Wallonia (French), while the German-speaking region in the country's east is bilingual – as is the capital, Brussels (Flemish and French). Most of Switzerland's cantons are monolingual but there are also a few bilingual cantons and one trilingual one. India has designated special status to a number of regional languages (the so-called 'scheduled languages'), which are official in the regions to which they are attached. As national official languages, Hindi and English can be used anywhere, so in all regions in India there is territorial multilingualism.

The territoriality principle has often been adopted when indigenous minorities have attained recognition and linguistic rights. In such instances, the outcome is territorial multilingualism in parts of the country and territorial monolingualism in the majority area. The territoriality principle is relatively straightforward to apply where only one language is used in a given territory, as long as there is consensus about where the linguistic boundaries should be. When there are two languages assigned to a given territory, for instance the national and the regional language, it becomes very important that measures are taken to avoid competition between the languages that could lead to pressure on the regional language. Other linguistic groups that might find themselves in the area, for instance new minorities, may be left with no language provision, no legal rights and no geographical space for their language. They have no choice but to use either the regional or the national language. If they choose the latter, this choice can weaken the linguistic equilibrium of the area and undermine the position of the minority language vis-à-vis the majority one. If the region pursues a policy that promotes its own language and uses it to the exclusion of the national one, then the linguistic burden for immigrants is doubled as they need to acquire two languages.

An alternative principle underpinning language legislation is the *personality principle*. It stresses the inherent emotional and spiritual connection between individuals and their language, which is why Myhill (1999: 34) refers to it as the 'language-and-identity ideology'. Linking these two has a long tradition going back to nineteenth-century philosophers who wrote about the importance of language to the individual as well as the nation. The principle has many advocates among modern linguists who have written about the mother tongue, for instance Tove Skutnabb-Kangas and Joshua Fishman. In one of his most enthusiastic quotes, Fishman says: 'This soul (the essence of nationality) is not only reflected and protected by the mother tongue, but, in a sense, *the mother tongue is itself an aspect of the soul*, a part of the soul, if not the soul made manifest' (1989: 276; emphasis in original). From this notion is derived the proposition that it is a person's inalienable right to use his or her language. For obvious practical reasons, it is only possible for a state to adopt this principle with respect to groups and not individuals. It is particularly helpful in those cases where a linguistic group cannot lay claim to a specific territory or where several groups share the same territory. It is a principle that underlies the language policy of states such as Singapore and Fiji Islands, allowing each of their major ethnic groups to maintain their own language and culture. It can be employed in monolingual countries, and in those that work on the basis of territoriality, to grant linguistic rights to specific immigrant communities hitherto not catered for. It can also be a useful tool for solving language problems arising from the application of the territoriality principle, for instance in areas where there are no neat linguistic boundaries and where sizeable numbers of speakers of two languages live together. For example, this is the case of some of the Swiss bilingual cantons along the Franco-Germanic linguistic frontier.

Useful though it may be to cater for specific groups, the personality principle may cause as many problems as it tries to solve. Once adopted, it may be claimed by any group, those aspiring to protection as well as those who feel discriminated by the territoriality principle. For, in effect, the two principles work against each other. The territoriality principle protects a nominated group who believe that a given area where they are concentrated is their homeland. However, it does so to the exclusion of all others. By affording personal linguistic rights to other groups, be they new immigrant ones or members of the national majority, the language meant to be supported by the territoriality principle is weakened. The ensuing competition for resources and public space can weaken the minority languages and ultimately work into the hands of the dominant majority language. Finding the right formula for a language policy that ensures a balance between conflicting ideologies and interests can take a long time, and it requires a great deal of sophistication. South Tyrol with its Ladin-speaking minority located within the German minority is a case in point; it will be discussed in some detail in the next chapter.

2.4.4 The dynamic nature of multilingual patterns

The practical application of the language-and-territory and language-and-identity ideologies frequently forces states to modify their language policies in response to changes in society and citizens' language behaviour that may have unplanned effects of multilingual patterns. For instance, the relative growth in the birth rate of different speech groups in multilingual societies affects their relationship vis-à-vis each other. Many immigrant groups in New York are becoming so numerous that private business and state authorities are responding by offering multilingual services. Spanish will become an increasingly important language in the United States as the number of its speakers is increasing considerably faster than that of the English-speaking majority. Similarly, the birth rate among Spanish speakers in Catalonia is higher than that of the Catalan speakers, which worries Catalan language planners, who believe that the only way in which the survival of Catalan can be guaranteed is to pursue monolingual Catalan policies, even though bilingual measures would be favoured by Castilian speakers. With time, not only the size but also the social composition of minorities tends to change. First-generation immigrants are likely to be socially homogeneous, as it is members of the poorer and less skilled sections of a country's population who emigrate in search of better living conditions elsewhere. Established immigrant communities are more heterogeneous and able to articulate claims regarding rights and support for their languages, and they lend status to the minority language by maintaining it.

Economic developments leading to migration can affect the linguistic pattern of a linguistic region profoundly. For instance, the traditional way of economic life of the mountainous terrain of the Romansh-speaking part of Switzerland used to be a combination of agriculture tended to in the summer months and other work done in the more industrial regions of neighbouring German-speaking areas during the rest of the year. But then bilingualism became the norm, and it continues to exist even though working practices have changed. Nowadays there is a great deal of immigration into the area, augmented in the summer and winter seasons, as the tourism industry has moved in and contact with employers and tourists requires a knowledge of either German or Italian. Today Graubünden is Switzerland's only trilingual canton. The spread of English as a preferred language of business in Asian countries such as Singapore and the Philippines is another example of language patterns changing in response to economic developments.

As we have seen, demographic changes inevitably affect linguistic boundaries. In states that are organised according to the territoriality principle, this may entail redrawing the official linguistic frontiers – an undertaking that can be fraught with problems. There was a time when Belgium saw a number of linguistic boundary changes carried out by unitary centralist governments, which deepened the long-lasting antagonism between Flemish and francophone Belgians. Only after the Flemish movement had become a powerful political influence was a situation reached where there was some degree of parity between French- and Flemish-speaking civil servants, institutions of higher education and members of influential political and economic bodies. Linguistic boundaries were fixed and special arrangements in the form of positive discrimination were made for vulnerable linguistic minorities in certain bilingual areas.

Also, changes in the political situation of a state, or its political system, or its language policy can lead to modifications of an established multilingual pattern. A new language may be added to already existing ones, for instance if, upon becoming independent, a state decides to promote one of its spoken vernaculars to the status of official language. Such is the case of Tagalog in the Philippines. Similarly, Papua New Guinea, a country with over 800 indigenous language varieties, kept English upon gaining independence and promoted two pidgin languages widely spoken in the country to official status: the indigenous pidgin Hiri Motu and the English-based Tok Pisin. The latter has become a main medium of communication and is now also spoken by many as a first language.

The case of Papua New Guinea also represents an example of how changes in people's language attitudes and perceptions may bring about a change in a country's multilingual pattern. As a result of the promotion and standardisation of pidgin varieties, these languages now take up official space in the country's linguistic repertoire and cover functions previously performed by other languages.

The nature of diglossia in Switzerland and in Greece, such as described by Ferguson in 1959, has changed, too. In Greece it has virtually disappeared insofar as the erstwhile High variety Katharévousa is hardly ever used any more. In Switzerland the functional distribution of H and L is becoming more blurred as Swiss German emerges as a favoured variety used for most functions of oral communication between German Swiss speakers. Fasold (1984: 56) refers to the demise of classical diglossia as 'leakage in function and mixture in form'. The influence of Standard German, and also of the Swiss variant of it, remains strong because of the omnipresence of the written word and the popularity of German and Austrian media. As can be seen, multilingual situations can remain relatively stable, but only as long as there is no competition between the different linguistic systems geographically, socially or functionally.

2.5   PERU: A SUMMATIVE CASE STUDY

A brief case study of Peru and its multilingualism is presented here, firstly to exemplify the use of certain terms, concepts and ideas examined in the more theoretical discussion of this chapter, and secondly to show how the country's language pattern has changed over the course of time in response to demographic changes and government intervention.

Peru is South America's third largest country. Its topography and cultures are varied, ranging from coastal lowlands, with most of the urbanised areas and the highest concentration of Spanish speakers, to the more isolated mountains and jungle. It is a nation with mixed ethnic origins of indigenous ethnic groups and Spanish. Peru's demography divides into some 45% Amerindians, 37% *mestizos* (i.e. of mixed Indian and Spanish descent) and 15% Europeans. Since 1940 Peru's population has more than quadrupled, from 6.2 million to approximately 28 million people, some 75% of whom live in urban areas (figures taken from the official government website); this represents a complete reversal of the proportion of rural to urban population. There is a marked contrast between the urban Hispanic culture and the subordinate Indian culture, and social stratification follows the same divide.

There are 106 different languages in Peru, 92 of them living languages. They belong to eleven different language groups, some of them spoken across national borders, notably Quechua and Aymara, and any one language may have dozens of different dialects. Over forty different varieties of Quechua have been identified, some of them mutually unintelligible, and there are six different dialects used for writing (spread over Peru, Bolivia and Ecuador). Some of the many jungle languages have so few speakers that they are on the brink of becoming extinct. In terms of speakers, the distribution of languages is very uneven: Quechua has approximately 4.5 million speakers and is found in twenty-one of the country's twenty-five administrative regions, although with varying degrees of density. Around 350,000 Peruvians speak Aymara, which also has a distinct territorial distribution as it is geographically confined to the country's south-west and the area around the capital, Lima. Aymara is the second most important indigenous language in Peru. When quoting statistics, the many other Amerindian languages are often referred to as 'other languages' (also *lenguas vernáculas* or *lenguas aborígenes*) and they are spoken by around 0.5% of the population, whereas 16.2% are Quechua speakers and 80.3% Spanish speakers. Census data collection in the mountain and the jungle regions has inherent and notorious difficulties; also, there is likely to be underreporting of indigenous language use. Therefore, all figures are best seen as approximations.

Against this backdrop of linguistic diversity, it is easy to see that multilingualism has been a constant feature of Peru's past. Languages have expanded and receded along with their communities, depending on the distribution and status of their speakers and the language policies imposed by the ruling powers, precolonial Indian as well as colonial Spanish. The Peruvian academic Cerrón-Palomino (1989) says that the typical sociolinguistic feature of present-day Peru is its diglossia, which involves a dominated and a superimposed language. Until 1975 Spanish was the national language and the only one used for all official purposes, including education. Spanish was, and still is, associated with literacy, higher social status and social advancement. Speakers of Indian languages were seen as backward and rural, perhaps not entirely without cause since the poverty incidence among those who speak vernacular languages is still considerably higher than the national average. Indian languages were stigmatised at a time when the main aim of those in power was to impose Spanish across the country. People affected and desperate to escape poverty ended up undervaluing their own cultural and linguistic background. Clearly, language was becoming aligned with social class and not with ethnicity. Not surprisingly, the number of monolingual speakers of Amerindian languages has steadily declined, while that of Spanish monolinguals has risen constantly – in 1990 over 72 per cent claimed to be monolingual. It seems likely that in view of the various pressures that are brought to bear on the individual in modern-day Peru, Aymara and Quechua are likely to survive as second languages, spoken alongside rather than instead of Spanish.

In the 1970s Peru experienced two revolutionary periods in the course of which language policies where formulated with a view to giving official recognition to its linguistic heritage. A change in the law named Spanish as the official language, alongside Quechua and Aymara in the regions where they predominate. The other indigenous languages were declared to be part of the cultural heritage. So, a territorial solution was adopted which enables Quechua and Aymara to be used for a number of official functions, but only in certain designated areas. These measures don't help the large number of Quechua and Aymara speakers who have migrated to urban areas. Coronel-Molina (1999) undertook a study of the functional domains of Quechua in Peru, following the typology suggested by Stewart (1968). He arrived at the following evaluation: Quechua is an official language, it has provincial function in designated regions; it has been used as a language of wider communication by the indigenous population and the Spanish administration in early colonial times. Today it is an international language spoken throughout several South American states where, in some regions, it enjoys the status of a promoted language. It is not a language spoken in the capital, although there it has group function among Indian migrants. It has minimal function as a religious language and as a school subject. However, it is used to some degree in bilingual education programmes, although these are not yet very well developed and often face resistance from the indigenous communities themselves, who still have to be fully convinced of the value of being educated in a language that carries so little esteem in society. Finally, Quechua does have a literary function as, since colonial times, a considerable amount of literary output of various genres has been produced. However, given the high illiteracy rate among Quechua speakers, much of this literature is inaccessible to many of them.

2.6   CONCLUSION

Migration, education and increased recognition of minority rights are three of the most important social trends that continue to impact on countries' linguistic patterns. These are interrelated and may affect a country in many different ways by creating new or additional layers of multilingualism that may require linguistic majorities and minorities to renegotiate power relationships and legal frameworks. With regard to the guiding principles and ideologies that underlie multilingual organisation, the following has been found:

- Few of the key terms and concepts used to refer to languages, their uses and their speakers can be seen to be straightforward; it is therefore necessary to clarify from which perspective and in what context they are being used.
- The organisation of multilingual countries is based on different guiding principles of governance and ideologies about the nature and role of language in society.
- These are subject to the political and social power relationships existing between the majority and minority groups.
- The citizens of multilingual states can be predominantly monolingual as well as multilingual.
- Societal multilingualism is never static: as a society changes, so do its linguistic patterns.

3   Old and new linguistic minorities

The limits of my language mean the limits of my world.

Ludwig Wittgenstein

3.1   INTRODUCTION

The concept of a linguistic minority is relatively easy to define because language is its main qualifying feature. As is to be expected, no two linguistic minorities are the same, because social groups are shaped and affected by various sets of geographical, political, economic and sociocultural factors in diverse ways. Even though language is the main qualifying feature of a linguistic minority (as opposed to any other kind of minority) it needs to be remembered that among its members there may be speakers who are predominantly monolingual, in either the minority or the majority language, while others may be bilingual or trilingual depending on their linguistic experience, opportunities and needs. The title of this chapter requires some elaboration before we discuss issues related to linguistic minorities such as official recognition, language use and survival in the modern global age.

A broad distinction between linguistic minorities can be made in terms of *age* and *origin* so that some minorities are referred to as historic (or old), autochthonous, indigenous, native or aboriginal, while others are described as new, allochthonous or non-indigenous. Old minorities are those that have inhabited a place or region from earliest times (admittedly, a rather vague attribution), whereas new minorities are seen as 'newcomers' to a region. Obviously, labels such as 'old' and 'new' are subjective and need to be re-evaluated as time and terms of reference change. An immigrant community, such as the Bangladeshis in Britain or the Kurds in Sweden, is still considered a new minority even though some of their members are now third-generation immigrants. When will they cease being considered new? And when will they stop being labelled 'immigrants'? These designations would certainly not be applied to members of the Amish community in the United States, whose forefathers arrived from Germany over two centuries ago, and probably not to those Hungarians in Canada who left their native country in the years immediately after the Second World War. Canada has seen more recent waves of large-scale immigration, for instance from Vietnam and China, who make up the new minorities now. In our exploration of linguistic minorities in multiple language contexts we are reminded of the inadequacies of certain descriptive labels as well as the diversity of multilingual contact situations within which they are found.

This chapter is divided into two main parts. The first contains a general discussion of linguistic minorities in macro-sociolinguistic terms, taking in terminological as well as theoretical considerations relating to speech communities and their languages. The second part presents two case studies that illustrate in context some of the issues examined in the first part. They highlight not only the linguistic complexity that shapes linguistic minorities but also their changing fortunes. They address the historical, the human geographical and the contemporary sociopolitical context, look into issues of language conflict and examine linguistic outcomes of language contact. In other words, we address questions such as: What factors and developments contributed to the formation of the linguistic minority? What is the territorial and social distribution of its speakers? What is the legal position of the minority and its status in relation to the linguistic majority? Which are the domains and functions of language use? Do they allow us to make any predictions as to the continued survival of the minority language?

Two criteria are applied in the choice of these case studies to allow the reader to compare the different ways in which minorities form part of, and play a certain role within, a larger polity's multilingualism. The first criterion is that only minorities that have received some form of legal recognition are included. The second is that they highlight the effect that social trends such as mobility and migration, renewed interest in minorities and internationalisation have had on the language behaviour of different groups. In their own ways, each of them also reflects the inherent dynamic nature of societal multilingualism.

3.2 LINGUISTIC MINORITIES: COMMUNITIES AND THEIR LANGUAGES

3.2.1 Indigenous and non-indigenous minorities

Two broad categories of indigenous linguistic minorities are distinguished in the literature, even though it is acknowledged that the distinction can be fuzzy and unsatisfactory. First, there are those whose language is autochthonous to the particular minority area and not spoken anywhere else, such as the Maoris in New Zealand, or Basques in both the French and the Spanish part of the Basque Country, or the Cherokees in the United States. Their speakers often form distinct ethnic groups with a strong sense of identity and loyalty to their ethnic homeland. The extent to which they have maintained their language depends on a variety of factors, among them the degree of group and language loyalty they have been able to foster in the face of pressure from the majority. The case of the Ladins outlined in the next section represents an example of such a group.

Second, there are linguistic minorities whose language is also spoken elsewhere as the dominant language of a national state. They are in a much stronger position as they can look to their linguistic homeland for status and support. Although speakers of the minority language may have been in the region for a long time, their status as a minority can be of more recent origin if they owe their position to border changes or to arbitrary frontier decisions which cut across speech communities, thereby turning the cut-off section into an adjoining minority. Occasionally, there are agreements offering special language maintenance support to the minority in exchange for similar measures on the other side of the border. This is the case with the German minority in the south of Denmark and the Danish minority in northern Germany. But such enlightened steps are rare and usually efforts to maintain contact with the mother tongue are organised by the minorities themselves. The Arabs in Israel and the Germans in Italy are examples discussed below.

Non-indigenous minorities, also referred to as immigrant minority groups, are the result of large-scale migration. Since most people leave their country of origin for economic reasons, immigrants and migrants often share the same underprivileged social background, which almost automatically puts them in a disadvantaged position in their new countries of residence. Traditional immigration countries have a history of accommodating immigrant communities that have subsequently become assimilated into mainstream society, although this may not have happened to all of them at the same pace. In Europe the phenomenon is a relatively recent one and is typically encountered in urban areas with their concentration of industrial activity (Extra and Gorter 2001; Extra and Yagmur 2004). The position of such communities has been made more complex by the fact that many governments were unprepared, if not unwilling, to consider large groups of migrants as potentially new citizens and have proved to be very slow in making legal, let alone linguistic, provisions for them that go beyond the UN International Covenant on Civil and Political Rights (1966), which protects the rights of minorities with regard to practising their own culture, religion and language.

The 1977 European Directive was an attempt to ensure Europe-wide legislation in support of language education for migrants' children. But since a directive does not bind member states to certain policies, it was left to individual governments to flesh out the recommendations. Very few did so, and where legislation does exist, it tends to concern access to language classes designed to help migrants' children acquire the language of their new environment. In most cases, efforts to help immigrant communities maintain their language have been left to the communities themselves. It is only relatively recently that national governments have begun to realise the potential capital these linguistic resources can afford and have initiated some concrete measures such as including some of the major immigrant languages in school curricula on an optional basis.

From a linguistic perspective, there is naturally great variation of language competence within immigrant communities, ranging from monolingualism in the immigrant minority language over several transitional bilingual stages to monolingualism in the host country language. Knowledge of vernacular forms rather than the standard varieties (in the minority and also the majority language) is often reported (Hoffmann 1991), as are all manner of cross-linguistic transfers. The case study of the Russian immigrant community in Israel discussed in Section 3.4 is a somewhat unusual example of a new minority: Israeli Russians are different from previous 'typical' immigrant communities in Israel in a number of ways as they are successfully maintaining their language, it seems, whilst also acquiring the language of their new country and, in addition, English, which is highly prominent in Israeli public life.

3.2.2 Some terminological considerations

The use of the term 'linguistic minority' reveals the perspective adopted in the description of a particular language community, namely one that takes the political entity of the state as a point of reference and implies that there is a national majority whose language is the dominant one. Thus, the linguistic minority represents a community of people who, among themselves, use a language that is different from that spoken by the majority of the state's citizens. Because of their minority status, most linguistic minorities have been shaped by political subordination and socioeconomic marginalisation – which, in turn, has affected their linguistic behaviour and their very languages.

Naturally, there will be considerable variation with regard to individual competence and frequency of use of the minority language and any other language or languages employed in daily interactions, just as the proportion of minority to majority language speakers will vary from one case to the next. In some minorities virtually every member is a minority-language user, and together they make up the bulk of the population of a given region and may account for millions of inhabitants. For instance, this is the case of the Catalans in Spain, especially when one disregards the region of Barcelona with its many Spanish-speaking residents and the more recent immigrant Moroccan and Algerian population. Large parts of Catalonia are solidly Catalan-speaking, and Catalans who aspire to a greater degree of autonomy resent being labelled a minority because of the negative connotations the term has and the way it positions Catalonia with respect to the whole of the Spanish state. Catalans are certainly not in a minoritised situation any longer as they were during long periods in their history. Today Catalonia is an autonomous region, Catalan is the official language there together with Spanish, and it is used by public authorities, institutions and in education (Hoffmann 2001b). In contrast, on the French side of the border, Catalan is spoken mainly by the older, rural population. The Catalan linguistic minority in the Roussillon area is geographically more dispersed and socially more homogeneous, and there is little protection for their language as French is the only official language.

'Language community' and 'community languages' are terms with more positive associations as they suggest social acceptance, vitality and active use in everyday life. A language that has a presence in the community is one that is likely to survive and keep the community together. The term 'community' is seen as being socially inclusive and, in the British context, the term 'community languages' is used in preference to 'immigrant languages' because the vast majority of speakers are second-, third- or even fourth-generation speakers (Edwards 2001). Therefore, community languages are typically those spoken by new immigrant minorities who have only relatively recently formed recognisable communities or been recognised as such (in a pragmatic rather than an official sense), and who cannot lay claim to a specific ancestral territory on British soil.

3.2.3 Some theoretical considerations

In order to secure the continued existence of its language and, by extension, of itself as a distinct group, a linguistic minority needs recognition and support. Indigenous minorities can base their case on the argument that their language and culture form part of the whole nation's heritage and are linked to a given territory, so special rights can be claimed on the basis of the principle of territoriality and linguistic equality. In contrast, new minorities must invoke the personality principle in the pursuit of language rights and protection, arguing that their language belongs to a living community of speakers (Baker and Jones 1998) who must not be discriminated against because of their linguistic background. The subject of language rights has become an area of growing interest in sociolinguistic discourse and has been examined from a range of different perspectives. For instance, proponents of linguistic human rights such as Skutnabb-Kangas (1981, 2000) and Skutnabb-Kangas, Phillipson and Rannut (1995) initially argued for greater institutional support for the education of minority children before widening the demands to include support for minorities at both national level and in supranational contexts against a backdrop of language endangerment. May (2012) refers to a more recent line of research around minority-language rights that also addresses 'social constructionist and post-modernist understandings of language that highlight the constructedness of language(s) and the contingency of the language identity link' (p. 131). The field of academic enquiry with regard to minority-language rights, among others, has widened from considering languages, speakers and language-planning policies to include critical theorisation of issues relating to ideology, power relations and identity.

In Chapter 2 the point was made that the terms 'linguistic majority' and 'linguistic minority' indicate a proportional relationship in terms of numbers of speakers and also imply their relative social status. Discussions of linguistic minorities often occur within the ideological framework of nationalism, where language is considered to be essential in the construction of a nation. This has been the nation-building practice in history and also in modernist discourse (Anderson 1983; Heller 1999). A common language helps create unity as it permits values and practices to be shared. At the same time it also provides legitimisation for the group's claim to nationhood. Those who are not part of the same majority-language group then find themselves in a peripheral position. 'Linguistic minorities are created by nationalisms which exclude them', Heller (1999: 7) writes, and he adds a further dimension to the argument: 'At the same time, the logic of linguistic nationalism is available to minorities as a way to resist the power of the majority. Language revitalisation movements are replications on a demographically smaller scale of the nation-building movements in Europe in the nineteenth and early twentieth centuries' (ibid.).

In many national contexts the majority–minority relationship is exemplified by one large group of inhabitants who all speak the national language alongside which exist one – or several – smaller groups that belong to a different language and culture. The state's ruling elite, as well as the political and educational establishment, use the majority language and therefore minority members usually need to be bilingual (Blackledge 2000). It is well to remember, however, that in many of the world's linguistically diverse countries none of the many component language groups are in a clear numerical majority. The dominating language usually is that of the ruling class, disregarding their relative size. Until the revolution in 1994, this was the position of English and Afrikaans during apartheid rule in South Africa, when only about a quarter of the population was able to speak these languages. In 1996 South Africa adopted a democratic constitution and launched a new language policy under which the nine most prominent African languages were declared official, alongside English and Afrikaans. The new language policy was complex, and it is taking time to be fully implemented. Meanwhile, English and Afrikaans continue to dominate. Another case is Swahili, a language of wider communication, in Tanzania. Since Tanzania gained independence in 1961, Swahili has been widely promoted as a national official language and is used in many official domains, even though it is estimated to be the mother tongue of less than 10 per cent of the Tanzanian population.

3.2.4 Language and ethnic identity

The terms 'linguistic minority' and 'speech community' encapsulate the idea that language binds people together. There are also a number of other factors, some of which are perceived as more significant than language itself, that foster group cohesion and serve as markers of belonging and inclusion. Common beliefs, shared traditions and rituals, forms of cultural expression, patterns of social organisation and racial features, or an attachment to a particular place through ancestral links, all contribute to feelings of 'groupness' or ethnic identity. At the same time, these factors establish boundaries vis-à-vis those who feel allegiance towards a different group. We speak of ethnic groups in this context, i.e. people who share objective characteristics such as language and religion, or more subjective features that achieve symbolic force (Edwards 1985).

Race, religion and language are the most easily observable features of any group. The interrelationship between these three can be more or less close, and they may carry different degrees of importance for individual groups. In Sri Lanka, for instance, about three-quarters of the population is ethnic Sinhalese and Buddhist. The largest linguistic minority are the Tamils, who comprise ethnic Tamils and Tamils of Indian descent (18%) belonging to the Hindi religion, and Muslims of Arabic descent (7%) who use Arabic and Tamil for their religious worship (1995 estimates; Baker and Jones 1998: 382). With different ethnic backgrounds and religious affiliations, it appears that language and the fact that they are in a minority position are the strongest group markers for the Tamils. In contrast, for the Jews, whether in Israel or in the Diaspora, the most important trait of common identity is religion, and although there are Jewish languages such as Yiddish and Ladino that are only spoken by Jews, it is not a prerequisite for Jews to have a knowledge of them. If anything, it could be argued that multilingualism is a notable Jewish characteristic, as throughout history, and also in modern-day Israel, daily use of more than one language has been part and parcel of Jewish life.

In the past, many Eastern European Jews would use Yiddish among themselves and know one or two of the languages used by the administration and the local population, for instance Russian plus Polish or Rumanian. Verschick (1999) describes Estonian Jews as always having been multilingual, speaking Estonian and Russian or German in addition to the Estonian variety of Yiddish. The writer and Nobel Prize winner Elias Canetti writes (1977) of his childhood spent in a town near the border between Bulgaria and Rumania, where, in addition to the two local languages, he also heard Ladino, the Spanish-Judeo language spoken by his family, who were Sephardic Jews. German was his parents' 'secret language', which he only learnt as an adult when he went to live in Austria. When he was a young boy his father had taken him to England to learn English, and for the largest part of his life he lived in England but always wrote in German. In their book on multilingualism in New York, García and Fishman (2002) refer to the published chronicle of an early twentieth-century Jewish immigrant, Harry Roskolenko, who recalls his childhood in the Lower East Side where many Jews had settled, calling it a small nation unto itself. 'My mother could talk Russian to the Russians, Polish to the Poles, and Yiddish to our own.' And of his mother's workplace he writes: 'They talked every language but English, and the foreman, when queried over some confusion in the work, answered in every language' (pp. 26–27).

There are many similarities of substance between ethnic and national groups, while the main differences tend to be of ideology or of scale. In the context of this discussion a national group is seen as one that usually identifies with its shared history, culture and language and feels strongly attached to its national territory, which may be a state or a part within a state. For instance, India can be considered to be a multinational state and the United States of America a one-nation state that encompasses many ethnic groups which may, or may not, use their own language – but all of them identify, at least to some extent, with the bigger entity of the American, English-speaking nation. This view, however, may not be shared by everybody, and conflict arises in those situations where several national groups are contained within a state and compete for autonomy for their territory and their language or for overall dominance.

3.2.5 Language and power

By their very nature, linguistic minorities find themselves under all manner of pressures (Heller 2006) that have linguistic consequences. For instance, dispossession and migration affect Aymara- and Quechua-speaking communities that are transborder minorities extending over several South American countries, notably Ecuador, Bolivia and Peru. Their ethnic identification is said to be more strongly linked to their land than to their whole group (Mariátegui 1973, cited in Mar-Molinero 2000: 59). Loss of land and subsequent migration to the cities are the main threats to the continued use of these languages despite their large number of speakers. Even in countries where the state affords official recognition and facilitates public use and educational provision in the minority tongue, there are internal forces at work that weaken the position, sometimes the very fabric, of the minority language. For example, in- and out-migration of minority members change the proportion of minority to majority speakers, as does intermarriage if the ensuing children are brought up in the majority language. Also, the establishment of new immigrant communities in a linguistic-minority area may lead to conflict if the law of the land allows them to claim the same linguistic rights for their own language as those enjoyed by established minorities and gives them access to already scant resources. The spread of English as a global language, too, can pose a dilemma: in many multilingual countries the learning of the other language(s) of the state is usually considered necessary for minority children and politically desirable for majority children. However, many parents consider it even more important that their children should learn English from an early age. In consequence, the learning of the minority language by majority-language children often falls by the wayside, while minority children can become burdened with a very heavy language learning load which may come at the cost of mother tongue teaching. For them, the acquisition of the majority language is not optional: in order to have access to many forms of employment, education and other facilities, minority members are under considerable pressure to know the majority language and conform to majority culture as well.

Multilingualism can therefore be considered a special feature of linguistic minorities. However, the nature of this multilingualism may be quite different in terms of linguistic outcomes and attitudes, as compared to that of majority children, for whom acquiring other languages may be largely optional and carries the promise of benefits that added linguistic capital may bring (Heller 2006).

In the context of language, unequal power relations and minority bilingualism we can also mention a linguistic outcome that may be the result of a minority's language being under pressure. Continued contact between languages of unequal status tends to weaken the non-dominant one, especially if the social status of their speakers is held to be low. Continued adaptation to the majority language may eventually lead to the minority one being impoverished or to speakers abandoning their language altogether. As argued earlier, language is an important element for a group's identity: not only does it provide a link to its past, but it helps to unify it in the present. Loss of the minority language can undermine this, and in extreme cases it may spell the end of the linguistic minority.

3.3   TWO MINORITIES AND THREE LANGUAGES: GERMANS AND LADINS IN SOUTH TYROL

3.3.1   General background

Südtirol, or the Autonomous Province of Bolzano-South Tyrol, a province within the region of Trentino-South Tyrol (Trentino-Alto Adige / Trentino-Südtirol), is situated in northern Italy along the border with Austria. It is a region that has two linguistic minorities (a German-speaking one and a Ladin-speaking one) and three languages, Italian, German and Ladin. Language contact between speakers of Romance and Germanic languages in the south of the region goes a long time back and has its origin partly in migration. In some instances, contact has been only sporadic as the mountainous terrain kept linguistic groups isolated. Egger (2001) lists twenty historic minorities for Italy, of which seven represent German speakers. The biggest by far is the South Tyrolean; the others are small linguistic enclaves along the borders with Switzerland and Austria (ASTAT 2004).

The Ladins are the oldest language group in South Tyrol, and an average of 90 per cent of the population of the two Dolomite valleys of Gröden (Val Gardena) and Gadertal (Val Badia) declared themselves in the 2001 census to belong to the Ladin language group. In South Tyrol, Ladin is spoken only in these two valley regions. The other three valleys where Ladin is found belong to three different provinces and thus fall under different jurisdictions, and this has prevented integration of the whole Ladin speech community, which is approximately 30,000 speakers strong.

According to the 2011 census, of the overall indigenous population (453,727) approximately 69% were German, 26% Italian and 4.5% Ladin. The distribution of Germans and Italians has always been uneven, with some more rural communities being almost entirely German-speaking and a higher than average proportion of Italians living in towns and bigger cities. In 1921, 23.4% of the population of Bozen-Bolzano, the region's capital, were Italian, and in 1991 the figure stood at 72.6%. Whereas the overall proportion of Germans to Italians has changed markedly (from 92:3 in 1910 to 69:26 in 2011 [figures have been rounded for clarity]), the Ladin population has seen a more moderate increase: from 3.7% to 4% (18,434 speakers) in 1991 and 4.53% (20,548 speakers) in 2011. These numbers prove the remarkable resilience of a small group under pressure from two different languages (all figures taken from Egger 2001 and ASTAT info. No. 38 on 2011 population census).

The Ladins are speakers of a Rhaeto-Romance language, and they form a minority within a minority. Their language is related to Rhaeto-Romansh, which is one of Switzerland's minority languages and is spoken in the canton of Graubünden (or Grisons). Just like Romansh, Ladin had no written standard in the past, as was typical for languages that for centuries had only been used for oral communication, by speakers who tended to be geographically isolated. At the beginning of the twentieth century, speakers of all five dialect groups of Ladin agreed to a single version of their language, which resulted in a common written standard form called 'Ladin Dolomitan'. Language development is an ongoing process, as Ladin is used nowadays in domains where it was not previously employed, such as education and administration.

The South Tyrolese dialects represent the southern end of the German dialect continuum. Tyrol, formerly entirely within Austria, was partitioned after the First World War when the largely German-speaking region to the south of the Brenner Pass was given to Italy. The fact that this was done without a referendum (which would probably have gone against the proposal) provoked considerable resentment and shaped attitudes for decades to come. A population who had been used to being part of the majority thus became a minority, although in a sociopolitical rather than numerical sense. German was used widely in the region until the establishment of Italy's fascist regime in 1922, which carried out a rigorous and much-resented Italianisation programme. Topographic names became Italianised, Germans were removed from public office, their schools were closed and a massive population movement was engineered, encouraged by a policy of rapid industrial expansion designed to shift the balance of power away from the traditionally agricultural German base. In 1939, a referendum was held in which German South Tyroleans were given the choice of either becoming Italian or leaving the region; many opted for leaving. During the Second World War the region was under German occupation for two years, but it was returned to Italy in 1945. The result of all these developments was a threefold increase of the Italian population, from approximately 10.6% in 1921 to 34.4% in 1961.

3.3.2 Language conflict and resolution

The new post-war Italian constitution of 1948 was committed to the protection of linguistic minorities, but it took many years for effective legislation to be passed and enacted. The Treaty of Paris of 1946 between Austria and Italy had laid the foundation for the so-called *Autonomiestatut*, or statute of autonomy, of 1948 that guaranteed the German minority in South Tyrol equality vis-à-vis the Italians and proclaimed measures to protect their economic and cultural development and their ethnic character. Some of these were easier to carry out than others – for instance, the re-Germanisation of names, the adoption of bilingual or trilingual signposts and the repatriation of those who had left between 1939 and 1943. But dissatisfaction soon started to mount, resulting first in civil unrest and terrorist activities which came to a head in the early 1960s as the Italian government was accused of dragging its feet about the implementation of the statute. Resentment was felt especially over the question of German representation in public administration and the legal system, schooling and equality in the appointment to employment in the public sector.

Meanwhile, strong links had been forged among the German-speaking community and also between them and the Ladins. A united front proved successful in demanding measures that would ensure equality between the different ethnic groups and the maintenance of their respective languages. A package of provisions was finally agreed after negotiations involving Austria and Italy as well as the United Nations. A second, heavily revised, *Autonomiestatut* was passed in 1972 giving the region a considerable degree of autonomy, especially linguistic autonomy and the right to call their region *Südtirol* officially. The statute took twenty years to be implemented. It ensures far-reaching protection for the German and Ladin minorities. The *Autonomiestatut* is held to be exemplary because of the involvement of an international body, the United Nations, in brokering a conflict solution which became respected by all parties involved, and because of the way in which it allows for official multilingualism. However, it has been pointed out that it may yet come under scrutiny from another international body, the European Union (EU), because certain regulations (for instance, regarding proportional distribution of jobs in public employment and the requirement of a language certificate as the only proof of linguistic competence) could be seen as interfering with EU anti-discrimination laws (Alcock 2000; Eichinger 2002; Egger 2001).

South Tyrol has done well, reaping considerable cultural benefit from the statute of autonomy. It has attracted financial investment from state and European funds and successfully established all-year-round tourism as an important economic pillar.

By adopting the territorial principle for the Ladin-speaking valleys and the personality principle for the Germans and the Italians, the law guarantees the use of all three languages in public administration and education. Important provisions include a greater degree of legal and executive autonomy for South Tyrol from central government and the adoption of three basic principles: (i) bilingualism in the administrative and justice systems, which guarantees linguistic equality, (ii) linguistic separatism of schools with regard to Italian and German, and (iii) *Proporz* (i.e. ethnic proportion) to be implemented as a sophisticated set of regulations designed to guarantee full equality by distributing public-sector employment in proportion to the relative size of the three language groups. Also required is a certain degree of bilingual proficiency, i.e. knowledge of 'the other language', tested by public examination. The issue of employment is of considerable significance in view of the fact that close to three-quarters of the South Tyrolean population are employed in the administration and service sectors and only about one-eighth in agriculture, the traditional domain of work of Germans and Ladins. Language examinations are required for entry, promotion and transfer to other institutions at every grade of employment; the higher the position, the more sophisticated the examination. The *Proporz* principle was initially seen as favouring the Germans and Ladins, but it has now come to be seen as being in the interest of all three language groups. The calculation of the proportional size of each linguistic group is based on regular censuses that include a declaration of language group membership. According to the statute of autonomy, schools in the Ladin-speaking region are for all children who live in the region, disregarding their linguistic background, and they use all three languages. The statute also confirms the system of separate German and Italian schools that employ mother-tongue-speaking teaching staff, first established in 1946. Because German schools were closed under the fascist dictatorship, a good deal of effort was required to re-establish both the schools and the higher education institutions, and to train teachers and develop resources.

3.3.3 Bilingualism and trilingualism

Four main linguistic varieties are used in South Tyrol. The South Tyrolean dialect is the spoken medium used by the German group. It is different in many respects from the Austrian-German Standard which is the formal variety used mainly in its written form. The difficulty for Italian and Ladin learners of German is that they have to acquire these quite distinct versions of German if they want to achieve oral and written competence and be accepted by local native speakers. As the region used to be predominantly German-speaking there is no indigenous regional Italian dialect. Italian immigrants came mainly from other north Italian provinces and brought their varieties with them; they generally show a strong influence of Standard Italian in their speech (Mayer 2000). This probably facilitates acquiring and using Italian for the Germans and Ladins, although the learning outcome is reported to be a greater familiarity with formal registers rather than informal ones (ibid.).

A recent investigation into the degree of bilingualism in South Tyrol describes the linguistic picture as one of institutional *versus* individual bilingualism (Angerer 2010), meaning that the relationship between the two languages is still an area of conflict. Most children from Italian and German backgrounds learn their second language at school, starting at primary level. But, whereas about 75 per cent of German children had contact with Italian outside school, the figure for Italian children was only about a quarter (Sprachbarometer 2006). As mentioned above, learners experience the added difficulty of having to deal with two very different varieties of German: in school they learn Standard High German, whereas in the community they hear the regional German dialect. Angerer found that ethnic separation between Italian and German Tyrolese people persisted in social, cultural and political life (apart from being institutionalised in education), and that there was a preference for Italian in specialised areas such as the legal system. So in numerical terms, the Italians in the region are a 'dominant minority' less likely to make active use of their bilingual competence than the German linguistic minority, who tend to use both their languages on a more regular basis.

Trilingualism is a feature of the Ladin community. The continuity of Ladin demonstrated by the statistics may in part be due to the relative isolation of the Ladin valleys, which made them less attractive to in-migration of Italians, and to the kind of social and economic developments that hasten language shift. Another reason may have been that the authorities had counted them as belonging to the Italian group and therefore did not target them specifically in their Italianisation efforts. Also, the more recent slight increase could be attributed to the language protection and revitalisation efforts of the more recent past.

A study of trilingualism in Ladin South Tyrol (Egger and Lardschneider McLean 2001) found that the region has institutional trilingualism, matched by almost universal individual trilingualism. Similarly, statistics from 1986 showed that all Ladins knew Italian and virtually all of them also knew German (cited by Egger 2001). In comparison, the incidence of bilingualism among South Tyrol's other two linguistic groups is lower but still quite significant, with 90.8 per cent of Germans being able to use Italian and 62.4 per cent of Italians stating that they knew German. However, while individual multilingualism is widespread among all three language groups, this is not matched by a high level of language competence (Lanthaler 2006). All three languages are nowadays used for oral communication, not least because of the region's tourist industry and contact with the media, and also because communication with administrative bodies and commercial contacts outside the area require the use of German or Italian.

Interestingly, most Ladin children start off as monolingual speakers: Egger and Lardschneider McLean (2001) found that most children (82%) grow up with just one family language (Ladin, German or Italian), as compared to 16% with two languages. But many children have access to the other languages before they start school, either in their natural environment or at kindergarten. The engagement with and official recognition of Ladin over the past decades have encouraged families in the Ladin valleys to use this language in the home, a trend verified by a rise in Ladin monolingual children and a fall in the number of bilingual ones entering kindergarten. Ladin plays an increasingly important role in school as a medium of instruction, and that is a further factor that sways parents towards choosing Ladin as a home language.

Ladin schools play a major role in developing trilingualism. In contrast with the South Tyrolean Germans and Italians, who can only choose monolingual schools for their children, there is only one school type for all children in the Ladin valleys, the so-called *paritätische Schule* ('parity school') that caters for children from all three language backgrounds. The school model encompasses teaching the Ladin language and culture as well as imparting a trilingual education. This means that all three languages are used as vehicular languages, starting with German for Ladin–German bilingual children and Italian for Ladin–Italian children in the first year of primary school. Ladin is used at all stages of schooling and all primary teachers have to be native speakers. From the second year onwards, education is imparted in equal measure in German and Italian, while Ladin continues to be taught for a couple of hours per week. This pattern of parity continues at secondary level, where each subject is assigned a particular language. Ladin continues to be taught as a subject, and English is introduced as the fourth language. This model of schooling supports the maintenance of Ladin while at the same time acknowledging two opposing sociopolitical trends: German is imperative for the maintenance of their Tyrolean culture, but Italian is instrumental for daily life. Ladin is closely related to Italian, which makes learning it easier, and the presence of the three languages in the community supports the language efforts made by the schools.

The implementation of the legislation designed to safeguard the position of German and Ladin in South Tyrol has required the translation of all manner of laws, regulations and documentation from Italian to German. Alcock (2000) reports that this fact led to an individual South Tyrolese legal and administrative language dissimilar to that used in other German-speaking countries because the legal and administrative systems are different. This, in turn, has led to South Tyrolese corpus planning in the form of the production of a first dictionary of legal and administrative terminology. But, although the legal position of German and Ladin has been assured, the linguistic reality of the administration of this Italian province is less secure as it does not, as yet, make full use of the possibilities open to it. For instance, Mayer (2000) points to the large amount of borrowing from Italian into German and remarks that over three-quarters of all court proceedings were held in Italian although roughly the same proportion of the population is German-speaking.

3.3.4 Language contact

The strong influence of Italian, as evidenced by the amount of language borrowing from Italian into German at all linguistic levels, has been widely commented on. Eichinger (2002) mentions the three lines of argument most often used in the description and evaluation of this type of language-contact phenomenon. First, there is a debate as to whether borrowings should be seen as habitual loans or instances of code-switching and whether South Tyrolean German is systematically affected by these processes. Second, there are those who distinguish between avoidable and necessary loans. He points towards a trend of systematically using techniques of loan translations and transfers but adds that 'the linguistic handling of the influence of Italian everyday culture on everyday life ... is much more complicated. There are lots of instances where the word coming from Italian fits much more naturally into the conversation than a German translation' (Eichinger 2002: 145). The third area of discussion considers the long-term effect of these cross-linguistic influences; here, pragmatists and purists concerned about the future stability of German pursue different lines of argument.

So far, neither the Ladins with their long experience as a linguistic minority nor the Germans with their shorter but more troubled minority history have been noticeably affected by language shift. It is now generally acknowledged that a successful formula has been found to end linguistic conflict in South Tyrol and that language protection measures for German and language vitalisation in the Ladin valleys have contributed to a stable linguistic situation. There has been a marked change in attitudes towards German and Ladin and towards multilingualism in general. There has also been a positive reinterpretation of Italian–German language contact, and speaking two European languages is now seen as an advantage that no longer carries a social stigma. Eichinger argues that young people in South Tyrol not only know the region's two languages, they also use their 'enlightened bilingualism' in a positive way. They embrace their Tyrolean dialect as a marker of group loyalty, they acknowledge the functional value of standard German and Italian and they can use all three varieties for code-switching to signal their local identity. 'Being bilingual and stressing the fact that they want to be locally recognisable by using regional markers, these people are well prepared for the challenges of globalisation and they fit well into the context of European communication', he declares (Eichinger 2002: 143). Similarly, Egger and Lardschneider McLean (2001) observed positive attitudes towards Ladin trilingualism and view the strengthening of Ladin regional identity as a kind of counter-movement to globalisation.

South Tyrol represents an example of a region that has been affected by the three common sociopolitical trends that carry multilingual repercussions: immigration, recognition of minority languages and internationalisation. What is special is that the immigration was state-sponsored and formed part of fascist language engineering designed to change the balance between the linguistic minority and majority in the region. With the acceptance and subsequent amendments of the statute of autonomy not one but two linguistic groups gained protection and promotion, and the Ladins in particular have profited from this. Internationalisation in this case is two-pronged: it involves bilingualism and multilingualism with two major European languages (Italian and German) and thus conforms to the trend towards the promotion of a greater degree of multilingual competence favoured by EU language policies and implemented by schools. Another aspect of it is the growing demand for English, a language deemed necessary to partake in wider aspects of economic enterprise and collaboration. For example, South Tyrol forms part of the Tyrol–South Tyrol–Trentino Euroregion, a designated EU hub. It fosters cross-border cooperation between the three neighbours in the Alpine region in areas such as traffic, tourism, infrastructure, social services and environmental issues, which requires the use of Italian and German; and it recognises that English may also be necessary for liaison with the EU Commission in Brussels.

3.4 AN AUTOCHTHONOUS MINORITY AND A NEW MINORITY IN A YOUNG STATE: ARABS AND RUSSIANS IN ISRAEL

3.4.1 General background

With the establishment of Israel in 1948, a largely Hebrew-speaking state was created for the Jewish people, who mostly came from outside

Figure 3.1 Multilingual plaque of the Ministries of Interior and Immigrant Absorption offices in Rehovot, Israel

the territory of modern Israel. Since its modern beginning, then, the Jewish state has been a country of immigration. It is considered a young state both because of the relatively short period of its exist- ence and because only a small proportion of the Jewish population are Israeli born. For half of Israel's approximately 7.5 million inhabit- ants (2008 census) Hebrew is not the mother tongue. Israel's popula- tion consists of a Jewish majority, comprised of many different ethnic and immigrant groups, and a large indigenous Arab minority. The country has seen a constant stream of immigration of people from all parts of the globe and also waves of large-scale influx of people from the same country of origin, the more recent ones from the former Soviet Union and from Ethiopia. Most immigrants did not establish themselves as distinct ethnic and linguistic minorities within Israel, and before the Russian mass immigration in the 1990s, there was no dominant group. As a result of the sheer numbers of newcomers and their special characteristics, previously established patterns of ethnic identity and language in Israel have changed. This has had knock-on effects on the autochthonous Arab minority, which has also suffered socially and economically because of Israel's unresolved question of Palestine.

Multilingualism in ancient Israel was mentioned in the first chap- ter of this book. Modern Israel has been multilingual since its founda- tion – evidenced, for instance, by multilingual institutional signs (as in Figure 3.1), especially used by those institutions charged with deal- ing with the country's multilingual populations. After the collapse of the Ottoman Empire, when the British took over the Mandate for

Figure 3.2 Trilingual street sign in Israel

Palestine from the League of Nations in 1920, Hebrew, Arabic and
English were all designated as official languages (English was later
dropped). Modern Hebrew had been used in the region since the late
nineteenth century by the Jewish population, and it was taught and
used as a medium of communication in the kibbutzim and newly
built towns such as Tel Aviv. It was left to the communities to determine education and with it language policies: many aspects of these
were aimed at replacing immigrant and heritage languages (such as
Yiddish) with Hebrew, presumably in the belief that this would promote nation building.

   In the absence of a constitutional framework (there is neither a
written Israeli constitution nor a language law), Israeli language policy has been described as being somewhat unclear as it leaves 'a
confusion of possibilities' (Spolsky and Shohamy 1999: 26). Stavans
and Narkiss (2003) discuss Israeli language policy with reference to
a language-planning typology outlined by Lambert (1995), which,
viewed from a national rather than a minority group perspective,
establishes three main types: (a) the 'homogeneous' category com-
prises states with a main majority language (for instance the USA,
the UK or Japan), (b) the 'dyadic' category has countries with two
or three main linguistic groups (e.g. Belgium or Canada) and (c) the
'mosaic' countries contain a substantial number of ethnic groups
whose needs have to be catered for by a national language policy. Israel does not fit into any of these three categories but represents a mixture of the three: (i) there is a strong force for Hebrew

hegemony; (ii) both Arabic and Hebrew have official status; (iii) in view of its strong presence in public life, there is de facto recognition of English, and the education system also allows a place for immigrant languages. This is well illustrated in the municipal street sign in Tel Aviv (Figure 3.2) where the two official languages of Israel (Hebrew and Arabic) appear together with English, and a second smaller sign in Hebrew only, which seems to have been affixed separately, perhaps privately.

3.4.2 Israeli Arabs

Before the creation of Israel, the Arabs made up the majority population in the region, but after the political events in 1948 they were turned into a minority. Today there are over 1.5 million Arabs (2008 census), most of them Muslims. Although there continues to be an exodus of Arabs from Israeli territories, their number has been increasing for demographic reasons and because Israel acquired new Arab territories as a result of the Six Day War of 1967. They tend to live in contiguous areas in towns and villages, mostly separate from the Jewish population. Many Arab men and an increasing number of women work outside their towns and villages and therefore mix with Hebrew speakers on a regular basis. 'In practice,' Koplewitz (1992: 34) writes, 'most Arabs in Israel have found it expedient to use Hebrew in their daily contact with the Jewish citizens of the country and with its official organs.' However, he points out, even though they may be fluent users of Hebrew they are clearly L_2 speakers and there has never been a question of either linguistic or cultural assimilation.

Arabic has full status as an official language of Israel. It is visible on money and stamps and official inscriptions, it can be used in the Israeli parliament and for official documents, and it is the language of instruction in Arabic schools. Arabic is therefore used in public, semi-private and private domains, i.e. in the community, in radio and television broadcasts, as a vehicle for a vibrant literary output and in the family. Nevertheless, in spite of this official equality, Hebrew is the preferred language in Israel. Knowledge of Hebrew is a requirement for Israeli citizenship and there have been repeated attempts, unsuccessful so far, by some parliamentarians to undermine the official status of Arabic. To be fair, it should also be mentioned that there have been calls for Arabic to be made a compulsory subject in Hebrew schools, as Hebrew is in Arab schools. The issue of any change to the formal status quo clearly remains a sensitive one (Koplewitz 1992).

Figure 3.3 Trilingual sign to a parking garage in Nazareth: Arabic, Hebrew and English

To understand the position of the Arab minority fully it is important to appreciate the nature of the Jewish state and also the relationship between ethnic group, language and nationality in Israel. The Declaration of Independence defines Israel as the 'State of the Jews', and there is general agreement among Jews around the world that Jewish identity cannot be separated from religion. This is illustrated by Israeli national symbols such as the national flag with its Star of David. In terms of successfully building a unified state that encompasses a population of so many diverse ethnic backgrounds, the emphasis on religion as the unifying factor must have been a powerful one. It has largely overcome tensions resulting from perceived inequalities and social divisions that have their origin in ethnic and cultural differences among the Jewish population.

So, on account of the very nature of the Jewish state and perceptions of Jewish identity, non-Jews are seen as separate. Coexistence based on equality of different groups has to be achieved by other means than integration – all the more so since Arab identity is closely linked to Islam and, similarly to Jewish identity, a close link to language also exists. This is the case for Arab communities inside as well as outside Israel. Clear ethnic and linguistic boundaries are thus perceived by both the minority and the dominant majority. The Declaration of Independence defines Israeli Arabs as citizens of a democratic country and equal to the Jews. Their linguistic and cultural separateness is accepted, they share the rights bound to citizenship and they have their own national identity recognised. But they do not share much political power, and 'state policies are not very responsive to their particular needs' (Ben-Rafael 1994: 166). Writing on issues of language, identity and social cleavages in Israel, Ben-Rafael characterises Israeli pluralism as allowing non-Jewish communities to retain, within an Israeli setting, their cultural, social and political identity, but he observes that 'the position of being a minority represents an alienating reality as such. What is more, the Arabs form concomitantly an under-privileged stratum' (p. 108). Israeli Arabs are Israeli citizens, but Arabs from the occupied territories of the West Bank and Gaza Strip are not. With the protracted *intifada* (Palestinian Arab uprising), many Israeli Arabs feel increasingly caught in the middle: discriminated against and treated with suspicion by Jewish authorities, while Palestinians and their Arab neighbours outside Israel view them with equal hostility, equating being Israeli with being Jewish. The use of each language in non-official signs is not always identical, perhaps reflecting different purposes or linguistic awareness on the part of the writer of these notices. For instance, in the sign illustrated in Figure 3.3 at the entrance to a parking garage, the name of the garage located to the left of the sign – counter to the typical right-to-left writing direction in both Arabic and Hebrew – indicates the name of the locality first in Arabic and then in Hebrew. However, the maximum height of the vehicle is indicated in Hebrew only but the warning about responsibility regarding damage or theft is in the three languages.

Although Arabic is held in high esteem by the Arabic minority, in the eyes of the dominant majority it appears to have less value. This is surprising in view of the fact that some 40 per cent of the Jewish population originate from Arabic-speaking countries and many of them speak Judeo-Arabic. Negative attitudes towards Arabic cause many young Israelis not to persevere with acquiring the language even though it is part of the school curriculum and the State is interested in having a bigger pool of Arabic-speaking employees. As many Arabs, especially those who belong to the younger and socially mobile sections of the community, acquire and use Hebrew on a regular basis and sometimes at the expense of their Arabic acquisition, the linguistic situation with respect to Israel's two official languages can be characterised as asymmetrical (or one-sided) bilingualism. In other words, whereas Arabs need to be able to function in Arabic and Hebrew, Jewish Israelis do not need to know Arabic. Given the prominence of English within Israeli society and the non-Hebrew language background of many of its citizens, the general linguistic situation is one of multilingualism for Jewish Israelis and also for the younger Arabs – for whom, however, the motivation and circumstances to learn English tend to be different.

The education system plays an important role in maintaining Arabic language and cultural values. As a rule, it is segregated at all stages except that there are no Arabic-speaking universities. There are

Figure 3.4 Arabic, English, Hebrew keyboard

colleges and higher education institutions, but most Arab students attend one of the Israeli universities where Hebrew and English are the mediums of instruction. This also adds pressure on Arab students to acquire a fluent command of Hebrew.

Education in Arab schools aims to promote Arabic language and culture while also acquainting children with Jewish culture and imparting common citizenship values. The Israeli education system is centralised in that the Ministry of Education prescribes the curriculum of every official education institution. Thus, Arab and Hebrew children essentially follow the same curriculum although with certain adaptations, for instance, with respect to the teaching of Arabic language, literature and history and Hebrew as a second language. So for Israeli Arab children the curriculum is more crowded than for their Hebrew counterparts. This, according to Koplewitz (1992), also implies that in relation to children in other Arab countries less time is spent on Arabic, especially countries where sciences, civic education and social activities do not feature as prominently on the timetable. As a result, Israeli Arab children's mastery of Arabic is said to be lower than that of other Arab children. Since one is obviously not comparing like with like, the question of comparable standards should not be such an important issue. It is quite natural for minorities to develop linguistic features that are different from those of their linguistic mother country. Also, the pluricentric and diglossic nature of Arabic makes it difficult to set up benchmark standards those all Arab children ought to achieve. Nevertheless, the perception of not knowing one's own language as well as other native speakers can have a negative influence on a minority's identity and self-esteem, as well as on their long-term cultural development and language maintenance.

More relevant, perhaps, are issues relating to quality of education and resources made available. The learning and teaching of Arabic is made more difficult because of the linguistic differences that exist between the spoken and written varieties; they are quite marked, as are those between the written classical and more modern literary versions. Modern Standard Arabic, though derived from the classical forms, has undergone lexical innovation and is subject to normative controls by the language academies of the various Arabic-speaking countries (the Egyptian and Syrian being the nearest to Israel and Palestine). Spoken rural and urban Palestinian dialects are said to show growing signs of convergence under the influence of Modern Standard Arabic and Hebrew (Shohamy and Spolsky 1999). However, they are still so different from the written form – with its morphological and syntactic richness – that Modern Standard Arabic has to be taught almost like a new language to children when they start their educational career. The computer keyboard available to any Arabic–Hebrew bilingual (see Figure 3.4) illustrates the coexistence of the two languages, as well as English, and the fact that the user has to deal with three different alphabets.

This teaching, naturally, requires well-trained teachers who should also be linguistically sensitive to the needs of minority children growing up in a bilingual environment. In addition, producing and updating teaching materials that are suitable for minority children and conform to the Israeli curriculum as well as Arab values is a costly and time-consuming issue. In fact, establishing a suitable Israeli curriculum for the Arab sector is a rather innovative enterprise which is still in its early stages and involves both Jewish and Arab scholars and practitioners (Stavans and Narkiss 2003).

Like the South Tyrolese, the Arabs in Israel are an autochthonous minority who owe their minority status to political developments that affected their region during the first decades of the twentieth century. But whereas, over the years, the Tyrolese have largely been able to overcome their inferior status with regard to language and social standing, the Arabs have been less successful. The position of the Arabs during the course of Israel's history as a linguistically distinct but socially inferior minority has not changed significantly; in fact, contemporary political tensions in the region seem to be making their lives more difficult. Their trilingualism may be seen as a matter of necessity rather than choice, it does not guarantee the same degree of success as that of the Jewish majority, and it is not accompanied by the same positive attitudes. One might argue that, in view of the troubled history of many Jewish communities throughout the world as well as in Israel, the success of their trilingualism may reflect a recognition of the usefulness of being multifaceted and multipurpose: knowing several languages is not only today's need but may be tomorrow's salvation. But, as we have seen, the Arab minority experience has been different. Furthermore, in more recent times the Arab minority have found themselves competing against certain new immigrant minorities (like the Russians) that – like them – are not assimilating quickly into mainstream Israeli society. This not only puts an additional strain on employment, housing and educational resources, but also weakens the position of Arabic as Israel's second official language.

3.4.3 The Russian immigrant community

In Hebrew, individual ethnic groups are not referred to as minorities unless they also belong to a non-Jewish religious community such as the Arabic-speaking Druze, who are a recognised autonomous religious community, or the Christian Arabs. Until the mid 1940s, the Jewish population was ethnically fairly homogeneous as the vast majority of its population came from Central European and Eastern European backgrounds. But since then the population has become ethnically much more mixed, with immigrants coming from Northern Africa, America, Asia and the Middle East. Another major demographic change was occasioned by a disproportionately large influx of Russian immigrants. Some 700,000 came after 1989, mainly from Russia, joining the approximately 100,000 Russian speakers already in the country. Although there has recently been a marked decrease of new Russian immigrants, they still account for over 50 per cent of all new immigrants. Today there are a total of approximately 950,000 Israelis of Russian origin, a figure that includes immigrants of second- and third-generation Russian origins.

Figure 3.5 Russian, English, Hebrew keyboard

They may not, in Hebrew, be called a minority, but they share features that are typical of a linguistic minority, such as a shared (Russian) language and culture. In the case of the immigrants who came in the 1970s, they also share a history of discrimination in their country of origin, and with regard to the 1990s immigrants a common immigrant experience that includes unfamiliarity with Jewish customs and traditions. Whereas the first wave of immigrants was motivated by Zionist ideals, the second had a more secular, non-Zionist character (Ohlstain, Stavans and Kotik-Friedgut 2003). Earlier Russian immigrants integrated socially and culturally into Israeli society, but because of their numbers and demographic heterogeneity, the later newcomers have been able to resist pressure to adapt to mainstream society. Many immigrants were highly educated when they arrived in Israel, and they turned into a politically attractive electorate. They achieved government support that enabled them to organise themselves into a micro-community structure and to establish their own social and cultural networks and activities where Russian is used and Russian language, literature and other subject matters are taught in Russian by former Russian teachers. In addition, keeping in contact with all things Russian is facilitated by visits to and from the old mother country, cable television etc. All this contributes to language maintenance while also enhancing the prestige value of Russian culture in Israel. Although Russian continues to be used in almost all domains, the younger generations who pass through the school system grow up to be tri/bilingual as they acquire Hebrew and English. The keyboard of the home computer of a Russian–Hebrew–English trilingual youngster (Figure 3.5) shows the complexities involved in learning to become computer literate in three different languages that each have their own alphabet.

In addition to these maintenance measures, which serve to create common bonds within the community, there are also other reasons why the Russians continue to be perceived as a distinct group. Their lack of Jewishness is one feature often commented on. Decades of external and internal pressures on Jews in the Soviet Union had led to loss of Jewish cultural and traditional traits rooted in both religion and language (i.e. Yiddish). 'Their remaining Jewish came to depend on nothing more than the bureaucratic fact that the "nationality" Jew was stamped on their documents' (Shohamy and Spolsky 1999: 235). The motivation behind their emigration was widely believed to be social and economic and not spurred by Zionist or Jewish core values, an argument reinforced by the fact that many immigrants brought with them non-Jewish spouses and other relatives. Ben-Rafael surmises that, in consequence of this lack of rootedness in Jewish culture, the Russian minority 'make their Russian background a central component of their identity' (1994: 151).

The point was made earlier that religious identity is the common bond that has held Jewish society together, however distinct the ethnic traits of different Jewish groups with North African, Middle Eastern, American or European backgrounds may be, and in spite of the social divisions these may cause. Now that the Jewish state has been in existence for over half a century and is ensuring the unity of the group, religion seems to be loosening its adhesive quality and alternatives may evolve. If the Russian immigrants remain a largely secular and culturally non-Jewish group but nevertheless an ethnically prestigious one, they are likely to present new challenges to Israel's self-image and policy decisions. Their willingness to learn Hebrew while simultaneously maintaining their loyalty to their ethnic language is starting to have an influence on Israeli language policy, both in terms of practice and ideology. In the school system and in public life 'there is as a result a new recognition of the possibility of plurilingualism and multilingualism', Spolsky and Shohamy comment (1999:

241–42). Indeed, they have put in question Hebraic hegemony to the point of recognising that the country needs to turn more pluralistic.

In the absence of an official Israeli language policy regarding recognition of pluralism, and on the basis of national consensus, one can so far discern only a few areas of development towards multilingualism. Important changes in education policy were initiated by the 1995–96 statement of the Policy for Language Education, which allows local education authorities to embark on initiatives designed to teach immigrant languages as second foreign languages (English being the first foreign language) for four to five hours a week during the intermediate stage of schooling. The significant step is that, whereas previously transitional immigrant language classes, for instance in Russian, were offered to children who had started their education in a Russian-speaking country in order to enable them to complete their education, Russian language classes can now be offered to Israeli-born children of Russian immigrant backgrounds. Clearly, this can be seen as a measure of state-sponsored immigrant language maintenance and endorsement of multilingualism.

To conclude, then, the Russians represent a linguistic minority that is both new (in the sense of recent) and non-indigenous to Israel. Within the Israeli context, they do not follow the pattern of linguistic adaptation of previous immigrant communities. Also, by comparison with many immigrant minorities in North America and Europe they stand out because of their social heterogeneity and status, and their commitment to language maintenance. Public attitudes towards the Russian immigrants may not be altogether positive on account of their manifest cultural and ethnic differences and accusations of their immigration being mainly motivated by economic reasons. New minorities in other parts of the world are often met with similar charges, and everywhere it is ultimately the majority who have to reassess the image of the society that is developing around them. Unlike other new minorities, the Russians appear to be exceptionally robust in resisting the loss of their language and, thanks to this, they have given Israel a novel linguistic dimension. Whether this new multilingualism will last for a transitional period only or become a lasting feature remains to be seen.

3.5 CONCLUSION

There are many factors that shape the character and vitality of linguistic minorities, among them their history and relative size vis-à-vis

the majority and other minorities; the demographic distribution and
social heterogeneity of their members; the prestige and legal status
they hold; and the extent to which their language and culture contribute to shape their identity. The nature of their relationship with the
country's majority and dominant elite tends to be one of inequality,
often marked by a history of discrimination and conflict. The main
points that have emerged in our discussion are:

- Linguistic minorities are under pressure from the majority to
  conform to their norms, and also from the minority community
  to maintain language loyalty. For the latter multilingualism is a
  necessity, whereas for majority speakers it is an option.
- When linguistic rights are afforded to indigenous minorities,
  others (for instance, newer minorities) may lay claim to similar
  measures on the grounds that in a democratic state the law should
  be applied equitably. Where several minorities exist within a
  state, there is likely to be competition for limited resources.
- The linguistic outcome of unequal power relations between the
  majority and one or several minorities may be a weakening of
  the non-dominant language(s) in terms of functions and the
  linguistic system itself, and this may be followed by language
  abandonment or replacement.
- Internationalisation may bring additional pressure to bear on
  the linguistic load of linguistic minorities, but it may also bring
  new opportunities and enhanced prestige to certain minority
  languages.
- The continued existence of linguistic-minority groups is fostered by pluralist policies embraced by the state that offers
  recognition, constructive measures to solve language conflict
  and a degree of support for language maintenance.

4 Globalisation, language spread and new multilingualisms

Postmodernity is the age of the multilingual speaker.

David Graddol (2006)

4.1 INTRODUCTION

In Chapter 1 we took a historical perspective to language contact and much of the discussion entailed an examination of factors that had contributed towards the spread of certain languages in the past. For example, conquests, religious crusades and colonisation led to the establishment of languages such as Arabic in parts of Africa and Spanish in Central and South America. By the eighteenth century, a whole range of political, economic and social developments that had been set in motion earlier started to gather momentum, most notably large-scale migration, overseas trading in commodities and slaves, the establishment of overseas colonies and plantations, and the beginning of missionary activities, all of which were to have far-reaching linguistic consequences. English was transported around the globe, to America and the West Indies, to Africa, Australia, New Zealand and the Indian subcontinent, as well as many of the islands in the Pacific Ocean. Wherever it was taken, it added another socio-linguistic layer to an already highly multilingual linguistic landscape. Other European languages, too, were spread beyond Europe as a result of colonial practices, although their trajectories followed a different course than English. In many instances, indigenous languages became threatened and, of those that have been able to survive, many are today seriously endangered.

Postcolonialism brought new linguistic challenges to newly independent states. In most cases, these states were not in a position to shake off the linguistic legacy bequeathed by the former dominant powers, as there were persuasive political arguments in favour of maintaining an official position for the former colonial language. At the same time, there was also a strongly perceived need to promote one or more indigenous languages that would symbolise independent nationhood. Nowadays a disproportionately high percentage of foreign aid from former colonising countries continues to be given to former dependencies, which helps maintain linguistic ties.

Not only colonialism but postcolonialism, too, has posed a threat to language diversity. Especially since the latter part of the twentieth century, powerful economic and social forces have promoted the widespread use of 'big' supranational languages in countries all over the world, in spite of any negative associations with their historical antecedents. The spread of English, above all, is indelibly linked with globalisation and internationalisation. However, although these trends appear to be unstoppable, it is not the case that international languages necessarily usurp all local ones. In many, if not all, postcolonial settings the ex-colonial language continues to play a role, while national language policies try to accommodate local and regional languages as well. Thus, multilingualism has remained a characteristic feature of these countries, on an institutional as well as societal and individual level.

The main concern of this chapter is the examination of some of the contemporary multilinguistic outcomes of nineteenth- and twentieth-century colonial rule and subsequent language change. A major topic is globalisation, a present-day phenomenon of supranational and transnational scope and one that is accompanied by a particular linguistic trend. To this end the chapter first clarifies certain theoretical concepts, and then exemplifies the phenomenon of language spread by discussing a variety of settings in which one language has gained ground vis-à-vis another or others. We outline three different types of language constellations that have emerged in the postcolonial period and highlight sociolinguistic situations in which a combination of official language policies, popular language practices and language spread have resulted in distinct patterns of multilingualism with the old colonial language. The final section looks at multilingualism with English within a European context in which English is not associated with a colonial past.

4.2   DECOLONIALISATION AND POSTCOLONIALISM

This section takes a sociolinguistic perspective of concepts that are pertinent to the discussion of the political, economic and sociocultural situation that many younger states that were formerly colonial territories have experienced since independence. Such situations can be viewed from different ideological stances and are thus open to diverse interpretations. The aim here is to offer some explanations within a linguistic context.

Typically, *colonialism*, and its power-political variant *imperialism*, has brought about the spread of the colonial or imperial language. For reasons of international expediency and also, partly, in response to present-day economic, political and sociocultural trends of global impact, patterns of multilingualism that developed during colonial rule have frequently been consolidated in states where English, French, Spanish and Portuguese were the colonial language. In other circumstances, such as in the aftermath of the fall of communism in the former Soviet Union, new linguistic constellations have emerged. For instance, in the three Baltic States the status of Russian has changed from dominant to linguistic-minority status, and in virtually all Eastern European countries Russian has been replaced by English as the first foreign language taught in schools.

Colonialism is an ancient practice propelled by different forces and motivations and resulting in varying linguistic impact patterns. Within the European context, colonialism refers to events that involved the settlement and dominance of territories with sparse population and loose organisation. One example is the settlement of north-eastern Europe (i.e. the region of the present-day Baltic States) in the twelfth century by the Knights of the Teutonic Order, which brought to the region a presence of German that lasted up till the end of the Second World War. Another example is the colonisation of Greenland, Iceland and the Faroe Islands by the Vikings (from Denmark and Norway), followed later by the formal incorporation of Norway and Sweden under the Danish Crown at the end of the fourteenth century. Throughout Scandinavia, Danish was the language of the administrators, educators and clergy until Sweden gained independence in the sixteenth century, Norway in the early nineteenth century and Iceland after the Second World War. After achieving home rule later in the twentieth century, Greenland and the Faroe Islands both elaborated their own languages, Kalaallisut and Faroese, for official use; and they have kept Danish as a second language. There is a notable presence of English as an international language in all of these Nordic countries, and competence in English is exceptionally high among many of their citizens.

Within Europe today there remains only one colonial territory, Gibraltar, a tiny outcrop on the Mediterranean coast that has a long history as a strategic melting pot of peoples from different linguistic and cultural backgrounds. Its official status is that of a British Overseas Territory, and English is the official language. Practically all Gibraltarians are bilingual or multilingual. Standard English and Spanish (which is taught as a second language in schools) act as a linguistic reference for the population, most of whom speak the Gibraltarian Spanish variety called *Yanito* (often written 'Llanito'), very similar to Andalusian Spanish; systematic code-switching is very widespread. Other varieties used in combination with these three are spoken by communities of Moroccans, Sindhis and Sephardic Jews.

In more modern times, colonialism has been associated with European power politics outside Europe, principally in Africa and Asia. By the end of the nineteenth century, major powers such as Britain and France, and also to a lesser extent states such as Portugal, Belgium, Germany and Italy, had secured territories that could be exploited economically if not politically. Even nations with small populations such as the Netherlands and Denmark were keen to secure a slice of the colonial cake. The exercise of power and the maintenance of economic and cultural links with the colonies always involved the use of the colonial language, certainly on the part of the ruling elite. This meant that the dominated people had to learn the language of the dominant power, whereas there was much less need for the latter to be multilingual. One may see a certain irony in the fact that many former colonial powers nowadays find themselves under pressure to learn and use one of the colonial languages themselves, i.e. English, and that immigrants from former colonies have brought multilingualism to their own doorsteps.

The process of *decolonisation* began to gather pace soon after the end of the Second World War, although it had started much earlier in the case of erstwhile Spanish colonies in Central and South America. It involved a range of processes whereby power from the departing colonial authorities was assumed by the newly independent nations. Invariably, decolonisation was followed by a period of adjustment of and experimentation with different political and economic systems and of cultural policies that included both ideological and practical decisions on language policies. The colonial language was an extremely powerful symbol of colonial rule that many were keen to see replaced by a language of their own. As it turned out, formal political independence has not been matched by economic or cultural independence. Close ties with the former colonial power have remained in the form of trade agreements and markets, military and foreign aid and cultural exchanges, which made it convenient, if not imperative, to hold on to the former colonial language at least in the form of a second official language. There were other reasons, too, that contributed to the adoption of such language decisions, such as financial expediency or the fact that no commonly agreed alternative could be found.

The terms *neo-colonialism* and *linguistic imperialism* have strong polemical overtones. They have been used to refer to continuing dependence through contemporary forms of imposition of western power, and indirect and irresponsible forms of control that reinforce economic and cultural inequalities. Invariably, English, the language with global currency, becomes drawn into such debates. There is no doubt that English is closely linked to globalisation and some of its more noxious ramifications, but it cannot today be seen only as the language of a dominant Anglo-American world power. Many peoples worldwide, be they in South, East or West Africa, on the Indian subcontinent or in the Pacific Ocean, have appropriated English as one of their own languages (with or without official status) and have developed varieties that diverge significantly from the American or British standard.

4.3 GLOBALISATION AND INTERNATIONALISATION

In the four decades following the Second World War the United States and the former Soviet Union were the main players on the world stage. For a variety of reasons, ranging from shared ideology to political and economic expediency to plain submission, many countries aligned themselves to one of the two ideological blocs in which English and Russian had important roles. But since the demise of communism from the 1990s onwards, the American-led socioeconomic model has achieved global dominance. As a trend towards dissolution of boundaries and integration, and the interdependence of economies and economic institutions, *globalisation* is commonly associated with changes in world politics and powerful effects on human society at many levels. People, goods and services are crossing borders, and as frontiers between countries become more permeable they lose their traditional function as economic, legal and cultural barriers that in the past provided frameworks for their societal organisation. Alongside the exchange of commodities, increased contact between people furthers the exchange of ideas and information, a trend greatly helped by modern technologies. Naturally, language is closely interwoven with the political and economic dimensions of globalisation, since such exchanges are most effective if there is a medium of communication that is widely accessible and accepted. The political scientist David Held points to the emergence of interregional networks and systems of interaction and exchange: 'Globalisation can best be understood as a process or a set of processes rather than a singular condition. It does not reflect a simple linear developmental logic, nor does it prefigure a world society or a world community' (Held *et al.* 1999: 27).

Globalisation has a plethora of ramifications and a profound impact on people's lives across the globe. Whether it is seen as a predominantly positive or negative contemporary force obviously depends on one's overall point of view. Opposing perspectives range, on the one hand, from the opinion that it offers unlimited opportunities, especially in the area of economic activity on world markets, to the view that it brings benefits for the desirable liberalisation of trade and social advances. The counter-argument is that globalisation has opened the floodgates to new forms of colonisation by the industrialised nations as there is an asymmetry of power and interests among the member states that belong to the so-called global village. The close link between globalisation and English is, however, an undisputed fact. The nature of this relationship is both complex and reciprocal: economic globalisation encouraged the spread of English and the spread of English also encouraged globalisation. It should not be forgotten that in the nineteenth century Britain had become the greatest overseas investor, exporter and importer, and English was already a lingua franca. Also, knowledge of English was necessary to access new technologies developed during the Industrial Revolution so that interested parties could read about them or come to Britain to experience them first-hand.

As regards cultural aspects, there is a sense that globalisation leads to homogenisation (alternative terms with negative connotation are Americanisation or even McDonaldisation) that will be followed by the destruction of traditional value systems and loss of national, regional and cultural identity – and consequently poses a threat to linguistic diversity. Yet while nations across the globe may experience the negative effects of globalisation, the sociolinguistic fabric of the United States and the United Kingdom remain largely unaffected. Both states are linguistic donor countries to the rest of the world, with little perceived need on their part to acquire foreign languages, at least at a popular level. Modern language learning at all levels of state education has been in decline, and in both countries there is a noticeable absence of effective government policies aimed at redressing the situation in spite of warnings that such parochialism can have serious consequences for economic activity in the longer term.

At the same time, the USA and the UK have growing immigrant populations among whom multilingualism is the norm rather than the exception.

The spread of English as a global language can also be examined from another standpoint. We can recognise the destructive potential of globalisation that may sweep away all manner of diversity. But with the greater flow of information, commodities and services there is also increased contact between different peoples and language groups. In this context new, more positive cultural trends are emerging, for instance in the form of greater cosmopolitanism and multilingualism and also as a reassertion of regional and local values and identities, a development highlighted in our discussion of linguistic minorities. Modern communication technologies may be dominated by English, but they also offer lesser-used languages new means of positioning themselves on the linguistic market, and this helps to encourage speakers to use their own languages in both spoken and written forms. For instance, there are both private initiatives and larger projects sponsored by bigger institutions to set up and maintain chat rooms, websites and blogs that help smaller languages to become more visible. Exposure to other cultures and languages can generate curiosity which, in turn, encourages tourism and commercial, educational and cultural exchange programmes.

A concept related to globalisation is *internationalisation*. The term can imply that control has been passed on to bodies outside and above the national entity, or it may refer to attempts aimed at transferring activities on to a wider global sphere by means of international cooperation. The focus does not need to be on economic activity; it might concern issues of a political, social or cultural nature. In the course of history, different languages have been chosen to act as vehicles of international communication in different parts of the world. After the end of the Roman Empire, medieval Latin remained the main written medium of western and central Europe, and it had a special role in the Christianisation process. Later, as literary works in the languages of Europe emerged, Latin retained an all-important position as the language of scholarship and organised religion (the Catholic Church being the most powerful international organisation at the time), and this made communication and dissemination of scientific ideas across Europe possible. At the time of the reign of the first ruler of the Holy Roman Empire of the German Nation, Charlemagne (747–814), Latin was used both as a written language and as one of the tongues spoken at his court. In the eighteenth and nineteenth centuries, French became the lingua franca of a socially defined group, the

aristocracy and educated bourgeoisie; it was the language of international diplomacy, which at the time was firmly in the hands of
the aristocratic elite, and of sophisticated social intercourse. Shared
interest in subjects such as the arts and literature, fashion and cui-
sine, and engagement in international relations developed in French
or in discourse heavily influenced by French. All European languages
bear witness to such language contact as they have adopted borrowings and loan translations from French, as indeed they did previously
from Latin, typically in registers relating to medicine, the law and
ecclesiastical matters.

Today, in certain parts of the world, Chinese and Arabic are of
major importance, while Russian and French can still have considerable influence. But English is commonly identified as *the* global language, used in national as well as international contexts and gaining
currency at considerable speed while at the same time enriching the
lexicons of many languages with new words and loan translations,
especially in fields relating to business, science, technology, pop culture and sport. It would be too simplistic to argue that this has been
brought about solely because of globalised market forces and power
politics. Ultimately, for a language to gain popularity it must win
users. People learn and use a language for a variety of instrumental,
personal and ideological reasons. Their motivation is influenced by
internal as well as external factors and cannot be seen solely in the
bipolar terms of free choice or coercion. Other mechanisms are at
work, too: some of them are discussed in the next section.

4.4   FACTORS AND FORCES BEHIND LANGUAGE SPREAD

Languages change both their form and function across time and
geographical space in response to internal and external forces that
impact the lives of their speech communities. Linguistic systems
undergo changes, for example in the morphological, syntactic and
semantic systems. Such changes go largely unnoticed by the majority
of speakers; others can be more visible, for instance in the form of
directed language intervention like spelling reforms or the influence
of other languages in the form of lexical borrowings, loan translations
and syntactic and semantic transfers. Furthermore, the sociolinguistic
situation of languages changes when they gain or lose users within
or beyond a given national territory. As a result of certain sociocultural trends, the functions for which a particular language is used
may increase or decrease and eventually new usages become formally

adopted. This is sometimes referred to as 'bottom-up change'. Change may also come about in response to imposed language policy measures ('top-down change'). Past linguistic history shows that those languages that have spread most successfully have had behind them the combined momentum from both bottom-up and top-down movements.

The classic definition of language spread is that of a process whereby 'the uses or the users of a language increase' (Cooper 1982: vii). The term itself appears neutral, but a language can be spread as a result of drastic measures such as one power assuming political or economic dominance over a speech community. For example, in their colonial contexts, Arabic, English, French, Spanish, Portuguese and Russian are languages that have been taken, far beyond their original frontiers, to places where most of them continue to play an official role today. In postcolonial times, Hindi and Swahili, further examples of languages that have spread, were promoted widely in India and Tanzania respectively, mainly for nation-building purposes. Language spread, in its more extreme interpretation, is expressed in the notion of linguistic imperialism illustrated by the hegemony of English on the international scene as imposed and maintained 'by the establishment and continuous reconstruction of structural and cultural inequalities between English and other languages' (Phillipson 1992: 47). On the other hand, Vaish (2005: 200) takes issue with the linguistic imperialism argument, saying that 'the spread of English in contemporary India has indigenous agency and voice'. She expresses the view that English enriches without endangering, as the way it is taught in schools adds to the multilingual repertoire that can help people to 'break the constraints of class and caste' (p. 204). So the argument is that the spread of English is not necessarily accompanied by language replacement but rather by an increase in multilingualism, since currently the vast majority of speakers of English use it as an additional language. It is the result of what Brutt-Griffler (2002) refers to as 'macro-acquisition', i.e. large-scale second language acquisition. In her study of the development of world English, Brutt-Griffler links the study of language spread to macro-acquisition and also to language change. This approach offers an alternative to the notion that people around the globe have adopted English as a result of economic and political imposition, as it shifts the emphasis to the more positive aspect of acquisition. According to this point of view, the spread of English occurs as speakers adopt it and become bilingual or multilingual. Then, when large numbers of such learners become habitual speakers of the language and use it in similar ways that display distinct linguistic particularities, a new variety of

English may emerge that is different from the American, British or Australian standard that was originally transported to that territory. In fact, these new Englishes, or world Englishes, are the subject of a vibrant research area that uses approaches and draws on insights from disciplines such as linguistics, language acquisition, language contact and language ecology; it has resulted in case studies as well as emerging theory development (e.g. McArthur 1998; Kirkpatrick 2007; Mesthrie and Bhatt 2008; Schneider 2007 and 2010).

In order to spread, a language must have a secure base. The languages that have spread in the last two to three hundred years, such as Hindi and Swahili, Arabic and Modern Standard Chinese, in addition to the major European ones mentioned above, have all had a solid linguistic foundation insomuch as they were varieties widely used for all functions, in both written and spoken form. They have enjoyed state promotion and protection, and as a consequence assumed prestige. However, the consequences have often been detrimental to smaller languages spoken within the same territory, particularly so if language promotion was propelled by the one-nation-one-language ideology. For language spread to occur on an international scale, additional features have to come into play.

A cluster of factors come together when a language becomes adopted by new speakers. Some of these factors are closely related to the nation whose language is spreading, others can be attributed to the individuals acquiring it, and yet others may be found in the nature of the language itself. Language-spread policies may gather momentum and continue to gain new users and uses even after the original instigators have ceased to exert their influence – English in postcolonial Africa and Asia is a prime example of this.

An obvious concomitant factor is a route, or 'geographical opportunity' (Wardhaugh 1987: 6), along which a language can be spread and become established, for instance through trade or migration. Towns and cities along these routes are important as they bring about improved communication, industrialisation and subsequent population expansion, which in turn is followed by further urbanisation. Commercial and cultural centres foster the spread of a dominant language, and they are instrumental in its diffusion into the surrounding regions. In the past, towns and cities were important for the spread of the standard variety that often assumed the function of lingua franca for speakers of different regional varieties. Today's capitals and major towns still play an important role in shaping linguistic patterns: on the one hand, they encourage the widespread use of the country's dominant language (or standard variety), while on the other, they

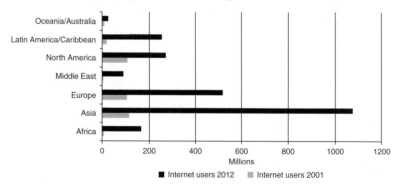

Figure 4.1 Total number of people in seven world regions who used the internet in 2000 and in 2012 (Data based on information provided at www.internetworldstats.com/stats.htm)

foment multilingualism because they attract immigrants who bring with them new languages which may include a lingua franca such as a pidgin or creole. Bilingual migrants from one part of the country may find that one of their languages, for instance a tribal one, is no longer of use in their new urban environment, where they need to acquire a different type of bilingualism. Studies from West Africa use the terms 'shifting bilingualisms', to describe the phenomenon of accommodation to more prestigious or dominant languages, and 'multiple bilingualisms', to refer to cases where the linguistic outcome is an average command of at least four languages (Bamgbose 2000; Dakubu 2000).

The virtual route provided by audio-visual and information technology has become a highway for language spread. There are very few places left in the world that are unaffected by film and television and, as Figure 4.1 shows, it is to be expected that an ever-increasing number of people will have access to the internet.

Approximately one-third of the world population in 2011 made use of the internet; there was a striking increase in a decade of 480 per cent, distributed in different continents to different extents, as can be seen in Figure 4.2.

It is, of course, not imperative to know English in order to use the internet or watch a film. But given the high profile of English in these media, as well as the way in which they promote contact between people, it is easy to understand how English enters the lives of so many people around the world and becomes recognised as the language of international communication.

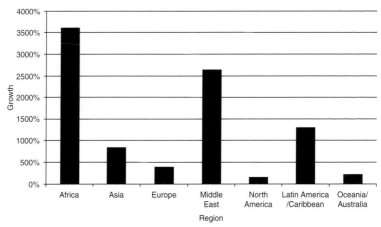

Figure 4.2 Percentage growth of internet users from 2000 to 2012
(Data based on information provided at www.internetworldstats.
com/stats.htm)

Political control of a territory is an obvious factor in language
spread. It is often the most important one, as it involves decisions
about which language or languages ought to be used in the fields of
law, education and administration. It is the means by which minority languages have been suppressed (in favour of the one sponsored
by the dominant state power) and colonial languages imposed in
many parts of the world. The manner and rigour with which specific
language policies are pursued depends on the ruling powers' political and cultural ideologies. Political dominance in a region is usually accompanied by other language-spread factors such as economic
influence and cultural missions: for example, the promotion of a particular political system or religion or literacy. A rough comparison of
British, French and Spanish imperial language-spread practices shows
such ideological differences. Spanish colonial policy in Latin America
was a three-pronged affair, combining the consolidation of political
power with the spread of Christianity and the Spanish language. The
British are said to have been more pragmatic in the pursuit of their
imperial ambitions (Wardhaugh 1987: 8), as they kept local vernaculars for lower level administrative and educational purposes, and also
in their missionary endeavours, although in parts of Asia and Africa,
English was associated with Christianity (mainly of the non-Catholic
varieties). French colonial policies were characterised by the ideal of
mission civilisatrice (civilising mission), which placed great importance
on the dissemination of the French language and French cultural

values. The French colonies were administered in line with metropolitan practices, and colonial schools and other cultural institutions mirrored those of France.

Contemporary economic factors continue to play a powerful role in the presence of the colonial language. The degree of interdependence can be gauged from the disproportionately high percentage of foreign aid (often with economic conditions attached) given by English- and French-speaking countries to their former colonies. Nowadays, many of the political and economic elites in these countries are still French- or English-educated, and the postcolonial education systems also favour these languages which are, or can be, used alongside national languages.

Languages attract prestige by virtue of the political power and economic clout attaching to their speakers. Knowledge of the language of the pacesetters of global markets brings with it the promise of social advancement and material gain. It can also bring independence and pleasure on a purely personal level, for instance in the form of study, work abroad, travel or taking advantage of virtual communication across national boundaries. The prestige a language enjoys is determined by the status of those who speak it, and also by the attitudes of those acquiring it. In colonial times, the status of English became established – or, as could be argued, imposed – by those who held power. In postcolonial times this prestige remains high, as English is acquired as an empowering tool of communication.

Sometimes positive attitudes appear to be directed towards the languages themselves, rather than their speakers, so that one can say that it is the nature of certain languages that contributes towards its spread. In Europe, French was traditionally considered to be the language *par excellence* for cultural pursuits of a literary, philosophical, artistic or culinary nature, as well as for social etiquette and sophisticated conversation. In the Maghreb, French was appreciated for its qualities of concept formation and appropriate terminologies, which Arabic was felt to lack. The classical form of written Arabic, on the other hand, continues to be admired for its inherent beauty, embodied in countless literary and religious texts and in works of art. Because of its global status, English today appeals – especially to third-party speakers, i.e. people who use it as a lingua franca – for its openness and because it is no longer tied to any particular race, creed, culture or sociopolitical system. As such, it is 'bound with utility and not with identity' (Wright 2004: 117). With regard to Arabic and English, Wardhaugh comments that they have taken on lives of their own: 'It seems almost as though certain languages acquire speakers rather than speakers acquire languages' (Wardhaugh 1987: 16). While usefulness is undoubtedly a driving force behind the expansion of English, the spread of Arabic is quite likely to be a combination of both utility and identity.

Some of the factors behind language spread are part of a planned political programme, for instance when a colonial power officially imposed its language in the territory over which it held sway. Similarly, when such territories acquired independence and decided to promote one or several of their indigenous languages, the spread of these languages was planned and pursued as part of a national political programme. When linguistic minorities gain recognition and a degree of autonomy, and subsequently embark on measures designed to counteract the decline of their language, these language-recovery efforts can also be seen as planned language spread even though such advance is on a small scale and always under threat of being scuppered by the hegemony of the majority language.

Remembering Cooper's definition of language spread, it is clear that a certain amount of increase in uses can be achieved through planned action. But behind every language that spreads are all those speakers of other languages who are willing to acquire and, most importantly, use it – and this cannot be achieved through planning alone. It is individuals who make decisions that impact on their language behaviour. The decision to migrate requires a subsequent decision as to whether or not the migrants take their linguistic and cultural baggage with them, and whether (and to what degree of proficiency) they want to acquire the language of the host country. One may continue to live with one's native tongue in the new community whilst also acquiring the host country's language and thereby become multilingual. Large numbers of migrants from the same language background may eventually become such a prominent linguistic force in their new country that part of its administration sees itself obliged to cater for them linguistically in some ways. So language spread can have different outcomes: it may lead to language replacement and shift, or it may result in a new kind of large-scale societal multilingualism that is relatively stable.

4.5 THE EMERGENCE OF POSTCOLONIAL PATTERNS OF MULTILINGUALISM

This section deals with the linguistic mosaic found in countries that have been affected by colonialism and subsequent developments, such as the extent to which the colonial language has spread; the robustness of indigenous languages at the time of independence; their status and perceived usefulness in terms of expressing national identity as well as the influence of day-to-day events in the new nation; and language contact between the indigenous languages and the colonial language. An outline is given of three broad types of sociolinguistic patterns that have emerged in the postcolonial era, each characterised by the mix of indigenous languages and the ex-colonial one, and the role that the latter still plays.

The first type consists of countries whose main language today is that of the original colonising power, even though there may be other languages also spoken, for instance indigenous languages and those of newer immigrant communities. Typical examples are the United States of America, Canada, Australia and New Zealand, and also virtually all the Latin American countries, some of which will be the subject of the first case study below.

The second type of sociolinguistic pattern to be exemplified is found in those countries that, after independence, decided to abandon the colonial language and promote their own language by using it for all official purposes. As will be shown, language replacement is a complicated endeavour that requires a sustained commitment in terms of allocation of resources and – in addition – a population that is willing to change old linguistic habits. The case studies will look at the linguistic policies of some of the former French colonies in the North of Africa and highlight a selection of their outcomes.

The third sociolinguistic pattern to be outlined is found in countries that, after independence, have partially maintained the colonial language by using it as an official language alongside other indigenous languages that may share official status. In many African states, French continues to be in use – for instance, Cameroon, Ivory Coast and Congo. English has official status, for example, in Pakistan and India, the Philippines and Malaysia, and in a number of countries in Africa where, over the years, new varieties of English have evolved and become officially recognised. The degree to which these countries have engaged in language planning aimed at promoting their own languages varies considerably, with Tanzania, Malaysia and the Philippines ranking among the most successful.

4.5.1   Type 1: (Almost) complete adoption of the colonial language

The case of Latin America

The term 'Latin America' is not a geographic one. It is used to refer to countries of South and Central America, and also to Mexico (which is part of North America), and it highlights the fact that a Romance language (i.e. one derived from classical Latin) is the predominant one. In the case of nineteen states, this language is Spanish, and in Brazil it is Portuguese. There are also three smaller territories where French is the official language: Haiti, the French West Indies in the Caribbean and French Guiana. The exceptions to the ubiquitous Romance languages are English in Belize and Guyana, Jamaica, Trinidad and several other islands in the Caribbean, and Dutch in Surinam.

Latin America has great linguistic richness, with over 1,000 languages, and it contains many more language families than Asia, Africa and Europe put together (Rajagopalan 2004: 77). However, many of these are endangered and disappearing at an alarming rate. Before colonisation, this linguistic diversity was considerably higher, and it is against this background of endangerment of indigenous languages that the present pattern of multilingualism must be viewed.

As we saw in Chapter 1, the colonisation of Central and South America dates back to the Spanish and Portuguese conquests of the fifteenth and sixteenth centuries. This colonisation followed a similar pattern everywhere: discovery and exploration led to oppression as the only means of consolidating conquest. Factors such as the unwitting importation of diseases to which the native inhabitants were not immune and forced dispersal from the ancestral land caused the demise of large sections of the population and deprivation of identity.

Initially, local languages, especially those that served as lingua francas such as Quechua and Aymara in the Andean region, Mapuche in Patagonia, Guaraní in present-day Argentina and Paraguay and Tupi (Lingua Geral) along the Atlantic coastline and present-day Brazil, were used by the colonisers for administrative as well as missionary purposes. But there was a growing body of opinion among the ruling elite, both secular and within the Church, demanding the sole use of Spanish or Portuguese. It was argued that the Christianisation of the indigenous population could not be achieved through indigenous languages, which were considered to be primitive and unfit to convey the Christian message. It is possible to trace such attitudes to the time at the beginning of colonisation, which coincided with the publication of the first Spanish grammar (1492) and dictionary (1495) by Elio Antonio de Nebrija. He sent out a clear ideological message when he put it to Queen Isabella of Spain that language had always been the consort of empire, '*siempre la lengua fue compañera del imperio*' – clearly implying that it should be. The superiority of Spanish could thus be demonstrated in terms of its advanced linguistic status, statesmanship and missionary endeavour. By the eighteenth century, a series of official language policies were decreed by the Spanish and Portuguese kings and viceroys forbidding the use of indigenous languages.

Many Latin American linguists have described colonial practices as 'ethnic-cum-linguistic' persecution because linguistic dominance has always been accompanied by racial and ethnic issues which, in turn, were linked to land rights. By the time the Latin American countries achieved independence in the nineteenth century, Spanish and Portuguese had been established as the dominant languages, and their status had been officially endorsed in the respective constitutions, which also proclaimed equality for all citizens. However, independence did not lead to the elimination of ethnic, social and economic inequalities. The plans for nation building were geared towards creating homogeneous monolingual and monocultural nation-states (as was the ideal in the USA and most of Europe at the time), and this was best achieved through assimilation of minorities into mainstream society, to be brought about primarily through education in the dominant language. In practice, this meant continued deprivation of rights and no recognition of the identity of the indigenous peoples, a process exacerbated by a number of other socioeconomic factors, such as industrialisation and urbanisation, that undermined the cohesion of their communities.

The combined social, political and ideological effect of colonial and postcolonial policies on the linguistic landscape was a massive decline in indigenous languages. Rajagopalan (2004) reports on the case of Brazil, where it is estimated some 1,175 different languages were spoken by an estimated 6 million people of different ethnicities when the Europeans invaded the continent. Today, among a population of approximately 203 million (according to an official estimate in 2011), only about one-tenth of these survive, and many of them are on the verge of extinction. Some countries started affording official status to certain of their indigenous languages in the 1970s (e.g. Peru), whereas others waited until the end of the 1980s (e.g. Brazil).

Questions of language have been taken up by national institutions advocating bilingual education, or, in more recent times, as a means of supporting national linguistic diversity. In other cases, language issues have been promoted by interested parties beyond the national context, as for instance linguists taking up the fight for beleaguered Amazonian tribes and endangered languages, or bilingual education programmes involving supranational cooperation. It is perhaps symptomatic that often the indigenous peoples themselves are not the prime movers in pressing for language maintenance measures;

for them, issues relating to survival, such as deforestation and land rights, are much more pressing.

Two case stories have been chosen to illustrate multilingual patterns in Latin America; one concerns a country, Mexico, and the other a language, Quechua, that is spoken in several Latin American countries.

Mexico has approximately 114 million inhabitants and over 100 different languages, of which 15 have more than 100,000 speakers. According to statistical work based on 2005 census material, Nahuatl was the language with most speakers, 1,376,026 or 22.89% of indigenous speakers, followed by Mayan with 759,000 speakers (12.63%). Altogether, a little over 6 million Mexicans, or 6.7% of the overall population, were recorded as speakers of indigenous languages (Schmal 2008).

In some parts of Mexico where there are high concentrations of indigenous speakers there are still many who are monolingual in their native language, but mainly there is individual multilingualism, especially in the eastern provinces of Yucatán and Oaxaca. However, the vast majority of the Mexican population speaks Spanish as their main language, not least because for many years there was complete linguistic homogeneity in the education system. Bilingual education programmes were introduced in the 1930s and initially they were of the transitional type. It was believed that they would help children to acquire literacy in Spanish, since indigenous languages were used as a spoken medium only. Mar-Molinero (2000: 135) points out that measures such as these inevitably lead to assimilation, and that this form of Castilianisation was not necessarily imposed by the state on the indigenous populations, but was often supported by them as they wanted to avoid segregation and were keen for their children to learn Spanish at the earliest opportunity.

Towards the end of the last century the state recognised the existence of fifty-six minority languages, and the amended constitution of 1994 now proclaims the right of Mexicans to use their mother tongues. As a result, language policies have shifted towards language preservation by adopting bilingual and multicultural objectives in the education system, and programmes have been organised by qualified indigenous staff. The long-term goals for the education of indigenous children, to achieve balanced bilingualism, are ambitious. A writing system for the Indian languages is to be promoted, with the Indian languages being used both as a subject and a medium of instruction. However, Mar-Molinero (2000) evaluates the bilingual education of the indigenous population in Mexico as marked by good intentions and little concrete achievement. It will require many years of status and corpus planning and, above all, a change in public attitudes and practices, before languages other than Spanish come to play some sort of official role. Mexican multilingualism continues to be a feature of the indigenous population, who are more likely to be literate in the country's dominant language only rather than in their mother tongue. This does not bode well for the maintenance of indigenous languages. Meanwhile, another non-indigenous language is making itself felt in the public sphere as well as in many individual Mexicans' lives, namely that of their mighty neighbour in the north, the USA.

The next example revolves around an indigenous supranational language and the attempts that are being made to stem, or even reverse, language shift. Quechua (or Quichua as it is called in Ecuador) refers to a group of very diverse varieties within a language family. Von Gleich (1994) likens it to a family that lacks the parental superstructure that would be provided by a codified norm acceptable to all speakers. Quechua is spoken by approximately 8.5 million people (von Gleich 1994), principally in Peru, Ecuador and Bolivia, but also in Argentina, Chile, Colombia and Brazil. Cerrón-Palomino (1989: 76) gives the following estimates for the distribution of Quechua speakers: Peru 4,402,023, Ecuador 2,333,000, Bolivia 1,594,000, Argentina 102,000, Colombia 4,402, Brazil 700.

Quechua was a lingua franca in the Andean region in times of the Inca Empire, and it was used by the early colonisers for administrative purposes and by missionaries for Christianisation. Over the past 400 years it has remained an oral language without a written tradition, marked by dialectalisation and cross-linguistic influence from Spanish. The loss of ancestral lands, urbanisation, industrialisation and migratory movements to the coastal towns are the main factors in the gradual language shift from Quechua to Spanish.

From the 1970s onward, indigenous issues have entered national politics in Latin America. In the case of Quechua, this has led to the adoption of language policies aimed at raising its status, providing bilingual education programmes and promoting efforts to standardise some of its varieties. The support for Quechua has been most effective in countries where powerful indigenous movements have coincided with positive government policies, such as in Peru in the 1970s and again in the 1990s, and Ecuador in the 1990s (von Gleich 1994). Many language-planning measures, such as standardisation of the six main varieties, together with elaboration of written norms, development of bilingual maintenance and literacy programmes, training of indigenous teachers and production of teaching materials, have been the result of supranational cooperation between Bolivia, Ecuador and Peru, often bolstered by the contributions of international agencies or the efforts of individual academics and practitioners. Among the achievements can be listed the establishment of Quechua schools run by local communities (which, however, as Hornberger and King (2001) point out, do not all teach Quechua), the foundation of the Academy of the Quechua Language in Peru, which 'affords access to symbolic capital' (Hornberger and King 2001: 178), and ongoing, community-based literacy programmes.

Von Gleich surveyed these efforts to reverse language shift from the perspective of what she calls language-spread policy. She did not observe a reversal in the language use of Spanish–Quechua bilingual speakers, although she highlights 'an improved complementary distribution of the functions of Quechua and Spanish in community life starting with primary education' (von Gleich 1994: 107). She found that the number of bilinguals has remained relatively stable, while that of monolingual Quechua speakers has been declining, and that of monolingual Spanish speakers continues to rise. Hornberger and King (2001) report similar findings from separate ethnolinguistic investigations into language use and language maintenance. Whereas the earlier studies showed a preferred use of Quechua for certain communicative functions, later ones indicate that shift is taking place domain by domain, as Spanish encroaches into all areas of communication. 'There is no longer a "safe" space, for instance, in the home, in the community, or among family, for Quechua to be used exclusively and therefore ensure transmission to younger generations', they conclude (Hornberger and King 2001: 168). Repeatedly, they make the point that the indigenous populations remain marginalised and their language is still excluded from the traditional channels of authority and power.

In their assessment of language-shift reversal in Latin America, Hornberger and King (2001) also refer to adverse reactions on the part of the Spanish-speaking majority, who resent the allocation of special funding to Quechua. It is obvious that language policy is intimately bound up with economic, social and wider cultural policy, and that the promotion of Quechua and bilingualism is dependent on improving the overall position of indigenous peoples within society. It has been argued that revalorisation efforts are more likely to be successful if they are targeted primarily at the hegemonic Spanish-speaking majority rather than Quechua speakers (Coronel-Molina 1999: 177). What is clear is that, if multiculturalism is to flourish, there has to be a consensus on cultural pluralism among large sections of society, and this will not be achieved so long as multilingualism is considered to be a characteristic of the underprivileged and marginalised sections of society.

The example of Quechua illustrates the difficulties involved in the maintenance of indigenous languages in Latin America. These stem from (a) the nature of the languages in contact, marked by orality and huge variation, pitched against the highly standardised dominant code that is also the language of literacy; (b) their contact with other languages, i.e. dominant Spanish and also other Indian and European languages, with which they compete for space and capital; and (c) the marginalised socioeconomic position of their speakers that is reflected in government policies which are often not in the interest of the indigenous population. The interplay of these factors makes any attempt to promote bilingualism extremely complicated.

Another linguistic development of the latter part of the last century, one that has been more successful and concerns the majority language, can be added to this account of the sociolinguistic situation in Latin America. The hegemonic attitudes by Spanish speakers must be seen against the century-old desire to assert their independence from Spain, including its linguistic norms. Thus, a number of Latin American countries have promoted their own national variety by means of status and corpus planning so as to raise the status of the non-Peninsular varieties of Spanish.

In summary, societal multilingualism in Latin America can be said to consist of a national standard of the former colonial language with some local variation (in both grammar, phonology and, more extensively, lexis) and a large number of indigenous languages – some of which, like Quechua and Aymara, are spoken transnationally and by a large number of speakers. Despite their recently raised status to that of 'national language' in some countries, provision for them is uneven and indigenous language issues remain controversial and closely bound up with politics. At the same time, language shift towards Spanish monolingualism continues to weaken indigenous languages. Clearly, multilingualism is a feature of the disadvantaged rather than the successful members of mainstream society, and being bilingual may well be considered a burden rather than a desirable sociocultural resource. Those sections of society that can afford it and want to move up in the world are now turning towards English, and this is fomenting a new kind of incipient elite multilingualism for the continent.

4.5.2   Type 2: (Incomplete) replacement of the colonial language

The case of the three Maghrebi countries in North Africa

The type of multilingual pattern we are now concerned with is typically found in some Arabic countries that have been under French colonial rule and for a shorter period of time than those of Type 1. They have made vigorous efforts to replace the colonial language which, nevertheless, continues to be used as an unofficial second language. Three North African countries, Morocco, Algeria and Tunisia, will be discussed here from the perspective of language spread – of both French and Arabic – and with regard to postcolonial language practices at an official level as well as a popular one.

The three countries have shared features such as the geographical similarity of bordering the Mediterranean and having had common histories, notably colonial experiences under the Ottoman Empire and then French rule in the nineteenth and twentieth centuries, and of Arabisation after independence. There are also significant differences – in size, geography, demography and economic development. Tunisia is the smallest, greenest, and economically most advanced nation (it has the highest GNP of the whole African continent), with some 9.6 million inhabitants of whom a high percentage (62%, according to Daoud 2001) live in urban environments. Morocco is very mountainous and demographically more diverse than the other two. Sixty per cent of its population of 31.6 million are considered to be of Berber or Berber-Arab origin. Situated between Tunisia and Morocco is Algeria, with a population of about 33 million. It is the second-largest country of the African continent, but more than four-fifths of its landmass is desert. The inhabitants are mostly classified as Arab-Berber; they live along the long coastline, approximately 45 per cent of them in urban areas.

The word 'Berber' is a European term employed to refer to the indigenous languages of the Maghreb and to their speakers. There are a number of varieties, not all mutually intelligible, and they are distantly related to Arabic. The three main varieties spoken in Morocco are Tamazight, Tashelhit and Tarifit; in more recent times Tamazight has been used as a generic name for the languages, while Amazigh is used to refer to ethnic and cultural features. Berber varieties have been used as oral languages for centuries, but some ancient texts in the language are extant. Efforts have begun to standardise some varieties and to restore the ancient script *Tifinagh*, said to be related to ancient Egyptian, with a view to using it in education programmes.

French colonisation of Algeria started in 1830, and by 1848 the country had been firmly integrated administratively into the French state as three *départements* (a subdivision of levels of government that covers both metropolitan and overseas French territory). Morocco became a French protectorate in 1912, whereas Tunisia had already become one in 1881. Altogether, French rule in the Maghreb lasted approximately 150 years. Morocco and Tunisia gained independence in 1956 and, after more than ten years of rural and urban warfare, the French were finally forced to leave Algeria in 1962. Yet close links with France continue to exist via international relations, trade, media and education. There is also a very large number of immigrants from North Africa who live in France and Belgium. Continued contact with their families' country of origin is a further element contributing to the maintenance of the former colonial language in the Maghreb.

In terms of their sociolinguistic past, Morocco, Tunisia and Algeria have much in common. Because of their geographical position, they share a long history of contact between indigenous languages and those that were brought to their shores by invading powers such as the Byzantines, Greeks and Romans, before they were introduced to Arabic with the spread of Islam in North Africa in the seventh century. Trade activity in the Mediterranean basin also brought contact with Maltese, Corsican, Spanish, Italian and an original pidgin called lingua franca (or 'language of the Franks') that had Frankish as a matrix language with lexical influences from different Mediterranean languages – and is said to have been used by the crusaders and Knights Templar who were based in Malta.

There are also many similarities in terms of how the three countries' colonial experience affected Arabic and Berber, and the way in which they pursued Arabisation in postcolonial times. As in the past, there continues to be widespread societal multilingualism; today it involves Arabic, Berber and French in Morocco and mainly Arabic with French in Tunisia and Algeria. The linguistic situation of the three countries with regard to Arabic is highly complex. It has variably been described as multidialectal, diglossic (with Modern Standard Arabic as the High and dialectal Arabic as the Low varieties) triglossic (taking in French as well) or double diglossic (with Berber and Arabic forming one layer of a diglossic relationship and French and Arabic another).

French colonial policy regarding language dictated that French was the only language to be used in all public spheres. However, it was not actively promoted (for instance, by means of establishing an effective French-medium education system), and therefore French spread

more slowly and less successfully than it might have done. This lack
of language support also meant that large parts of the population had
no direct access to the administrative system of their own country.
Arabic, the language of the majority, and the minority Berber languages had no official status or use. French was reinforced through
French settlement, especially in Algeria, whereas Arabic was actively
discouraged. It is said that no interpreters were available in government offices, although some use of Berber was made in an attempt to
win Berber support against the Arabs in Algeria (Wardhaugh 1987).

By the time the French were forced to withdraw from the Maghreb,
the French language had become firmly established in the administrative and educational infrastructure of the three countries. The people
who took over the government and administration of the newly independent states were an Arab elite, French-speaking and with little
experience of literacy in Arabic. Among the general population in
all three countries literacy rates were low, and those who could read
and write had learnt to do so in French. French was not only the official written medium; it was widely spoken among educated Arabs,
and many sections of society who had little formal education spoke a
pidginised form of French. In the 1960s over one-third of the population in Morocco were reported to be able to speak French (while one-
fifth could read it). About half the inhabitants of Tunisia and Algeria
spoke French, while one-third and one-sixth, respectively, could read
it (Gallagher 1966). On the whole, even after independence, attitudes
towards French are said to have remained positive.

Knowledge of spoken Arabic in its many different dialects was
widespread. However, oral competence was not matched by knowledge of the written form, a problem that continues to exist to this
day in much of the Arab-speaking world. Arabic had not been taught
in schools or used as a medium for literacy and learning. There were
attempts at educational reform in the latter years of colonial rule, but
they came too late and ignored the needs of the population, namely,
that Arabic should be taught as a mother tongue and not as a foreign
language. For a variety of reasons, school attendance rates stayed low
and illiteracy high.

In the absence of a standardised form of Arabic that could be used
to replace French, what linguistic tool could the newly independent
states use for the purposes of development of their state and nation
building? Classical Arabic was known by those who had learnt to read
the Qur'an and classical texts but, with the highly selective functions
attributed to it and its considerable linguistic distance from spoken
varieties, Classical Arabic could not be considered an appropriate

candidate to fulfil the needs of a modern state. So, for some years after independence, and out of necessity, the three countries continued to conduct their affairs in French, while language policies were developed that aimed to introduce Arabic into all spheres of national life.

This objective was the main plank of Arabisation, the term used to describe postcolonial policies in Morocco, Tunisia and Algeria aimed at language replacement. A prerequisite for the wider social and educational objectives was to develop a standardised version of Modern Standard Arabic that could be used to supersede French and raise literacy. The task was considerable: to agree a norm that was based on written Classical Arabic and at the same time was accessible to speakers from a wide range of geographical backgrounds. Initially, the aim was to find a standard acceptable to the wider North African Arab world, and administrators and educators from Egypt and Libya were drafted in to assist Arabisation programmes for the three Maghrebi countries. But it proved difficult to reach consensus, because of the many divergent spoken varieties in use.

Arabisation has proceeded at different rates in the three countries, and it has followed different trajectories. It encompasses standardisation of Arabic; extending this form to functions previously occupied by French; turning monolingual Berber speakers into speakers of Arabic; and tackling illiteracy. There now exists a standard form that is used for written purposes (and can be employed for educated spoken discourse), which is referred to as Modern Standard Arabic, although other labels are also used, such as Literary Arabic (used by both Daoud 2001 and Youssi 1995) and Educated Arabic (Daoud 2001), or even Middle Moroccan Arabic (Youssi 1995). In the three countries primary education is now conducted entirely in Arabic and many government ministries and agencies use Arabic only. There are considerable differences between Modern Standard Arabic and the various dialectal forms in terms of vocabulary, grammar and phonology, and it has been recognised that this causes problems for children learning to read and write and thus slows down their progress – which may explain, at least in part, why the literacy rate is still quite low (Marley 2004).

Arabisation has brought Berber speakers (about 40% of the population in Morocco and 20% in Algeria) into contact with Arabic, and over the past fifty years or so a marked shift from Berber to Arabic has taken place, especially in Tunisia. In Morocco there is still a sizeable number of Berber speakers among the population, and the language is seen to be an important component of the Amazigh cultural identity. Towards the end of the last century about a quarter of Morocco's

Berber speakers were estimated to be monolingual – mainly women and children – and three-quarters were users of Arabic as a second language (Youssi 1995). The degree to which Berber speakers are fluent bilinguals depends very much on personal circumstances. As primary schooling is in Arabic only, monolingual Berber-speaking children have an uphill struggle during the initial years of their formal education, since the system is not geared towards the needs of budding bilinguals. They learn to read and write Modern Standard Arabic, a language they are unlikely to have encountered in their daily linguistic environment. In the absence of Arabic immersion programmes or bilingual education schemes, it is easy to see why many children either drop out of school or stay mainly monolingual and illiterate. The more successful children who develop bilingual fluency will have literacy skills in Arabic only. There are, thus, a whole bundle of historical and ideological factors and practical problems that are slowing down the process of Arabisation. The linguistic upshot of all this is that multidialectism and diglossia remain the defining sociolinguistic forces that allow French to continue to feature in the region's multilingualism.

Tunisia has come closer to achieving functional literacy than the other two countries. Since independence, its language policy has followed the dual objective of promoting Arabic and improving functional competence in French and, more recently, in English. French has given way to Arabic in certain areas of public life, but it still plays an important role, for instance in academic and professional circles. As Daoud (2001) points out, French is considered the language of modernity, better education and information, and in addition it is seen to be useful for accessing original material. Even though French is losing out to Arabic, especially among the younger generations, it is still firmly established as part of the country's bilingual language policies. It is taught for several hours per week in schools from the third year onwards, and some say that French is more widely present today than it was in the colonial period when it was the language of the elite only (Kefi 2000: 31). According to Daoud, there is today, also, a greater interest at both national and individual level in learning English, in addition to – not at the expense of – French, in order to use it for business, especially tourism, and for access to scientific and technological sources.

Arabisation is not only a matter of replacing one language with another. As a counterpart to independence, it touches upon power-political, social, cultural and economic issues, and it has consequences for individuals and public life in general. It has contributed to nation building by asserting Arabic-Islamic identity and thereby offering a powerful alternative to western cultural influences. Invariably, it has been accompanied by tensions that have arisen between the Islamists' goals about the whole project and the views of the modernists who regard the maintenance of French as a necessary requirement for future development. Also, many people feel that Arabisation ignores the multilingual nature of the region: the Berbers are largely bilingual but, while they are Muslims and share Arab religious values and traditions, they see the disregard for their language as a threat to their identity.

Possibly in response to such anxieties, in 2000 the Moroccan government published its Charter for Educational Reform, which signalled a significant change in language policy with three objectives: that Arabic teaching should be reinforced and improved, that there should be recognition of Tamazight and that there should be diversification of languages for teaching science and technology. As regards the latter, the most appropriate language for teaching these subjects appears to be French, as it is still the case in much of higher education; the Charter also recommended that English should be introduced (Marley 2004). Marley undertook a study of attitudes to the Charter among teachers and older students at school, and he found that an overwhelming number of those questioned considered French to be very useful in a number of domains and generally came out in favour of bilingualism as long as the other language was a European one. Whereas the Amazight culture was accepted as part of Morocco's heritage, the informants were less sure about the benefits of introducing an indigenous language into the school system. As so often is the case, attitudes towards multilingualism are influenced by the perceived social prestige and instrumental usefulness of the languages involved, rather than their intrinsic cultural value.

4.5.3 Type 3: Partial maintenance of the colonial language

The case of many former British or American colonies

This type of multilingual pattern can typically be found in many states that once formed part of the British Empire, many of which today belong to the Commonwealth of Nations. During colonial times, English was widely used for higher-level administration and education, which meant that those members of society who aspired to higher positions in their country's political and economic life needed to acquire it, with the result that by the time independence was achieved, English had become adopted by the indigenous political and economic establishment. In countries that had the necessary economic means and enjoyed suitable sociolinguistic conditions, national language policies were geared primarily towards the promotion of major vernacular languages or indigenous lingua francas. Such measures represented a powerful indication of independence and a break with the colonial past. In Chapter 2 we presented examples relevant in this context, for instance the promotion of Swahili in Tanzania and India's decision to declare Hindi as an official language at the federal level. However, while the replacement of English by an indigenous language seemed desirable initially for ideological and nation-building purposes, the practical side of the task was hugely demanding. Not only were political will and popular support required, financial resources and time had to be found for language standardisation and elaboration to suit modern technological and administrative needs; teachers had to be trained and materials developed; and it was necessary to promote the new national language in education, the media and public administration. Thus, many African and Asian states adopted a pragmatic approach when deciding to keep English as an official language: they would do so, often, alongside another vernacular language, or even more than one. In the case of India, as we saw, almost twenty years after the formal adoption of Hindi, the state acknowledged the continued widespread use and usefulness of English. Originally it had been stipulated that English would be phased out, but continued linguistic rivalries between Hindi, Urdu and Tamil contributed to an erosion of national consensus for Hindi. In 1968 a constitutional amendment declared that English was the second official language and that it could be used nationwide. Thus, in the conflict between nationalism (in the sense of exalting the ideals on which one's nation is built) and nationism (prioritising efficient government), English was seen as contributing to the latter (Dua 1993), i.e. as a tool that helps maintain cohesion among ethnically diverse members of the state.

In countries that are characterised by the Type 3 multilingual pattern, English is typically used in areas such as higher-level administration, education (especially higher education), international relations, business and technology, although the range of domains where English prevails differs from country to country. Access to English depends on demographic and social conditions, as does the extent to which the language is used in its written and spoken forms. Speakers may be monolingual, bilingual or multilingual with different degrees of fluency in each of the languages they speak. Whilst not being fully fluent in languages other than their mother tongue, they may still make use of mixed codes which have emerged as a result of borrowing and code-switching in many contexts.

In some multilingual settings, mixed varieties have become widely adopted. They often involve more than two donor languages, such as, for instance, Sheng in Kenya and Camfranglais in Cameroon. Sheng is a mixed speech form that contains Swahili and English elements as well as words borrowed from local languages. It is an oral, non-standard form of language that originated among urban lower-class speakers, but it is now more commonly used by young people and in popular culture. Camfranglais is said to have emerged in the 1970s after the unification of francophone and anglophone Cameroon. It may have its origin in typical language-contact situations in urban areas such as markets, ports and sports venues. It also has become more widely adopted by young people and popular culture. These mixed speech forms are interesting phenomena: as multilingual repertoires, they reflect the multicultural orientations of their respect-ive speakers, and as mixed varieties they pose challenging questions as to whether, how and when they might turn into languages in their own right.

In our discussion of societal multilingualism in Chapter 2, refer-ence was made to a number of countries that represent the kind of multilingual settings under discussion here, such as Singapore, Cameroon and Malta. The Republic of the Philippines, though not a member of the Commonwealth, can serve as a further case illus-trating postcolonial language policies that tried to strike a balance between the seemingly conflicting aims of putting an end to the colonial past, furthering national identity among a multiethnic and multilingual population, and maintaining the advantages that English provides. First claimed as a colony by Spain in the sixteenth century, Spanish rule in the Philippines lasted for over 300 years and left behind a legacy of Catholicism as the dominant religion (reflected in the Spanish names of most Filipinos) and, in sociolinguistic terms, thousands of Spanish loan words in many of the country's large number of indigenous languages. Following the Spanish–US War of 1898, the United States bought the Philippines from Spain for 20 mil-lion dollars and brought English to their new colony, decreeing that English become the sole language used in both public and private education (Gonzalez 1998). The aim was that English should replace the use of Spanish and become the common unifying language. Only gradually, after independence in 1946, was vernacular language teaching officially introduced for initial literacy instruction. At inde-pendence the new state adopted Tagalog, an indigenous variety used mainly for oral communication, to be promoted as its main national language. The standardised form is nowadays known as Filipino: it is spoken in all domains of public life by about a third of the population as a first language and it is widely used as a second language by most of the rest (who are speakers of a very large number of mostly Malayo-Polynesian vernaculars). English was, however, kept as an important second language and its status as the country's second national language was formalised in the amended constitution of 1987.

Education uses vernacular languages as auxiliary teaching languages alongside Filipino and English, especially in the earlier stages of education. This trilingual system is normally available as a transitional arrangement at primary level of education, and bilingual education is the norm at the secondary level. According to Gonzalez (1998), since the 1960s there has been a shift towards Filipino as a medium of instruction at all levels of the school system. This arose as a result of demands from nationalist-oriented students and teachers, and it led to the introduction of both Filipino and English as mediums of instruction from first grade onwards. Changes in language practices take a long time to be fully implemented, as the production of suitable teaching materials and the training of teachers is both lengthy and costly. Evaluations of the bilingual programmes introduced after the switch from a monolingual English to bilingual education system found that measures of achievement were often disappointing. The main gain for Filipino has been a growing pride in the national language accompanied by increased general use in school, outside the classroom and in the wider society in domains such as entertainment, media and business. Also, with regard to English, Gonzalez (1998: 199) mentions a perceived decline in language skills since the language is now in direct competition with Filipino in terms of allocated time and resources. He points to socioeconomic rather than pedagogical causes for this development, such as a general decline in the quality of teaching professionals owing to economic conditions that deter aspiring teachers from entering the profession and the uneven distribution of resources for teaching content in a variety of languages. A further factor is a sociolinguistic change due to a more restricted role for English in education and public life in the wake of the advances of Filipino. However, English is still used in international business, tourism and certain areas of education such as mathematics, science and technology. Private schools place much emphasis on English, and thus children from urban and more affluent backgrounds tend to acquire high standards of proficiency, which affords them advantages when entering both higher education and employment.

To sum up, in many countries in the developing world, a Type 3 sociolinguistic pattern has surfaced after independence. The former colonial language, typically English but also French or Portuguese, has been maintained as a matter of expediency, while one or more indigenous languages have been promoted and, in many cases, are still undergoing status and corpus planning. English, with its history of administrative and academic usage, plays a significant role alongside vernacular languages that may lack the linguistic means to enable such usage. English may function as a neutral lingua franca within a linguistically diverse country, it facilitates international communication and it helps maintain links between Commonwealth countries. Whereas in colonial times only a small elite had access to English, the language is now acquired as a second language as a matter of course by a much larger section of society, and it is habitually used in certain domains of public life by large segments of society, or at least by those who have had regular access to education.

It will have been noticed that, in most cases of Type 3 multilingualism, English is one of the languages. What happens to this language when it is developed and acquired in these contexts?

Naturally, there is considerable variation in the proficiency attained by different people, both within and between Type 3 countries. The vast majority of the world's one-and-a-half to two billion speakers of English are bilingual or multilingual and speak English either as a second or a foreign language. Trying to measure the spread of English is fraught with difficulties for practical reasons and also because it raises the question of who should be counted as a speaker of English and what criteria of use and proficiency should be applied. In contrast, the linguistic outcome of the spread of English has been well documented, even though fully articulated theoretical explanations may still be outstanding (Brutt-Griffler 2002). As English has been adopted by speakers in different regions of the world and become part of the sociolinguistic context, the language has been adapted to local sociocultural conditions. This nativisation has produced new varieties that are referred to collectively as 'New Englishes' and individually as, for instance, Sri Lankan English, Singapore English or West African English – the latter, a variety that may emerge as an agreed standard used in West African countries such as Nigeria, Ghana, Liberia, Sierra Leone and Western Cameroon, where English is an official language. These new varieties serve as target standards for English learners in Africa and Asia. They reflect local identity and help deflect the previously held association of English as the language of the colonial power. Wherever a New English variety forms part of a country's linguistic pattern, it usually enjoys government promotion, often as part of the country's language policy. It is used in education both as a subject and a vehicular language, and it serves as a neutral language in multiethnic contexts. Because of these and other reasons, it is seen as a high-status language, not least because it affords access to communication with a wider global community.

4.6 MULTILINGUALISM WITH ENGLISH

The twentieth century witnessed a spectacular spread of English, not just in countries that had a past colonial history which brought English to their shores, and not only promoted by British expansionist activities. When, towards the end of his life, the nineteenth-century German statesman Otto von Bismarck was asked what he thought was the most decisive event in modern history, he is said to have replied that it was the fact that the North Americans speak English. Quite what he had in mind we do not know, but perhaps he was fore-telling one of the most remarkable linguistic developments ever.

'It is a phenomenon which lies at the heart of globalisation: English is now redefining natural and individual identities worldwide; shift-ing political fault lines; creating new global patterns of wealth and social exclusion; and suggesting new notions of human rights and responsibilities of citizenship', Graddol (2006: 12) writes. It is a bold statement, yet he also argues that the role of English as *the* global language is not guaranteed and that a shift of economic domin-ance from West to East may see other languages such as Arabic and Mandarin assume greater importance while English becomes some kind of universally acquired skill. However, until they acquire suf-ficient proficiency in Mandarin and Arabic, countries in the Middle and Far East will have to communicate in English with China or the Arabian states. China has been setting the pace for English learning since it decided to make English compulsory in primary education. In 2005 an estimated 176.7 million Chinese were studying English and, as a result of the new policy, over 200 million students are learning English each year (Graddol 2006: 95). Graddol writes from the per-spective of English language learning, and he is concerned with inev-itable changes that affect both the teaching and the very language itself that is imparted. 'The new language which is rapidly ousting the language of Shakespeare as the world's lingua franca is English itself – English in its new global form' (2006: 11). Increasingly, English is no longer taught by native-speaker EFL teachers, who use their own traditional standard forms, but by those who have become proficient users of English as a second or foreign language.

In his work on world English, Kachru (1992) developed a model to represent different types of language and users of English. It consists of three concentric circles where each ring represents the kinds of spread pattern, acquisition and functional domain of English language use typical for that category. First there is the 'inner circle' of native speakers (e.g. the British, Americans, Canadians and Australians) for whom English is the mother tongue and also the only language that they use. Then there is the 'outer circle' comprising those who use English as a second language alongside another language in everyday communication, for instance in contexts discussed in the previous section. And thirdly there is the 'expanding circle' of people who may live in monolingual, bilingual or multilingual countries and learn English as a foreign language and use it for certain purposes. Fishman (1992) refers to this phenomenon as 'use of English by third parties'. While there is some disagreement about the norm-providing aspects of the model, it has been widely accepted.

Another theoretical work that has been highly influential is the Dynamic Model of Postcolonial Englishes developed by Edgar Schneider (2007) in an attempt to account for the emergence as well as the structural features of new varieties of English. He characterises them as language-shift varieties that differ from creoles in that they are largely 'the product of educational systems' (p. 156), yet are similar in that they evolved through language contact. He considers sociolinguistic determinants such as the histories, social conditions and identity constructions of both the indigenous populations and the settlers that influence contact settings and have an effect on how English is acquired and used and on the linguistic forms that eventually emerge. The model adopts a language ecology perspective and includes insights from second language acquisition and language-contact research.

In the following, we use Kachru's simpler and more graphic model with its focus on language users. Thus, if we apply it to our discussion of multilingualism with English, we can distinguish the following three types: (a) countries where English is the majority language and multilingualism only a feature of certain new immigrant linguistic minorities mostly in urban areas; (b) countries where English is used habitually by sizeable sections of society for a range of functions and as such contributes to the multilingual pattern of these countries, as in the Philippines and other places referred to in the previous section; and (c) the 'expanding-circle' type of multilingualism that has come to many countries as part of socioeconomic and political developments in the twentieth and twenty-first centuries. It is found in countries where large numbers of speakers, rather than entire communities, have acquired English and use it as a lingua franca for communication with people from a variety of different geographical and linguistic backgrounds.

4.6.1 Multilingualism with English in inner-circle countries

Before they experienced large-scale immigration in the second half of the twentieth century, inner-circle countries already had multilingual elements in the form of indigenous non-English minorities. However, the indigenous language tended to be ignored, so that many years of neglect led to the demise of many native varieties in Canada, the United States and Australia. While earlier immigrants, primarily from Europe, had brought considerable linguistic diversity to North America, Australia and the UK, this was of a transitory nature. Both the indigenous populations and newcomers experienced increased pressure to conform linguistically.

The 1960s and 1970s saw significant social changes heralded by falling birth rates, increased economic prosperity and political liberalism. A range of factors, including legislative measures concerning anti-race discrimination, working conditions, minority rights and movement of labour facilitated immigration and brought about the recognition of minority cultures and languages and subsequent measures to protect and support them. For instance, in Wales legislation started to promote Welsh in the 1960s; in Scotland and Ireland the profile of Gaelic was raised; and resources were made available for the use of these languages in education. In Canada the Official Languages Act was passed in 1969: it made French official and promoted bilingualism, especially through a series of bilingual education programmes that later became models for similar programmes to be used in other settings, for instance in Wales and the Basque Country. Unusually, the Canadian programmes were targeted at the children of majority-language English speakers, not those of the francophone minority. Although they did not, on the whole, establish long-term bilingualism among the anglophones, they did help promote positive attitudes. For the first time, at any rate while the economic situation permitted it, Australia embraced its multilingualism following a policy that was designed to promote 'unity within diversity'. In comparison with the other inner-circle countries, 'Australia has shown by far the most radical and progressive approach to multilingualism', Edwards commented (2004: 39), as the country committed considerable resources to the institutional support of both indigenous and immigrant languages. Even the United States showed some recognition of minority languages, especially Spanish, and in areas of high demand some education programmes were made available. However, they were usually of the transitional kind, and in the absence of a national languages policy, there was limited commitment to minority languages and considerably more support for the 'English-only' stance. Nevertheless, with some 45 million speakers of Spanish (Morales, 2008) and the Hispanics representing the fastest-growing population group, it is difficult to imagine that they will not make a more permanent sociolinguistic impact.

As economic fortunes have changed in more recent times, all inner-circle countries have reined in some of their original commitment to multilingualism and everywhere there have been demands that immigrants should speak and use English. Edwards speaks of the 'monolingual backlash' evident in a campaign such as the 'English-Only' movement in the USA, and he reminds us that 'language is often the focus of hostility' towards newcomers (Edwards 2004: 45). He also points to a deep-rooted suspicion of bilingualism, to which we could add the frequently voiced opinion by native English speakers themselves that they are no good at language learning (a spurious argument for which there is no evidence). So, for the time being, mainstream inner-circle speakers remain largely monolingual, but attitudes towards minority cultures have become more accepting. It is the members of these minorities who are multilingual with English.

4.6.2 Multilingualism with English in outer-circle countries

This sociolinguistic pattern was described in Section 4.5. The discussion of Type 3 multilingual patterns centred on postcolonial English-speaking countries of considerable linguistic diversity where English represents an additional linguistic layer. As we saw, English is acquired as a second or subsequent language, and attitudes towards English and multilingualism are, on the whole, positive. There is variation in the degree of proficiency in English attained and the use made of it by individuals and whole communities but, because of the role the language enjoys on the national as well as the international level, it can be expected that the number of fluent speakers of English will continue to increase.

4.6.3 Multilingualism with English in expanding-circle countries: Europe

There are many countries with a wide range of different sociolinguistic patterns that fall within the category that Kachru labelled as the expanding circle. We have chosen to exemplify this type of multilingualism with reference to Europe, i.e. to a group of different countries that show similar sociolinguistic practices as regards English. In many instances, the term 'Europe' equates to the member states of the European Union that, it must be borne in mind, harbour significant economic inequalities, as well as demographic and sociocultural differences, which impact on their access to and use of English.

In contrast to other continents, English is a relative newcomer in many European states, where it only began to make sizeable inroads from the second half of the twentieth century onwards. Graddol (2006) suggests that in these postmodern times Europe is providing a new source of ideas about how to adapt to a globalised world, and he lists the pooling of sovereignty, free movement of goods and citizens, standardised approaches to the teaching and learning of languages, and new forms of multilingualism. Our discussion of linguistic minorities in Europe, especially the example of South Tyrol (Section 3.3), gave an indication of how speakers from linguistic minorities embrace regional and international languages alongside the majority national ones as part of their linguistic repertoire. Positive attitudes towards multilingualism exist among majority speakers, too; as national boundaries are becoming more permeable and cooperation between European member states has become a visible element in ordinary life, being able to communicate in more than one's mother tongue is an advantage, if not a requirement.

English is used as a lingua franca among many thousands of members of international communities that have sprung up in Europe where there are transnational political, military and non-government organisations, multinational commercial concerns and scientific institutions. Apart from these groups of people, there are many ordinary European nationals for whom the use of English has become an indispensable part of their linguistic repertoire. English has become visible throughout Europe in a growing number of domains that involve knowledge transfer and international communication, for example in commerce and the leisure industries, and above all in telecommunications and information technology. It is evident in the media and particularly dominant in advertising, especially for consumer goods. In many managerial, technical and professional environments, a knowledge of English is considered an essential requirement for careers with a European or global component, be it in international organisations or national ones with multinational links. For many academic careers English is an indispensable prerequisite, as it is used for the dissemination and exchange of scientific material in research publications and at conferences and workshops. This development has created its own momentum in higher education where English is securing an ever-increasing foothold.

English is at the core of virtually all major social trends and techno-logical and business developments, from the rise of the urban middle classes and associated cultures of leisure activities and consumption, the growing use of the internet and other forms of communication systems, to the internationalisation of business and financial institu-tions. Education policies in all European countries have responded to this demand, often urged on by parental pressure, by giving English prominence over all other foreign languages on the school curri-culum: English is most frequently the first foreign language children learn at school, increasingly it is introduced at primary level and it is very often studied throughout secondary education. In a number of EU countries, bilingual programmes with English as a medium of instruction are offered at school level. Similarly, a growing number of universities use English on all manner of postgraduate programmes and also on certain undergraduate courses of study, for instance in business and communication studies, and in medicine and the natural sciences.

English is acquired in a variety of settings and from many differ-ent sources that may use native or non-native-speaker models. Apart from regular schooling and courses for adult learners offered by mainstream and private institutions, many learners take the oppor-tunity of visiting an English-speaking country, often for study pur-poses, and make use of language resources easily accessible in the media. In many of the smaller European countries which do not dub foreign films and entertainment programmes, English is promin-ent on national television channels as well as through cable televi-sion, it figures in popular culture and sport and it is highly visible in public spaces in the form of publicity and advertising. Thus, learn-ers of English benefit from non-formal, extra-curricular contact with the language they are acquiring, and their learning is enhanced by the association of English with high status, instrumental reward and usefulness as a means of international communication. As regards language teaching, it is clear that English enjoys advantages that no other foreign language can compete with and, for many learners, acquiring English goes far beyond what was traditionally seen as for-eign language learning. Naturally, the learning outcomes vary consid-erably, and only those who continue to use the language on a regular basis beyond school can be classed as multilinguals.

The European Union as an institution has an explicit language policy that specifies the status and use of the languages of its member states. French and English are the two main working languages and thus a prerequisite for EU employees; permanent staff at the Commission tend to use French, while English is used by delegates from member states attending meetings. It has gained considerable ground as a result of several rounds of expansion of the Union, not so much because of political decisions but simply because members prefer to use English.

The EU and the Council of Europe are committed to multilingualism and language diversity, goals that are to be achieved through the promotion of teaching more than one language in schools and continued support for minority languages. Thus, the study of more than one foreign language is pursued by two-thirds of EU upper secondary education students: in some of these countries, such as the Baltic States, Finland and the Scandinavian countries, Slovakia and Slovenia, the figure is much higher. In contrast, the equivalent figures for the UK show that over half of upper secondary school students were not studying any foreign language at all.

It should be mentioned that in many European countries there exists a long tradition of learning languages for their instrumental as well as their intrinsic cultural value. This is borne out by the results of a Eurostat survey published in 2010, in which almost a third of adult EU citizens declared that they spoke at least two foreign languages. On the other hand, the same survey also showed that a third of those questioned did not speak any other language. This suggests that multilingualism in Europe has a close link with levels of education, degree of social mobility and cultural openness; it is not a general feature of society or of whole communities.

So far we have traced the spread of English in Europe in terms of uses and users, i.e. at the sociolinguistic level. This trend has also made a mark at the micro-linguistic level in similar ways to those described above for 'inner-circle' users of English. On one hand, we can observe it in the English that is used and, on the other, we cannot fail to notice the impact English has had on the European languages themselves. The term *International English*, or the more precise denomination *English as an International Language*, describes the kind of English that is used for international communication by expanding-circle users. Cross-linguistic influences, especially at the phonological level, can be observed, as well as the use of either American or British standard pronunciations or a mixture of the two. Adherence to grammatical and pragmatic norms may be less strict in spoken (and cyber) discourse where 'a kind of suspension of expectations regarding norms seems to be in operation' (Seidelhofer 2003: 15), while, for instance, academic writing tends to show fewer variations from standard norms.

All European languages show evidence of contact with English, for example in the form of loans and all manners of lexical, semantic and syntactic transfers – and even pseudo-transfers, i.e. new creations that look English but are not authentic or do not have the same meaning in English. The Germanic languages seem to be particularly susceptible to lexical as well as syntactic and semantic influences from English, which are facilitated by the structural similarities between the two languages and possibly also reflect perceived affinities and positive attitudes towards the language and its speakers.

To sum up, multilingualism with English in Europe is very varied in terms of when, where, how and to what degree of competence the language is acquired, and also in what domains and for what functions it is used. Multilingualism is an attribute of individuals, yet it also has a significant presence at societal level. Many Europeans need English for a limited range of specific, perhaps highly technical, contexts outside which they may feel uncomfortable or at a loss. English brings the promise of material gain, higher status and further prospects of mobility, so there are powerful reasons for learning and maintaining it. An additional feature of this type of multilingualism is that being proficient in English does not require developing feelings of shared identity or the necessity to delve into Anglo-Saxon culture, because English for international communication is neutral and culturally non-specific. It is a sociolinguistic phenomenon which is quite unique and which, for the time being, is likely to continue to spread.

4.7 CONCLUSION

This chapter set out to examine certain twentieth-century socio-political developments and their linguistic repercussions. The effects of colonisation went far and deep, affecting not only the political and economic structure of the colonised territories, but their very cultural and linguistic fabric, too. Here we list some of the most salient issues discussed:

- The most significant linguistic effect of colonialism was the transportation of one language to a territory where the arbitrary drawing of territorial boundaries by the colonial powers resulted in multilingualism of the superimposed colonial language over and above the already existing local sociolinguistic mosaic.

- Postcolonialism frequently brought a rearrangement of sociolinguistic patterns, either by elevating the status of one or several indigenous languages, replacing the former colonial language or taking up a place beside it. These measures were often motivated by ideology, and they were frequently not followed by practical steps leading to an increase in use of native languages.
- Internationalisation and globalisation have gathered momentum in the economic sphere. Their linguistic concomitant, the spread of English, has touched the sociolinguistic situation of every continent. English has assumed an unprecedented presence and evolution (the emergence of new varieties) around the globe and is being acquired by an increasing number of people as a second, additional or international language. New types of multilingualism with English have developed in different parts of the world.

Part II
Construing individual multilingualism

5   Individual multilingualism

Those who know nothing of foreign languages know nothing of
their own.

Johann Wolfgang von Goethe

5.1   INTRODUCTION

Language contact, as we have seen, is brought about in many different ways. Depending on prevailing circumstances, societies and their
individual members are affected differently in terms of whether they
become users of several languages or not. In theory, it is possible for
citizens of multilingual states to remain largely monolingual, especially if the country has adopted the territoriality principle and there
is a fair degree of equality between the languages involved, or the
different language groups are isolated from each other without much
need for communication between them, or the population is too poor
to participate fully in the country's social and economic life.

There is no inherent correlation between societal and individual
multilingualism. But in reality, in a multilingual sociopolitical context the likelihood that more people have contact with several languages is greater, simply because of the increased opportunities for
interaction. The resulting multilingual language competence may,
however, be of a kind restricted to only a limited range of functions
and competencies, whereas people who live in monolingual countries may achieve a wider range of knowledge of several languages
by, for instance, having been schooled within a multilingual education programme. There are, on the other hand, also societies with a
rigid social stratification that allows only limited contact between the
constituent social groups, such as the caste system in Indian Hindu
society, where very marked variation has developed even within language. Ultimately, the occurrence of multilingualism on a personal
level and the degree of language proficiency achieved depend on

personal circumstances, patterns of social interaction, mobility (both social and geographical) and motivation.

People become multilingual for a variety of reasons. For many, the acquisition of several codes is part of becoming socialised into a particular group that requires the use of different languages to fulfil different functions, such as communication within the family group, between different social groups or with official authorities. For others, becoming multilingual is a matter of education or of personal choice and ambition. The citizens of multilingual states who want to partake in the state's affairs at all levels, whether for ideological or professional purposes, are usually highly motivated to learn the languages that will provide access to their desired goals. When two people with different native languages marry, one of them will need to speak the language of their spouse, or both partners may opt to communicate in a third language: for instance, in the case of Amazonian tribes (small in number but famously mentioned in sociolinguistic texts!) communication between spouses in a lingua franca is the social norm. And there are families from mixed linguistic backgrounds who settle in a third country and may decide to raise their children to become trilingual (they account for a relatively small number of the world's plurilinguals, but they are the source for most of the case studies of trilingual children that have been published to date). Children who are born into multilingual families, or into multilingual communities, or who are sent to bilingual schools, do not have much choice in becoming multilingual, but whether they maintain active use of their linguistic repertoires in later life may well be a matter of personal decision for some.

This chapter focuses on the individual as the smallest unit in the multilingual mosaic. If we want to understand the sociolinguistic patterns of a given society, it can be illuminating to look at the incipient stages of their formation. Who is multilingual? How does one become multilingual? What factors play a role in shaping the plurilingual's linguistic repertoire? What is involved in managing several languages at the same time? Studies into bilingualism and second language acquisition have suggested a variety of answers to this kind of questions. Many researchers say that their findings are applicable to children acquiring 'two or more languages', although in most cases the data used is taken from bilinguals. The only reason why this claim may be upheld with some confidence can be seen in the argument that it has been demonstrated that, in terms of processes and strategies, monolingual and bilingual first language acquisition essentially proceed in the same manner. Therefore, one may assume that, qualitatively, plurilingual acquisition is similar and that, quantitatively, the presence of several linguistic systems and functions in a variety of different linguistic contexts makes plurilingualism more complex and variable.

5.2 MULTILINGUAL INDIVIDUALS – WHO ARE THEY?

For most of us it is easy to think of someone who knows several languages and can speak them in appropriate contexts, but we might not be prepared to call them multilinguals. In countries that are largely monolingual certain myths often surround the phenomenon of bilingualism and, by extension, multilingualism. In those contexts, multilinguals are people who live in multilingual countries, or are children who grow up with different languages, and bilinguals are regarded as equally fluent in both their languages. The reality is quite different with regard to bilinguals as well as plurilinguals. Some children are multilingual because they grow up in a monolingual family and in a multilingual community, for others the situation may be the reverse. Some people grow up with just one language and become highly competent users of several tongues at a later stage in their life, whereas others may abandon their childhood multilingualism and end up using only one of their languages in their daily lives. There are also those who remain multilingual but the languages that they use at a later stage in their lives are not necessarily the ones they were brought up with. In any case, how would one go about measuring 'equal competence', in quantitative as well as qualitative terms? Most people use different languages for different purposes, and therefore they are bound to have unequal language knowledge and fluency. Also, their need to use their various languages may change over time, as may the functions for which they use them.

From an ethnological and sociological point of view, the multiplicity of languages and cultures constitutes a basic frame of analysis, while in psychological approaches binary models (comprising modes of contact between two languages or two cultures) are clearly prevalent. The distinction between *pluri* on the one side and *bi* on the other involves methodological considerations such as the difference in perspectives taken and subjects studied. *Bi* (duo, dual or couple) inevitably evokes dichotomous distinctions of balance or imbalance, similarity or difference, dialogue or opposition. These dichotomies suggest a binary relationship of the languages and/or cultural domains and may convey the notion of an unattainable ideal of 'perfect' bilingualism, as in concepts such as 'mother tongue / foreign language' and 'source language / target language'. *Pluri*, understood as 'more than two', has revealed itself in many analyses as a concept of unmanageable and uncontrollable complexity. In immigration countries, where the population has a number of languages of origin, the language of the majority is the language of schooling, transaction and socialisation. *Multi/pluri* (many) sometimes entails an appeal or return to *mono/uni* (one), as manifested in widely asked questions about the possible (dis) advantages of early bilingualism in terms of the cognitive health of individuals or the good governance of a country. Another variant that comes into play when considering plurilingualism is *inter*, an indicator of relationship and not of simple juxtaposition that oscillates between the *bi* and *pluri* modes. Coste *et al.* (2009: 10) state that:

> while the concept of *interlanguage* is governed by duality, the *intercultural* concept operates sometimes in the mode of 'two' (relations between two cultures, or existence of a mixed culture, or appearance of a stage in-between), and sometimes in the 'more than two' mode (interception, interpenetration, interference or inter-construction and inter-definition of several cultures).

Our discussion and consideration of trilingualism as a form of plurilingualism (or multilingualism) will be expanded in the following chapters, especially those dealing with competence and education.

We use two labels that go some way towards meeting the popular perception of bilingualism and multilingualism, leaving the intractable notion of competence aside. We refer to someone whose dual or multiple language acquisition occurred in a largely untutored or informal manner as a 'natural multilingual', as opposed to those who mainly learn languages in a classroom or formal context. Plurilingual children are, obviously, prime candidates for natural multilinguals, but so are immigrants, refugees and displaced persons who find themselves immersed in a new linguistic environment and 'pick up the language' in the course of time. A 'regular multilingual' (an extension of Grosjean's notion of the 'regular bilingual') is someone who uses more than two languages in his or her daily life. Both these concepts must only be seen as general labels for relative states that cannot be assigned definitive delimitations. Consider the following examples of multilinguals:

> The Moroccan immigrant in France, who is from a Berber-speaking background, acquired Moroccan Arabic during his childhood in the community and at school, where he also learnt a little French. He now runs an import business in Marseille. His

clients are Arabic- and French-speaking and so is his wife. Over the years, his French literacy skills and knowledge of French vocabulary have increased considerably, whereas his Berber has become rather rusty as he only uses it occasionally. We might call him a natural bilingual as regards his Berber and Arabic; he is now a regular bilingual in two languages, neither of which is the one he first acquired as a child.

The child in Guinea-Bissau, who is fortunate enough to have attended school for several years, acquired first the indigenous community language of the region. She subsequently acquired Kiriol, a lingua franca used in a small town where the market is a meeting place for people from other ethnic backgrounds. Her mother is a successful trader and her father an official in the regional administration. The family can afford to send her to school, where Portuguese is the medium of instruction and children are immersed into that language. She can read and write in Portuguese but not in her other languages, which are occasionally used by teachers when classroom communication in Portuguese breaks down. She is certainly a natural and regular bilingual with regard to her tribal language and the lingua franca and with Portuguese, which plays an important but restricted role in her life.

The Malaysian employee, who works in a call centre for a big international company in Amsterdam, grew up with Malay, and then started to learn English at school and later at university, where she also learnt some Chinese. She uses her three languages for work. English is used for formal and informal communication on the firm's premises. She is learning Dutch, as she intends to stay in the Netherlands for some time. She spends her free time with other Malay speakers and her Dutch boyfriend, with whom she uses English and some Dutch. It is easy to see that she is a regular multilingual, although the amount of use varies for each of her languages.

Translators and interpreters become multilingual and expert users of their specific skills through training in adulthood. They continually increase their linguistic repertoires, acquiring new technical terminology and registers in all their languages. Often, natural multilinguals make poor translators and interpreters unless they undergo formal training. Highly competent translators may never become brilliant interpreters, nor do interpreters necessarily produce elegant translations. Many translators and interpreters reach native-like competence in their working languages, yet many hesitate to consider themselves multilinguals.

The point about these examples is that they illustrate how, for many people, the acquisition (and also attrition and/or maintenance) of languages can occur at various times during their lives and is determined by different circumstances. The proficiency they have includes being fluent in written as well as oral skills, but it is quite rare for multilinguals to be equally fluent in speaking, understanding, reading and writing in all their languages, unless they are trained linguists and practise professionally. Writing about bilingualism, Grosjean proposes the notion of the 'complementarity principle': 'Bilinguals usually acquire and use their languages for different purposes, in different domains of life, with different people. Different aspects of life require different languages.' (1997: 165) This principle applies to multilinguals, too, and the greater number of languages is likely to produce even more variability in linguistic competence. Each individual manages his or her own individual language and linguistic policy, social needs and multilingual identity, much as happens in the family language policy discussed in Chapter 7.

How do linguists deal with this variable phenomenon of plurilingualism? In the early studies of bilingualism a number of definitions were put forward; they referred explicitly to two languages and to the kind of language contact studied. The general belief seems to have been that what could be said about bilingualism was equally applicable to multilingualism. Einar Haugen's pioneer work described multilingualism as 'a kind of multiple bilingualism' (1956: 9). Other scholars make allowances for more than two languages in their definition of bilingualism: for instance, Grosjean defines bilinguals as 'those people who use two (or more) languages (or dialects) in their everyday lives' (1997: 164). Oksaar's fairly detailed definition of bilingualism is: 'the ability of a person to use here and now two or more languages as a means of communication in most situations and to switch from one language to the other if necessary' (1983: 19). Towards the end of the twentieth century interest in third language acquisition and trilingualism became more widespread, but few definitions were proposed. Hoffmann's work on trilingualism takes it to be 'the presence of three languages in one speaker' (2001a: 14), where 'presence' refers to the instant availability and potential use of all three codes in appropriate contexts.

The term 'multilingualism' has been in use in the sociolinguistic literature for a long time, because it encompasses the idea that not only more than one language but also several other kinds of linguistic varieties may be present in a particular sociolinguistic situation. It is only in recent years that the term has been employed in the psycholinguistic treatment of language contact and in applied linguistics work on third or multiple language acquisition. Thus, Cenoz and Genesee (1998: 16) clearly see multilingualism as an attribute of the individual when they describe it as the final result of the process of acquisition of several non-native languages. A similar view is taken by Herdina and Jessner (2002: 52), who propose 'the command and/or use of two or more languages by the respective speaker' as a general definition. All in all, we converge on the definition of a multilingual as someone who is able to draw on his or her linguistic resources, consisting of two or more linguistic systems (and combinations of these systems), at any given moment in the appropriate context, and who does so as part of their normal daily life. We distinguish between multilingual and plurilingual, with the latter describing someone who has isolated command of each linguistic system and keeps and uses them separately, whereas multilingual is one who has a complex linguistic system consisting of multiple options.

Because of the diversity of contexts and manners in which people become multilingual, it is tempting, for methodological reasons, to establish typologies of multilinguals. In the following we have used two criteria together, age and sociocultural context of acquisition and use; both are given a general interpretation (in Chapter 6 we elaborate on this typology from a psycholinguistic perspective). For the sake of simplification, we are restricting the present description to trilinguals. With every additional language, the combinatory possibilities – and with them the numbers of types – will increase.

We distinguish the following types of multilinguals:

(i) children who are brought up with two home languages that are different from the one spoken in the wider community;
(ii) children who grow up in a bilingual community and whose home language (used by either one or both parents) is different from the community languages;
(iii) children and adult third language learners, i.e. either monolinguals who learn two languages in a school or other study context, or bilinguals who learn a third language primarily in an academic context;
(iv) children and adults who become trilingual through immigration, i.e. either monolinguals acquiring two new languages or bilinguals acquiring another new language in a natural context;
(v) children and adults in trilingual communities.

For each of these types one could identify subgroups if one distinguished between simultaneous and subsequent acquisition, which
can be an important psycholinguistic factor determining manner
and, possibly, quality of acquisition. Several constellations are possible: simultaneous acquisition of three linguistic systems by the
child, simultaneous acquisition of two languages followed by subsequent acquisition of a third language, or monolingual acquisition followed by subsequently acquiring two more languages either at the
same time or subsequently, either in childhood or later. Similarly, the
identification of languages that are acquired 'naturally' as opposed
to 'tutored learning' may be considered significant although, as the
examples above have shown, the two often follow each other or go
hand in hand: the trilingual child is likely to become educated in
one or more of her languages, immigrants may learn some of their
host country's language before emigrating and afterwards pick up a
lot more from their new linguistic environment without undergoing
formal tuition. These perspectives are taken up in the next chapter
when discussing the development of trilingualism and trilingual language processing.

In sum, typologies and classifications may provide a framework
for scholars involved in unravelling the intricacies of multilingualism at large and trilingualism in particular. Any classification and
typology aims at generalising the knowledge we have, yet there are
individuals who straddle the categories (especially types (iii) and (iv),
which are somewhat fuzzy). Just as language is dynamic in nature, so
are its use, learning, acquisition, development and appropriation by
the individual throughout a lifespan. In the following sections of this
chapter we deal in a descriptive manner with two consequent issues:
the study of multilinguals (which is elaborated in the next chapter
by adopting a more psycho-sociolinguistic perspective) and a brief
survey of studies reporting on the development of multilingualism
(which is also taken further, from a language development perspective, in simultaneous multilinguals in Chapter 6).

5.3 THE STUDY OF MULTILINGUALISM

Like bilingualism, multilingualism research is multifaceted and multidisciplinary, as it draws on fields such as psycholinguistics and linguistics, applied linguistics, especially second language acquisition,
neurolinguistics, sociolinguistics and education. Contributing to the
literature is also a growing body of writings by 'interested parties',

namely parents of multilingual children and multilinguals them-selves. Whilst their accounts may sometimes lack a certain scientific rigour, they may nevertheless provide interesting data and insights into 'real life with several languages'. Not surprisingly, the research tools and methodologies used to explore trilingualism are essentially the same as those used in bilingualism studies. Moreover, the theoret-ical models used to explain both bilingual and multilingual research findings rely heavily on monolingual ones (we will come back to this topic in the next chapter).

For many years research into bilingualism, second language acqui-sition and education proceeded in parallel fashion (more on this in Chapter 8). More recent times have seen a rapprochement of the three fields and also a widening of scope to include situations where more than two languages are being developed. Projects that involve children, community languages, schools and minority communities are good examples; their outcome may be publications that highlight the linguistic resources in schools or particular educational needs of multilingual children. They may spur language planners, education-alists and teacher trainers into action, and they also have an impact on attitudes of minorities and mainstream society alike. Another area of research that has benefited from interdisciplinary cross-fertilisa-tion has resulted in studies that try to ascertain whether – and if so, to what extent and in what way – bilingualism has an effect on the acquisition of a third language. When disseminated, such work can inform policy makers and educators and may influence pedagogical decisions regarding curriculum planning.

The studies currently available cover predominantly the multilin-guals of types (i)–(iii) outlined earlier. In quantitative terms, it has to be said that, to date, studies in third language acquisition (i.e. relating to type (iii) multilinguals) far outnumber those dealing with the other types. Whilst there are a growing number of research studies examin-ing types (i) and (ii), there are hardly any studies on type (v) multilin-guals. This is ironic, because the incidence of the latter is far greater than that of the former. But it is easy to see why this should be so: most of the accessible research into language acquisition of trilingual children involves children who acquire combinations of two or three European languages in European (English-speaking), North American or Australian contexts. Type (v) multilinguals are found in the many linguistically diverse countries of Africa and Asia. For linguistic and practical reasons, not many western academics have access to these settings and the indigenous languages concerned and their users. The kind of language-contact research that is carried out by scholars in these countries tends to be written from a sociolinguistic or educational perspective rather than with the focus on the individual. It is important to keep this bias (European and Anglo-Saxon) in mind, as any generalisations made with regard to individual multilingualism should be seen, in the main, as globally restricted to the developed countries of the world.

5.4   HOW DO CHILDREN BECOME TRILINGUAL?

There are, broadly speaking, two types of sources to consult for an answer to the question of how a child becomes trilingual: the more research specific and the more general. We focus on the former, surveying and referring to findings from linguistic studies that address issues of language development and behaviour in children between one and ten years who – counting family, community and school exposure – came into contact with three languages. Earlier work tends to cover several aspects of child trilingualism in a fairly general way and is based largely on observational studies, diaries and occasional recordings, whereas in the last two decades studies have focused on specific issues, above all code-switching, and they have relied on more substantial and systematic collections of corpus data that recorded input as well as output. The significance of non-linguistic factors that appear to influence acquisition and use features in all of these studies. One of the most notable differences between the conversations of monolingual children and those of bilinguals and trilinguals is that multilinguals can draw on more than one linguistic repertoire. They will do this, for instance, in the form of borrowing or coining in order to fill a lexical gap which may be either a momentary one (see the first two examples) or for which an equivalent has not yet been acquired (see the third and the fourth). All four examples (borrowed items in italics) are from a young English–Spanish–German trilingual child (Hoffmann 1991):

(a)   English (age 3;10): Will you play *mit* me? (German preposition *mit* used instead of English 'with')

(b)   Spanish (age 3;8): Nina pinta *mit* lápiz (German preposition *mit* used instead of Spanish 'con')

(c)   Quiero más *grapas* 'I want more grapes' (noun based on English 'grapes' instead of Spanish 'uvas')

(d)   German (age 3;7): Tee schon *gepourt!* 'tea has already been poured' (English 'to pour' morphologically adapted as a German past participle)

Multilingual children are also able to code-switch when quoting somebody in order to achieve a particular effect or to be more precise.

Naturally, this is likely to occur more frequently if the interlocutors share the child's languages and also if they code-switch themselves. As indicated earlier, there are few systematic long-term and in-depth studies of trilingual language acquisition comparable to those that have been carried out with bilingual children, notably in the areas of syntactic development, mixing and language differentiation (e.g. Deuchar and Quay 2000; Lanza 1997a, b; Meisel 1990, 1994, 2001; De Houwer 1990; Fantini 1985 or Taeschner 1983).

For half a century we have witnessed a wealth of studies on bilingual first language acquisition (BFLA, Cunningham-Andersson and Andersson 1999). Scientific journals have devoted special issues to it; conferences, symposia, and colloquia specifically themed around BFLA have been held throughout the world; textbooks on this particular topic have appeared in bookstores; academic programmes and specialised courses as well as worldwide networks and websites have increased in volume and accessibility. BFLA researchers (see Genesee and Nicoladis 2007 for a review) have shown that bilingual children go through language development milestones at the same age as monolinguals; they acquire language-specific properties of the target languages early in their development and similarly to monolingual peers; and they differentiate their languages from their earliest productions (*Dual System* hypothesis, as coined by Genesee 1989). Evidence for language differentiation has been found in the area of phonology, lexis, word-order patterns and language choice (see, again, Genesee and Nicoladis 2007) as well as in language-contact situations (e.g. Lanza 1997a, b, 2001). At the same time, evidence of cross-linguistic transfer of specific features from one language to the other has also been widely documented (see Yip and Matthews 2007 for a review) and it is now accepted that, although BFL learners develop separate languages, the development of these languages is not autonomous but interdependent.

Unlike BFLA, the study of early trilingualism has not received much attention, at any rate until very recently, and research on the simultaneous development of three languages is at a relatively early stage (Barnes 1997, 1999, 2011; Chevalier 2011; Kazzazi 2011; Montanari 2009a, 2009b, 2010, 2011; Quay 2001, 2008, 2011a, b; Hoffmann 1985; Hoffmann and Widdicombe 1999; Stavans 1992; Hoffmann and Stavans 2007; Ivir-Ashworth 2011). Most studies on trilingualism deal with the acquisition of a third language later in childhood (such as through schooling) or with the role bilingualism plays when acquiring a third language (see Cenoz 2003a; Cenoz and Jessner 2000, to name a few). Studies on Trilingual First Language Acquisition (TFLA), that is, on the development of three languages from birth, are either

Table 5.1 *Studies of Trilingual First Language Acquisition (TFLA)*

Researchers (year)	Participant's age	Languages (parental and other)	Country of residence during the study	Topics studied
Murrell (1966)	2;0 to 2;8	Swedish, English, Finnish	Sweden, UK	Morphology, word order, interference
Oksaar (1977)	3;11 to 5;8	Estonian, Swedish, German	Germany	Language acquisition, separation and interference
Hoffmann (1985)	First 5 and 8 years respectively	German, Spanish, English	UK	Phonology, morphology, syntax, interference, socio- and psycholinguistics
Mikes (1990)	0;11 to 1;11	Serbo-Croatian, Hungarian, German	present-day Serbia	Lexical development and differentiation
Stavans (1992)	2;6 to 3;9 and 5;5 to 6;8	Hebrew, Spanish, English	USA	Trilingual code-switching
Hoffmann and Widdicombe (1999)	4;4 to 4;5	English, Italian, French	France	Trilingual code-switching, coining and interference
Quay (2001)	0;11 to 1;10	English, German, Japanese	Japan	Language choice, parental discourse styles
Barnes (2006)	1;11 to 3;6	English, Basque, Spanish	Basque region of Spain	Acquisition of questions in English
Stavans and Swisher (2006)	2;6 to 4;2 and 5;5 to 7;1	Hebrew, Spanish, English	USA	Language switching and trilingual competence
Wang (2008)	birth to 11	Chinese, French, English	USA	Acquisition, language use, language awareness, identity formation
Kazzazi (2011)	1;5 to 4;9	German, English, Persian	Germany	Speech interaction and language contact
Ivir-Ashworth (2011)	1;4 2;1 and 2;9 3;6	Croatian, English, German	UK	Language mixing
Chevalier (2011)	2;1 to 3;1	English, French, and Swiss German	Switzerland	Language dominance
Montanari (2013)	Birth to 2;6	Tagalog, English, Spanish	USA	Development of phonology, lexicon, word order and language choice

not very systematic in how they report input characteristics, data collection, analyses etc. (see Quay 2001, 2011a, and Hoffmann 2001a for reviews); or they amount to a few case studies that explore specific themes such as cross-linguistic influence (Kazzazi 2011), code-switching after age three (Edwards and Dewaele 2007; Hoffmann and Stavans 2007; Stavans and Muchnik 2008; Stavans and Swisher 2006), the relationship between input and development in one language (Barnes 2006, 2011); or else they are anecdotal reports of individual cases of trilingual acquisition at times addressed to the general public (Maneva 2004; Wang 2008). In sum, systematic, longitudinal analyses of early trilingualism are scarce. The following is an overview of case studies of TFLA.

The scarcity of studies on trilingual infants could be attributed to their time-consuming nature and, more specifically, to the taxing methodological issues involved in studying the development of three languages. Notwithstanding arguments by sceptics who claim that TFLA is an extension or a variant of BFLA and that the results from trilingual studies do not contribute anything to what we already know from BFLA studies, we believe that this is not the case (Hoffmann 2001a, and emphasised by Quay 2011a). These studies have argued that TFLA is not the sum of three first languages, nor the addition of a third language to bilingualism, but rather it is a unique phenomenon with its own characteristics and features that should be studied in its own right. Studies that have aimed at understanding the nature of trilingualism and trilingual development have focused specifically on incipient and simultaneous trilinguals for whom TFLA is similar to monolingual and bilingual development in some aspects yet different in others. The great contribution of the studies which have emerged is in the perspective taken, namely TFLA as a natural linguistic path rather than an extraordinary or problematic linguistic situation imposed, for instance, by immigration. In this vein, these studies provide a unique window to the acquisition of more than one language and as an exemplar of how language acquisition, in general, works.

Studies by Hoffmann and Stavans (2007), Quay (2011b), Barnes (2011), Kazzazi (2011), Montanari (2011) and Navracsis (1998) compellingly show that, unlike many bilinguals, trilingual children are not balanced and do not use their languages equally; rather, there are always dominant and weaker languages depending on the interactional conditions, the exposure to input, the situation upon which a language is called in, the stage of acquisition and the need the child has to communicate. Dominance in some languages, or what might be taken to be lack of proficiency in others, has been proven in these studies to be transient and dependent on the quality of the input in each language as well as language-internal properties, regardless of input amount or frequency. Also, not all children who experience trilingual exposure develop and become productive in three languages. For example, Chevalier (2011) observed two developing trilingual children longitudinally from approximately two to three years of age. These children grew up in Switzerland in mixed-language families where the language combinations were English, French and Swiss German (the local language was French for one child and Swiss German for the other). Chevalier found that, while one child was productive in all three languages from the start of the study, the second child understood the two minority languages but spoke the community language (Swiss German) predominantly. Other case studies of early trilingual development have also shown uneven management of the three languages (Barnes 2006; Wang 2008; Stavans and Swisher 2006) or infelicitous production in the development of the three languages (Kazzazi 2011; Stavans and Muchnik 2008) on the path to achieving productive trilingualism.

The case studies mentioned above differ from each other with regard to their subjects, languages, special focus and methodologies. Still, it is possible to extract some features which are typical for trilingual language acquisition. For example, in most cases the trilingual children had two first languages which they acquired from their parents. In the case of some children, the third language, that of the community, was added before the child began producing speech (in Hoffmann and Widdicombe's and Stavans and Quay's studies, for instance), while in the case of others, exposure to the third language occurred after that milestone (as in Oksaar's study). Different languages were clearly associated with different persons and/or contexts, and the children would address their interlocutors in the appropriate language. Invariably, the language of the community, even if added after the first two, developed into the dominant one. Initially, all parents had decided to use their own language with their children but, with time, many became flexible in their language choice when interacting with their children, particularly when they got older. Many of the studies confirm that trilingual acquisition is highly complex because of the interplay between the social, emotional and cultural factors that influence the establishment of the linguistic systems in different ways (this will be explored further later). The same can be said of the assessment: the larger the number of languages involved, the higher the number of possible interpretations.

How trilingual did the children turn out to be? There are some studies that set out to prove that children can acquire three languages just as well as comparable monolingual or bilingual children, and there are others that pass a general judgement on the language proficiency achieved. There is agreement that successful separate development is related to the quality of input and to the caregivers' discourse strategies. Also important are those factors that contribute towards a non-conflictive acquisition context: the amount and quality of support; positive attitudes towards the languages, their speakers and multilingualism itself; an attractive cultural embedding for each of the languages; varied sources of linguistic input; and realistic expectations of what can be achieved in terms of language proficiency and cultural identification on the part of the families and other caregivers.

The children described in these case studies represent only a relatively small, privileged number of children. Another case of self-report is worthy of mentioning because it illustrates how many children grow and learn to speak the languages of their environment in a much less structured manner. Huber (2001) recalls her childhood spent in a large, extended family of Italian origin in Tunisia. Italian was the family language, Arabic was spoken in the street and French was the language of the school she attended. She claims that their use of language was primarily aimed at effective communication, and she adds: 'There was no rule. Whatever the listeners would understand faster, whichever language conveyed the message accurately, whichever was funnier, we used' (2001: 4). This kind of language practice in multilingual families is bound to be widespread. Stavans' (1992, 2001) account is more comprehensive in its discussion of this kind of language use. Research in TFLA as a socio-interactional asset of multilingual families in general and children in particular is in its early stages; there are many questions which have only been answered partially, findings that await confirmation, and theories and models that need to be developed further on the basis of case studies as well as experimental research.

What emerges quite convincingly from the studies thus far is that hearing, interacting in, and choosing from three different languages increases the complexity of early language development. The studies mentioned here provide a base to investigate further and answer more robustly questions such as: what leads some children but not others to develop and become productive in different languages early on, especially when exposure to the three languages is available and, up to a point, balanced? To what extent and how are the three languages kept apart? Are they stored differently from one language in monolinguals?

5.5   *ACQUISITION OF A THIRD LANGUAGE THROUGH SCHOOLING*

There are many children who become trilingual when they are a little older and start schooling. Two broad distinctions can be made here: either the third language is introduced as a school subject or it is the medium through which schooling is carried out. In some contexts, such as the European Schools or the Luxembourg education system, the language is first introduced as a subject and then, as the children become more proficient in it, it is gradually used as a medium of instruction. But more often than not, it is a case of sudden and total immersion into a new social and linguistic environment in which the child is expected to somehow acquire the new language through exposure, contact and osmosis.

Typically, this is the case for migrant, immigrant or refugee children in bilingual areas who enter a formal education system that uses two languages, for instance the children of Kurdish–Turkish parents in Germany or of Vietnamese or Iranian parents in Montreal or Vancouver. In the case of children from multilingual backgrounds from ex-colonial countries in Africa or Asia, they may already have acquired some English or French, although it is unlikely to be the kind of language they need for communication with their peers.

Canada is a country with an enlightened, supportive approach to the education of children of immigrants and refugees, positive attitudes towards multilingualism and considerable experience of bilingual programmes. Consequently, there exist a number of studies of multiple language acquisition among indigenous and new minorities where the focus is on sociocultural aspects, attitudes towards their own multilingualism and the use that minority members make of their languages. Lamarre (2003) reports on research carried out with trilingual youngsters in Montreal who had acquired a minority language at home plus English and French at school. She found that there was a strong commitment to maintaining the spoken home language, although not necessarily literacy in it. In most cases, the spoken home language and also English or French were used in the family. Schooling affected the use of the home language because siblings who started out using the home language to each other switched to using the school language as they grew older.

A similar situation exists for foreign children entering schools in various countries of the European Union who already know two languages and are faced with having to learn the language of the school system for purposes of communication and education. Often, their previously acquired languages are of little value in this process. In contrast to Canada, there is not much language support offered in such countries to these children to ease their entry into the school environment. The development of their home languages stagnates owing to lack of support and opportunity to acquire literacy skills, and this may adversely affect their acquisition of the school language, which leads to subtractive bilingualism.

For these new-minority children, school is not only the place where the third (or even fourth) language is acquired, it is also where they experience socialisation through that language and where their multilingual identity develops further. Playground and other activities play an important role in their social development through communication with peers and teachers. Furthermore, school is the place where the third language is needed for carrying out complex tasks associated with the development of academic and literacy skills in the new language – often leaving behind the development of those skills (if they exist prior to this schooling) in the other languages. Whether a child succeeds depends to a large extent on the kind of support he/she receives, as just being submerged in a new linguistic environment is unlikely to lead to full linguistic competence. Whilst much has been written about the specific psycholinguistic issues concerning these children, and the kind of bilingual or trilingual education that should be made available for them and related language policy issues, little detailed longitudinal work has been undertaken on the linguistic aspects of the acquisition processes in such minority children.

There are other contexts in which children acquire their third language through schooling. In many African countries where an ex-colonial language is used in education, children from multilingual backgrounds often start school with no prior knowledge of this language. Frequently in these cases, little thought is given to facilitating the acquisition of the school language, as described previously by the example of Guinea-Bissau. Moore's (1999) ethnolinguistic investigation reports on language acquisition and use in a village in the Mandara Mountains of northern Cameroon where there is widespread multilingualism due to traditional norms of exogamy. In this context, a woman marries outside of her primary language group, moves into the compound of her husband's parents and raises her children in the language of the paternal household, while the children also have considerable contact with their mother's language from contact with her family and friends. In addition to the various local languages, villagers also have exposure to non-community secondary languages through religious practices. Qur'anic schools offer Arabic instruction through the medium of one of the fifteen local languages, Wandala.

The various Christian missions offer literacy training in the local language, Fulfulde, and in French. The focus of Moore's study is on the contrast between the children's considerable experience of multilingualism and L$_2$ learning in a natural context and the instructional practices of classroom acquisition of French, the country's official language.

Moore describes features of secondary language socialisation in this community, which is characterised by language input that is richly contextualised in everyday activities. Language accommodation is frequent, and there is no pressure to perform linguistically. Learners are aware of the second language acquisition strategies they employ and they have a clear idea of their language learning preferences. In stark contrast to this were the French-medium classroom norms and rules of interaction. No other language was allowed, either in the classroom or the playground, and violations were punished; classroom communication was teacher-centred and the teaching of literacy became decontextualised. 'Several aspects of classroom practice are incongruent with community practices', and actually hindered the children's successful acquisition of French, Moore concludes (1999: 148).

Africa offers various models of trilingualism, not all of them as structurally neat as this one. For example, trilingualism in Mali may be an asset of the wealthier population only. Muslim conquests from the southern part of the Sahara into northern Mali have resulted in a considerable influence of Arabic on the local language spoken and, most importantly, in its use for religious rituals. Nearly 90 per cent of the Malian population claims to practise Islam. Places of worship such as mosques exist side by side with animist structures within a given village, and children attend the madrasa (Islamic religious 'school', or rather, class) – some at the mosque and some at the schools. These lessons consist of chants of Qur'an verses which are given to the children from as young as six or seven years of age on wooden tablets. The children sit and chant verses, at times repeating what the instructor recites. Children in these settings – like in others known from other religions (e.g. the 'Heder' Bible lessons in Judaism) – are far from being literate in Arabic; nor are they speakers of Arabic, for they cannot communicate in the language beyond reciting prayers in the mosque. The other language in which children are schooled in Mali (these children belong to the more educated and affluent part of the population in the bigger cities) is French, the colonising language and in fact the language in which daily transactions and routines are conducted. Only the fortunate ones get to learn reading and writing in this language. The others learn the language informally and seldom become literate in French. The third language is, of course, the indigenous/tribal/regional language. The upper socioeconomic class can afford English for their children who attend bilingual French–English schools or morning school at the madrasa and afternoon schooling at the English school. Whichever way we look at it, every child in Mali is raised trilingually, and the result is varying degrees of competence in each of the three languages.

Numerous studies are available on a variety of different topics relating to third language acquisition in a classroom context where the language is a subject rather than the school medium and where the pedagogical philosophy dictates a communicative approach to language teaching. More often than not, the subjects under examination are bilinguals acquiring their first foreign language as a school subject, or monolinguals learning a second foreign language. The learners tend to be older children and young adults from linguistic majorities or recognised regional linguistic minorities such as the Swedes in Finland, Frisians in the Netherlands or the Basques and Catalans in Spain. Invariably, the third language is English, because it tends to be the first foreign language offered by schools. The research topics that have been pursued concern a broad range of issues, for instance learning strategies, instructional conditions and teaching methods, the teaching of particular skills such as reading or writing, learners' attitudes and motivation, learning outcomes and cross-linguistic influences found in learner output. Third language acquisition is similar to second language acquisition in many ways; however, there are also significant differences, because the learner already has language learning experience and possesses linguistic knowledge of two different codes – which may interact with the third or be used as a kind of default code for items not available in the new L_3. Also, the general effect of bilingualism on cognition is likely to influence third language acquisition in the case of regular bilinguals, who are said to have an advantage over monolingual learners (Cenoz 2003a, 2003b).

According to studies of Russian first and second generation immigrants in Israel, learners acquire English not only as a school subject but also as a medium of instruction and learning, especially at the higher level of education such as university (Aronin and Toubkin 2002). Learners realise that the language they are studying is an indispensable tool for further study and career purposes, and this immediacy has implications beyond the range of language they have to learn, as it is likely to affect their motivation and attitude (Stavans and Goldzweig 2009). Also different from the studies mentioned in the preceding paragraph is the work undertaken with the children of recent immigrants to bilingual Canada, in which the focus has frequently been not so much on linguistic aspects but rather on learning conditions (e.g. Cummins 2001), on what the acquisition of a further language means to young people and on how they react to the language (or languages) of mainstream society or their immigrant community (e.g. Lamarre 2003).

An enduring research topic concerns the 'age factor', i.e. finding out whether there is an optimum age for introducing a third language. Some research in bilingual contexts seems to suggest that older primary children – rather than the very young ones or young adolescents – are more successful L_3 learners, but this cannot be taken as a general truth. Language learning is influenced by a variety of psychological, social and educational factors that interact in complex ways. These factors are dynamic in that attitudes and motivation change over time and in response to what is taught, the methods employed and the personality of the teacher. It is therefore quite likely that, depending on the linguistic, social and educational contexts of particular education systems, different optimal ages and various conditions of acquisition and perseverance in the introduction of a third language can be identified (Bialystok and Shapero 2005).

5.6 CONCLUSION

Individual multilingualism can be seen to be a very diverse phenomenon. For adults and children alike, there are different ways of becoming multilingual. Here we list some of the most salient issues discussed regarding the development, competence, processing and maintenance of individual multilingualism:

- Language use is determined by a range of factors relating to why, where, how and with whom one is communicating. With regard to acquisition, language mixing is commonly employed to fill linguistic gaps in the child's still incomplete linguistic repertoire. Mixing also contributes to efficient communication in interactions among multilinguals. When talking to other multilinguals, trilingual children code-switch, as do adults, although they may also use this strategy for other reasons and purposes.
- Multilingualism is dynamic. It changes in the course of one's life depending on one's linguistic needs and opportunities and

on social and personal circumstances. The complementarity principle applies to multilingualism as well as to bilingualism, and it explains why multilinguals might not always have equal linguistic competence in each of their languages and why one should not assess their linguistic competence in terms of their knowledge of each individual language.

- The establishment of a third language through schooling may be highly varied in terms of sociolinguistic context, amount of exposure to the L_3 and attendant pedagogical considerations. The third language may be one that is spoken in the wider community or be limited just to the school environment.
- There is no evidence to suggest that the processes involved in second and third language acquisition are substantially different; but their operations may become more complex because of the number of different systems involved.
- As is the case with all human learning, the interplay of many different social, psychological, maturational and emotional factors is just too intricate to allow individual elements to be isolated, clearly delimited and deemed of particular significance vis-à-vis the others.
- Our understanding of multiple language acquisition and development is still in need of a good deal of empirical and systematic research.

6 Multilingual language competence and use

D'you know what, 'te' is a letter in German and it's a word in Spanish. That's funny.

Luis (6 years, incipient trilingual)

6.1 INTRODUCTION

We have argued earlier that individual multilingualism is a very diverse phenomenon. Adults and children have different ways of becoming multilingual and developing multilingual competence. At the same time, multilingual language use – which, on the one hand is the outcome of multilingual competence and on the other is the driving force that refines this competence – is determined by a range of factors relating to why, where, how, about what and with whom one is communicating. We have thus concluded that different types of multilinguals and various ways of developing or acquiring multilingualism provide a range of ways to define and classify multilingual individuals. Such a classification is a rather complex task because multilingualism is dynamic – and not only at its inception, since it changes across the multilinguals' lifespan depending on linguistic needs and opportunities within social and personal contexts. In the previous chapter we laid out the general issue of who is regarded as multilingual, how children become trilingual, the different research perspectives taken in particular studies concerning the development of trilingualism in infancy, and how formal education can generate trilingualism. Unlike the general concepts and ideas underlying Chapter 5, in this chapter we delve into more specific matters concerning the question: *how* do trilinguals do it (acquire and use three languages)? How can we explain it? What is the evidence we have? Knowledge of the processing and use of languages in trilinguals provides a window to understanding language processing in general and the limits of cognitive capacities where language load is concerned.

156

The multilingual's lifelong use of different languages and the pattern of mixing or switching between these can be taken as illustrative evidence to distinguish the various types of language behaviour and linguistic competence that are different from monolingual output.

The dynamic nature of multilingualism is best accounted for by the complementarity principle, according to which the languages available to the multilingual are used for different purposes, in different domains of life, with different people, to discuss different topics. New interlocutors, interlocutionary acts and linguistic systems require constant restructuring of language constellations, often resulting in the stronger language taking over the weaker one. Assessing multilingual competence as consisting of a 'strong', 'weak' or 'balanced' language repertoire is a complex task that requires caution. To this end, assessing multilingual competence aims at outlining overall language competence rather than specific knowledge in each individual language.

The language constellations and underlying forces are ruled by individual as well as societal processes. These, in turn, have an impact on acquisition or learning of the languages and the resulting linguistic competence, leading to differences in the multilingual competence of children and adults. For instance, a second or a third language gained through formal education usually depends on sociolinguistic context, amount of exposure to the new language, the influence that the L_1/L_2 exerts on the language(s) acquired and additional pedagogical considerations.

How can we measure the different types of multilingualism? Measures that try to account for an ultimate native-like proficiency in all the languages assume that the multilingual is the sum total of the native-like monolingual competence in each language. The problem with such measures is that comparing the performance of a multilingual to that of a monolingual only tells us 'how monolingual' that multilingual can be. It does not tell us anything about 'how multilingual' the individual is. On the other hand, measures that assess performance according to language use might be indicative of a different ability, namely one which does not include multilingual or alternative communication strategies. Measures of multilingualism are usually driven by educational, political and economic forces rather than socio-psycholinguistic ones. Such tools, especially within the formal educational system, often consist of language tests construed according to monolingual paradigms of the language structure. In fact, the so-called measurements of multilingualism follow a binary scale of 'correct' or 'incorrect' according to monolingual language standards.

Thus, the multilingual is assessed as two monolinguals rather than as a multilingual.

Some theorists conceptualise bilingualism as a 'spectrum or continuum' from the relatively monolingual to the highly proficient bilingual speaker who functions at high levels in both languages (Garland 2007; Hornberger 2002). One of the pioneer proposals for such models had its roots in Grosjean's (1997, 2008) BIMOLA (Bilingual Model of Lexical Access) model. In this model, the bilingual continuum expands from 'more' to 'less' monolingual (or bilingual). There are three modes establishing the relationship between the two languages and the need that arises out of the situation of using them. The model covers psycholinguistically and sociolinguistically motivated needs, providing 'gradability' and 'calibration' of language competence and use. Its suitability will be considered further in subsequent sections in this chapter.

In what follows in this chapter we first offer an account of multilingual competence, paying special attention to what constitutes such competence by reference to what is known about monolingual and bilingual competence. It should be noted that our use of the term 'individual multilingualism' is based on studies on trilingualism, because of the scarcity of studies on individuals acquiring more than three languages. We then present an account of multilingual language use at the individual level borne out of multilingual competence, using models of multilingual processing. Finally, the intersections between languages, competence, and processing will be illustrated by examining multilingual productions involving language alternation or code-switching.

6.2   MULTILINGUAL COMPETENCE

It has been said previously that the term 'multilingualism' encodes a wide range of meanings. These meanings were discussed in the work of scholars such as Haugen, who included multilingualism under bilingualism and suggested that the term 'bilingual' includes plurilingual and polyglot (Haugen 1956: 9). In contrast, in more recent research looking beyond the study of two languages, bilingualism is treated as a variant of multilingualism (Haarmann 1980: 13; Herdina and Jessner 2002: 52) and multilingualism is used exclusively to refer to the learning of more than two languages (e.g. Hufeisen 1998). This conception of multilingualism includes any kind of language acquisition resulting from the number of languages involved

4

4

4

4

4

4

4

4

4

4

4

4

4

4

4

in multilingual development and use (Jessner 2008). This approach does not allow for the use of the terms 'bilingualism' and 'multilingualism' as synonymous.

The meaning of multilingualism adopted for our purposes in this section focuses on the knowledge and use of more than two languages. On this basis, we discuss multilingual processing as a unique phenomenon that to some extent is different from monolingual processing. The dynamic nature of multilingualism, which involves more than one or two linguistic systems, is affected not only by changes within the single language system but also by the interaction of the systems and by the cognitive processing resulting in interactions between and across the systems. In this sense, multilingualism, unlike monolingualism, changes in the course of time with regard to language proficiency, language dominance and language competence in the multilingual's repertoire.

The view that multilingualism is an extended version of bilingualism has recently been challenged. In parallel, those who are convinced that bilingualism differs from trilingualism have been supported by scholars who claim that second language acquisition (SLA) is different from third language acquisition (TLA) in various respects (Cenoz and Jessner 2000; Cenoz *et al.* 2001, 2003; Herdina and Jessner 2002; Flynn *et al.* 2004; Hoffmann 2001a; Hoffmann and Stavans 2007). These studies share the view of the development of a third language consecutively to the development of the first or second language. The question of when a person can be considered multilingual has been pivotal in much of the recent TLA research, in studies that provide incipient steps away from the traditional monolingual-based view, although multilingualism is still considered exceptional and its development often seen in terms of the competence in each of the individual languages. In TLA research, the interplay within and across the three systems is sometimes considered as unintended or even undesirable language behaviour, reflecting poor language competence in need of improvement.

According to the *Common European Framework of Reference for Languages*: 'Plurilingual and pluricultural competence refers to the ability to use languages for the purposes of communication and to take part in intercultural interaction, where a person, viewed as a social agent, has proficiency of varying degrees in several languages and experience of several cultures. This is not seen as the superposition or juxtaposition of distinct competences, but rather as the existence of a complex or even composite competence on which the user may draw' (European Language Portfolio (ELP) 2001, Council of Europe, English version: 168).

One feature that commonly characterises plurilingual and pluricultural competence is its unbalanced nature, consisting of either: (a) proficiency that varies according to the language; (b) language ability that differs from one language to another; or (c) a pluricultural profile that differs from the plurilingual profile. This is also the reason for the imbalance in the *strategies* used in carrying out *tasks* that redefine or reshape the linguistic message according to the resources available to the speaker as well as his/her perception of the interlocutor's resources, depending on the language or language combinations employed.

Another feature that is typical of plurilingual and pluricultural competence is that it is not the result of a simple addition of two (or more) monolingual competences in several languages. It permits combinations and alternations of different kinds. It is possible to switch codes during a message and to resort to bilingual forms of speech. A single, richer repertoire of language varieties and available options thus allows choices based on this interlinguistic variation. This combinatorial ability leads to: (a) a complex exploitation of pre-existing sociolinguistic and pragmatic components in communicative competence; (b) a better perception of what is general and what is specific in the different linguistic repertoires; and (c) the need to refine knowledge of how to learn and the ability to form relations (i.e. construct a linguistic and cultural identity incorporating a diversified experience of otherness) and to deal with new language-driven social situations.

A third feature that is often attributed to plurilingual and pluricultural competence and derives from the above mentioned (imbalance and alternation) is its incomplete form or *partial competence. Partial competence* in a particular language does not mean being satisfied with a limited mastery of a language but, rather, seeing this mastery, imperfect and dynamic, as part of an evolving multiple plurilingual competence. This 'partial' competence is at the same time a *functional* competence with respect to specific communicative objectives that are propelled by *language activities* shaped by a particular *domain* and specific *tasks*. The concept of partial competence has to be reframed as part of a plurilingual competence that encompasses it and qualifies the speaker of a given language in accordance with the language activities and language use in certain contexts.

We have previously discussed the differences and similarities between bilingualism and plurilingualism. Bilingualism is ordinarily understood as the bilingualism of any individual who, as a result of various circumstances (mixed marriage, travel, migration, language policies of the region of residence), develops the ability to communicate in more than one language in order to achieve his or her daily communication needs. The term 'bilingual' has been used to describe the individual as a speaker of at least two languages, as well as institutions and societies in a wider geopolitical space; it embeds dichotomous categorisations (Mackay 1978), resulting in unclear divisions and a focus on certain aspects of language-contact phenomena. It is evaluated through competence in the languages as ranging from one extreme of native-speaker fluency in two linguistic codes ('the native-like control of two languages', Bloomfield 1935), through possessing a minimum competence in at least one of the four language competences, i.e. comprehension, speaking, writing and reading (McNamara 1967), to the more holistic view proposed by Grosjean (1982, 2010) as dual language usage in daily communication. Plurilingual competence was formerly often equated with semilingualism in one or all languages, but this has been proved to be fallacious: 'If only one of the speaker's two languages is inadequate by monoglot norms, there is no case for semilingualism. If both languages are marked as different from monoglot norms, there is still no case for semilingualism, since such norms might be irrelevant in a society where everyone shares the bilingually-marked speech patterns' (Baetens Beardsmore 1986: 14).

Most plurilingual individuals use their languages for specific and differentiated communication needs, as it is often unnecessary for a person to develop equivalent competences in each. This results in *different competences* in each language, which are neither equal nor totally similar to those of monolinguals. The plurilingual competences fulfil a range of different *functions* that depend on different communication needs. Partial knowledge in one language should not be confused with lack of (or reduced) competence. A distinction should also be made between mastery of the language and knowledge about language that can be acquired through the medium of one or the other language and can be transferred from one to the other. Moreover, learning a new language does not imply starting anew but reorganising linguistic and language knowledge through different linguistic tools. The competences of a plurilingual individual are complementary, because the use of one component of the repertoire or another (or their alternate use) is a matter of strategic development of communicative competence. A typical feature of plurilingual competence is the unevenness of language and linguistic knowledge, which is characterised by simultaneously complex and dynamic occurrences, rendering original language production phenomena unique to plurilingual speech. The linguistic assets of the plurilingual individual operate according to the situation and the interlocutor. In some situations, plurilinguals may choose to conceal a language repertoire, while in others they may choose to activate all languages, moving from one to another, in order to select their interlocutors and include or exclude them from the conversation, change the level of discourse, speak more forcefully, quote other participants or mark a distance from their own words.

The study of multilingual competence can be challenging in the collection and interpretation of data, and also because of the absence of explanatory theoretical models. The rewarding side, however, is that multilingualism provides a platform for fascinating glimpses into the human capacity for processing language and the linguistic resourcefulness of multilingual individuals. The study of bilingual development and use, undertaken from a variety of linguistic, psycholinguistic, sociolinguistic and pragmatic perspectives, has provided ample evidence of language processing, formal preferences and discourse strategies in speakers of two languages. We can expect linguistic versatility to be even more enhanced when there are three languages in constant contact and use.

The linguistic adjustments bilingual and trilingual speakers make according to new situations, environments and perceptions does not mean that their overall communicative competence is affected. Rather, a redistribution of functions is assigned to each of their languages, and changes in the proficiency in one or two of their languages may be the result of increased or reduced use of the languages concerned. Active bilinguals and trilinguals can become passive ones, or vice versa, particularly those individuals at either end of the age range. Yet, in spite of these changes, they remain communicatively competent speaker-hearers within their linguistic environment. Dominance in one language may not hinder communicative competence in the others: the speaker's output might be less perfect (by absolute standards) but communicative nonetheless. Grosjean 2001 proposes that the bilingual's speech modes are 'end points' on a scale. A bilingual may move from a monolingual speech mode when talking to a monolingual person, where she/he uses one language only, while the other remains deactivated, and then change along the continuum to the bilingual speech mode, where use is made of both languages when speaking to another bilingual, in the form of frequent switching and borrowing.

The notion of speech modes also applies to trilinguals. Their three speech modes, monolingual, bilingual and trilingual, would then, at least in theory, have seven different constellations as compared with the monolingual's one and the bilingual's four: the monolingual modes of languages A, B and C; the bilingual modes A + B, A + C and B + C; and one trilingual mode involving all three languages A + B + C. That is, 3 + 3 + 1 = 7. Available research does not mention the use of seven different speech modes, and it is reasonable to suspect that trilinguals rarely make use of all seven. Our own observations indicate that trilinguals tend to have two languages activated at any one time, rather than all three. Apart from some cases of borrowing, the majority of trilingual output involves interplay of two languages rather than three. Yet there are studies that report on trilingual mixing at morphosyntactic levels and at the phrasal levels that indicate the use of particles and structures from three typologically divergent languages such as Hebrew, Spanish and English (e.g. Stavans 1990; Stavans and Swisher 2006; Stavans and Hoffmann 2007; Stavans and Muchnik 2007); Chinese, French and English (Wang 2008); Basque, Spanish and English (Barnes 2006); German, English and Farsi (Kazzazi 2010); and Croatian, English and German (Ivir-Ashworth 2011).

The complex and different features involved in multilingualism encompass competence, cognitive processes, awareness and complementarity. Understanding how these features come together is paramount to appreciating the differences between monolingual, bilingual and trilingual competence. The understanding of these features sheds light not only on what the multilingual knows and can do (i.e. their competence), but also on how multilinguals 'do multilingualism' (i.e. the processing).

6.3 EXPLAINING MULTILINGUAL COMPETENCE: MULTILINGUAL LANGUAGE PROCESSING MODELS

For multilinguals, the habitual use of several languages as opposed to only one makes both a quantitative and a qualitative difference. When trilinguals communicate they have to make decisions as to which language to use, what are the appropriate linguistic means to employ and whether switching between languages is a communicative option or not. This section provides an overview of theoretical models – mostly from the psycholinguistic perspective – that account for what it takes to juggle between and within the multilingual's linguistic systems. The main concern in this section is to look at models that explain the similarities and differences between monolingual, bilingual and trilingual processing while keeping as a central motif the question: how do multilinguals do it?

6.3.1 From monolingual to bilingual models ▬▬▬▬▬▬

One of the most influential models of language processing, which has
had a considerable effect on the outlook on multilingual processing,
was proposed by Levelt (1989) as a monolingual speech processing
model. Inspired by other cognitive processing models within the con-
nectionism paradigm, Levelt proposed an autonomous and stage-based
model consisting of three information stores: the conceptualiser, the
formulator and the articulator. The conceptualiser is responsible for
turning communicative intentions into preverbal messages that the
speaker can access through extralinguistic knowledge in individual
communicative situations. The formulator encodes the utterance,
and the articulator churns out speech. This account of monolingual
processing falls short of explaining bilingual production, in which a
wide array of possibilities are provided by each language and its linguistic system. De Bot (1992), on the basis of Levelt's model, describes
how selection and control works in bilingual processing by means of
a 'monitoring' function. This function shows the state of activation
of various languages and acts as a monitoring device between the
intended language and the actual language used. This adaptation to
bilingual processing deals with three issues that are unique to bilingualism and trilingualism: language separation and code-switching;
language assignment; and cross-language differences in lexicalisation
patterns.

Similarly, Perecman (1989) sees language processing as taking
place on different levels: a prelinguistic conceptual level, which is a
property of the human mind that is common to both the bilingual's
languages and independent of each language, and then the functionally different semantic-lexical level. In monolinguals, the conceptual
system feeds into only one linguistic system, and the processing routines from the conceptual down to the phonological forms are auto-
mated. In bilinguals, on the other hand, there are two options for
encoding, drawn from two different linguistic systems. Perecman's
suggestion is that the processing routines are less automatic for the
bilingual, and that the distinction between levels of representation
will be more marked.

Bates and MacWhinney (1989) regard language processing as a series of competitions between lexical items, phonological forms and
syntactic patterns. Competition Model studies suggest that learning of
language forms is based on the accurate recording of frequent exposure to words and patterns in different contexts. If a pattern is reliably
present in the adult input, the child picks it up quickly. Rare and
unreliable patterns are learned late and are relatively weaker, even

in adults. According to MacWhinney (2001, 2007), this model of language learning should account not only for the acquisition of a first language by children but also for the learning of second languages or the development of bilingualism both in adults and children.

For a Spanish–English bilingual, the Spanish word *libro* competes with the English word 'book'. A Spanish–English bilingual child, then, will not have a single clear way of deciding when to use *libro* and when to use 'book'. However, from exposure to the two languages, the bilingual child receives reliable cues that help separate the two languages. Hence, exposure to these cues enables the child to learn to use *libro* when speaking to a Spanish speaker and 'book' when speaking to an English speaker. When these two parallel forms compete, the one that receives additional input from the activation of relevant supporting contextual cues will win. However, reliance on contextual cues to resolve a competition in the choice between two words may be problematic, because contexts are not fully transparent. For example, a child exposed to Spanish from one parent and English from the other might also be exposed to visitors who will shift back and forth between languages. So interlocutionary contextual cues may be misleading, and the child's further control of the competition must also rely on language-internal resonance. Consider the case in which the child has activated English forms such as 'park' and 'go' to produce an utterance such as 'We are going to the park.' These forms co-activate each other through so-called resonant interactive activation. As active forms within English they activate other forms within English, and the entire English lexicon becomes resonantly activated, while the Spanish lexicon remains available but deactivated.

The case is slightly different when it comes to adults or adolescents who are L_2 learners. Figure 6.1 is an illustration of the trajectory of an L_2 word acquisition.

In Figure 6.1 Case A, the new L_2 form begins as a word association dependent on the L_1 form (e.g. the learner of Spanish receives the lexical cue *rana*, which is associated with the word 'frog' in the L_1 English), and is then associated with the concept. In Figure 6.1 Case B, as the L_2 form gains in strength, it forms new direct links to meaning, shown by the broken line from *rana* to the concept of the frog (depicted by the picture), and the translation route from L_1 to L_2 becomes stronger: the line between *rana* and 'frog' thickens, indicating that this association is strengthened. Also, the routing of the L_2 through the L_1 has established a more solid dependency from the word *rana*, through 'frog', to the concept depicted by the picture. Then, as L_2 resonance grows, the asymmetry between the two languages decreases. However, as

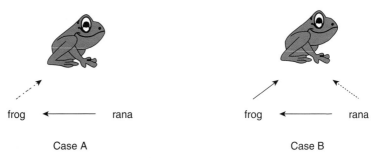

Figure 6.1 Trajectory of L_2 word acquisition

L_1 becomes more deeply entrenched and L_2 remains dependent on L_1, the strength of L_2 links to concepts will never 'catch up' with the strength of L_1 links. As a result, L_2 will remain partially 'parasitic' or dependent.

The Competition Model of bilingualism sets the two language systems one against the other and explains the development of bilinguals in terms of the creation of competition between the two language systems on every level of analysis. This then leads to the conclusion that children with less balanced or later L_2 input will perform like native speakers on many tasks but will show residual asymmetries, suggesting that L_2 is still partially dependent on L_1. Adult second language learners might recruit non-language means to promote L_2 resonance in their attempts to control the effects of L_1 entrenchment.

Much of the scholarly work on multilingual processing draws on concepts and theories developed and described primarily with regard to monolingual processing, with the necessary data-driven adaptations into bilingual processing theories. The outcome of such adaptations has resulted in explanatory bilingual processing models: some of them are outlined in the following section.

6.3.2 Bilingual models

Green (1986) proposed a model of bilingual processing consisting of two coexisting independent monolingual systems that are activated or inhibited. The activation of the linguistic system of the bilingual does not switch one of the languages on or off but operates different degrees of activation. For example, one of the bilingual's languages may be more active in a given speech situation involving the speech processor, while the other may be less active or dormant in long-term memory and thus not be involved at all with the speech processor. This concept suggests coexistence between the languages rather than an absolute separation, resulting in synchronised language activation. Similarly, the language mode hypothesis (BIMOLA) proposed by Grosjean (1998, 2001) describes the language mode as a 'state of activation of the bilingual's languages and language processing mechanisms at a certain point in time' (Grosjean 2001: 2). Depending on the language mode, the speaker chooses a base language (for a bilingual situation) or base languages (in the trilingual case) to be activated depending on factors such as the participants' language-mixing habits, the usual mode of interaction, the presence of monolinguals, the degree of formality and the form and content of the message uttered or listened to, as well as the socioeconomic status of the communication partners. The model constitutes two networks that are set up with both independent (monolingual mode) and interconnected (bilingual mode) features that result from language contact. Each network operates at three linguistic levels: features (i.e. 'shared' system of sounds from all the languages in question), phonemes, and words (i.e. 'separate' repertoires for each language), activating or inhibiting features at all three levels. Thus, a strong activation involves mostly the monolingual mode for one language and weak activation involves the bilingual mode for both languages. There are three states of activation/inhibition between a base language and another language: 'the monolingual mode', 'the intermediate mode' and 'the bilingual mode'.

Although the BIMOLA model is an interactive model of bilingual processing, it is also influenced by socio-psychological needs, as is the M-factor (Multilingualism factor) model first proposed by Hufeisen (1998), which stipulates five initial stages of language acquisition with regard to the bilingual's two languages. Each of these stages is controlled by one of five factors: (i) the neurophysiological factor, i.e. the core mechanisms and requirements for general language learning, production and reception; (ii) the learner-external factors, i.e. the sociocultural and socioeconomic background, learning experience and traditions, and learner's exposure to the language; (iii) the emotional factors, i.e. anxiety, motivation and attitude toward the languages and their learning; (iv) the cognitive factors, i.e. language awareness, linguistic and metalinguistic awareness, learning awareness, the implementation and exercise of learning strategies and techniques; and (v) the linguistic factors as included in the learner's L_1s. Therefore, bilingual processing is the amalgamated 'factor-complex' that is unique to each bilingual. This factor-complex may consist of some predominant factors that have a strong impact on the language

learning situation and other non-dominant factors that may become
irrelevant for the individual learning process.

Metalinguistic awareness has just been mentioned in relation to
the competence of multilinguals. Metalinguistic awareness also has
an important role in bilingual processing because it refers to: (a)
tasks, e.g. making grammaticality judgements or repairs; (b) skills,
e.g. the ability to focus on language forms; and (c) levels of awareness,
e.g. when a learner is aware of the forms and functions of the language being manipulated. Bialystok defines metalinguistic awareness
as involving all three aspects and proposes to apply it to language
development in bilingual children, assuming that language processing can be described in terms of the 'analysis of linguistic knowledge' that enables mental representations to become more explicit
and structured; and the 'control of linguistic processing' (Bialystok
1991). Bialystok's experiments have shown that the abilities of monolinguals and bilinguals differ significantly (the latter outperform the
former) in problem-solving tasks in three different language domains:
metalinguistic awareness, resolving conflicts and exercising greater
control of executive function. She claims that 'the development of
attention control that is part of executive functioning and is used
to selectively attend to target cues in conflicting situations is more
advanced in bilinguals than in comparable monolinguals' (Bialystok
et al. 2008: 91).

Explaining bilingual development in simple terms by comparing
it to monolingual development has not been productive. The complexity is such that comparing the development of bilingualism both
in adults and children across two individuals who are bilingual in
the same languages, or across individual bilinguals in different languages, has produced quite a few experimental studies and theoretical
explanatory models within a dichotomous (i.e. with two dimensions)
framework. The nature and impact of bilingualism as dichotomous
must be further explored, because it may also shed some light on the
major processing differences between bilinguals and trilinguals.

6.3.3 The binary notion

In line with the inhibition and activation control of the languages
discussed so far, the study of bilingual development assumes that if
one language is used the other is not, thus creating a binary choice
between the available systems. For instance, Bialystok (1999) argues
that treating bilingualism as a single independent variable and cognitive flexibility, metalinguistic development or acquisition of literacy
as dependent variables leads us to conclude that speaking more than

one language is an objective, identifiable and binary notion. Although one can think of variables such as gender, age, or attending school or not as binary, valid and reliable independent variables, being bilingual cannot be classified in such an easy way. Bilingualism, and by extension trilingualism, are not discrete states of affairs, they are relative notions.

There are many reasons for this. First, the assumption that languages are homogeneous is rather weak. While there may be universals in natural languages, there are also radical differences across the structures and the functions of any languages. For instance, word order in English strictly imposes meaning, while in Spanish word order is more flexible.

When a young bilingual learns the word 'dog' in English and *perro* or *perra* in Spanish, gender distinction is more immediate in Spanish than in English. In consequence, the word 'bitch' for a female dog in English is likely to be acquired much later. The structural or formal 'penetrability' to and from one language and the other is not the only reason why bilingualism cannot be dichotomous. The users of the languages, the contexts and content of the messages and the purpose of delivery are some additional layers of complexity that seem to be in conflict with a dichotomous view.

There are many factors that affect bilingual acquisition, notably the parents' language, their level of education, reasons for exposing their children to more than one language, the degree of support from both inside the family and the wider community, and the literacy environment that the child is exposed to. It is easy to see that bilingualism is not a linear construct but a complex one with multiple dimensions and shades that yield overlapping possibilities, as illustrated in Figure 6.2.

The multiplicity of variables influencing bilingualism makes it impossible to establish a simplistic dichotomous choice regarding bilingualism. In any system binary choices are brute mechanisms (Bialystok 1991). Yet there are studies (Stavans 1990; Stavans and Swisher 2006; Kazzazi 2011) that show that at the initial stages of multilingual development, when children are sorting out the multiple language inputs, they resort to some kind of binary classification. Binary choices are brute mechanisms in the sense that they seem to work only at a very superficial level or at the final stages of production, rather than at the multiple-layered processing paths that lead to such productions. That is to say, binary choices reduce us to stating that such and such production is language A or B if – and only if – we consider the phonological, morphological, syntactic

Figure 6.2 Continuum of bilingualism

or semantic variants of each language. This fact poses further difficulties, especially when the final product originates in a similar language typology and thus the starting point may not have been genu-
inely binary to begin with.

If bilinguals do not make binary choices, this would presumably
also be true for trilinguals. If, in fact, bilinguals juggle two linguistic systems and these have an effect on human cognition, then do
trilinguals act like bilinguals or are they different? There is a growing
number of studies that claim that trilingualism is not bilingualism
with one more language added on (Stavans 1990; Stavans and Swisher
2006; Montanari 2013; Hoffmann 2001a; Barnes 2006; Kazzazi 2011).
Trilingualism is far from being dichotomous, taking into consideration that three languages come together, different features converge
or diverge, both structurally and functionally, and often the languages
in question are typologically different.

6.3.4 Trilingual models

Several scholars, among them Grosjean, have been working in the
past two decades or so on developing suitable models to explain multilingual and, more specifically, trilingual processing, taking a holistic
view which shares the basic premise of regarding the bilingual as a
competent – or multicompetent – yet specific speaker/hearer whose
mind (and thus processing of languages) is not the same as that of the
monolingual.

Clyne (2003) presented a model of plurilingual processing (i.e. one
that goes beyond bilingualism) that integrates linguistic and social-
psychological dimensions such as the speaker's multiple identities.
In an attempt to answer how a plurilingual utilises the resources of
his/her languages when alternating between them and how the activation of each language is controlled, he offers a model that consists
of three options: separation, adaptation and mixing. Each of these
options involves processing strategies of convergence, facilitation,
transference and transversion ('crossing over') from one language
towards the other. While this model draws on connectionist models
such as Levelt's and De Bot's, Clyne addresses novel language-contact

issues integrating linguistic features from two languages with consciousness and intentionality. Clyne's proposals are discussed further in Section 6.4.

Herdina and Jessner (2002) propose a multilingual processing model following this holistic view, and they emphasise the dynamics of multilingualism as a necessary condition. This model was inspired by the dynamic systems theory (DST) developed in the exact sciences, which explains interactions between the subsystems of a complex system as non-additive ways of influencing overall and individual development. Herdina and Jessner adapt this scientific framework to multilingual analysis and coin their model DMM – Dynamic Model of Multilingualism – to explain the development of a changing multilingual system within a non-linear yet reversible complex one. The dynamic nature of this model generates great variability in processing, since the model is highly influenced by social, psycholinguistic and individual factors, apart from the different forms of contexts in which language occurs. At its core, the DMM model assumes that each of the multilingual's language systems ($LS_1/LS_2/LS_3/LS_4$ etc.) is an open system affected by psychological and social factors. These systems are interdependent and stable because they are anchored in the language maintenance, communicative needs and language choice of the multilingual speaker. The model explains multilingual proficiency as the outcome of the dynamic interaction between the various psycholinguistic systems LS_1, LS_2, LS_3, LS_n, cross-linguistic interaction and the multilingualism factor. Combining not only the elements but also the different degrees within each element produces a dynamic multilingual processing model where seemingly identical phenomena of transfer can lead to different multilingual productions by the same speaker. Hence, the DMM provides a conceptual framework that explains that multilingual systems include certain components which monolingual systems lack; and even those components that the multilingual system shares with the monolingual system have a different significance within the multilingual system.

Another model explaining processing in multilinguals is the multilinguality model proposed by Aronin and Ó Laoire (2004). This model draws on Hamers and Blanc's (1989) distinction between bilingualism and bilinguality – the former being a societal phenomenon and the latter an individual one. According to Aronin and Ó Laoire, multilinguality constitutes one of the most defining attributes of the individual; but, unlike Hamers and Blanc, they also distinguish between multilinguality and individual multilingualism: whereas individual multilingualism refers only to the psycholinguistic processes and results of trilingual hearer/speaker productions, multilinguality concerns the ability of the multilingual to communicate in a social and physiological environment with a communicative goal. This model signals a new approach to multilingual processing as influenced mostly by variables external to the individual's cognition.

In summary, following the models of processing for monolingualism and bilingualism described thus far and extrapolating them to trilingualism or multilingualism, the three key issues of activation, inhibition and control should be considered to generate three possible states as a function of the language used at any given moment. Adapting this paradigm to trilingualism, the three languages of the trilingual can be in one of these *activation* states: (i) one selected, one active and one dormant, (ii) one selected and two dormant, or (iii) one selected and two active. The *inhibition* paradigm – the opposite process to activation – in bilinguals has four functions in language processing: (i) to prevent repetition, (ii) reduce interference, (iii) realise language choice and (iv) enable switching. The inhibitory process (i) occurs following the production of a word with the highest activation level: inhibition may reduce this activation level, preventing its repetition and allowing the production of the next word; (ii) is used to suppress irrelevant and interfering distracting information; (iii) applies the inhibitory control model, allowing language choice that enables production in one language while inhibiting the other selected language; and (iv) involves the cooperation of both activation and inhibition; there is switching between languages when the previously spoken language must be inhibited and the previously inhibited language must be activated. The amount of inhibition which is necessary for a language to be suppressed is relative to the speaker's proficiency in that language. For instance, an unbalanced bilingual may exercise more inhibition to suppress the dominant over the weaker language. The *control* paradigm regulates inhibition or activation, monitors the correct selection of intended words and oversees retrieval and fluent errorless production of the intended message. Processing in trilinguals requires – to a greater extent than in bilinguals – that the language systems be highly controlled, as complexity increases according to the number of languages, their structure, typology, usage and availability.

The models surveyed regarding trilingual processing build on those of bilingualism. One of the major questions that is raised, is whether in fact trilingualism involves a different kind of processing. If the answer to this question is yes, then one would have to accept that trilingual processing may be slower than bilingual processing, because

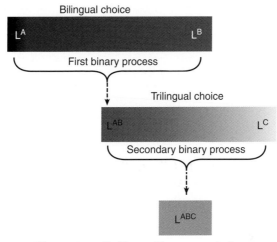

Figure 6.3 Illustration of trilingual language choice

there is an additional step that involves a third language, as illustrated in Figure 6.3.

Following Figure 6.3, the choices drawn from the different language modes will yield, at a first stage, a degree of binary decision between language A and B to render a bilingual production labelled language 'AB', which then will lead to a second degree of binary decision between the bilingual production and the third language, namely language C, to render a trilingual production called language ABC. This would require longer processing time for trilingual productions, which could vary depending on the languages' forms and functions, the user's competence, the interlocutor and the illocutionary setting. Presumably, the more divergent the characteristics of the languages are, the longer it will take the trilingual to process the three languages. However, this is not the case, trilinguals are not slower language producers than bilinguals. The most illustrative trilingual production to examine is one in which alternation between the three linguistic systems yields evidence of both language competence and language processing.

The actual 'intersection' of trilingual production that best captures trilingual processing is evidenced in code-switching. Stavans and Swisher (2006) argue that looking for a suitable analytic framework to explore trilingual switches inevitably takes us to existing explanatory models developed to account for bilingual code-switching. In general, the models provided for analysing language mixing, code-switches or code-mixes from a structural point of view are of limited

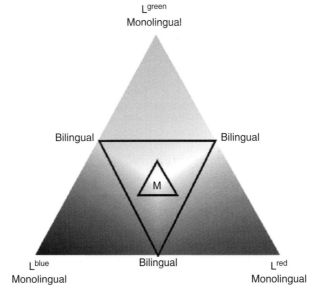

Figure 6.4 A model of multilingual production

validity because they: (a) are based on adult productions, (b) regard bilingual code-switching as a binary system, and (c) often involve languages with a similar typology, rendering a natural convergence of patterns.

Studies of morphosyntactic switches show that they are binary at certain levels of analysis. In conversational interaction, these switches may combine elements of two out of the three languages. Most studies report combinations that involve two languages at the lexical, morphological and sentential levels, but we also find switches at the discursive and pragmatic level that involve all three languages. In the following section we discuss a model of trilingual processing proposed by Stavans (2005) with some examples of trilingual switches.

The model, shown in Figure 6.4, allows a two-dimensional representation illustrating both the origin and confluence of trilingual productions (an additional dimension could be visualised if the diagram showed shades of green, blue and red, instead of different shades of grey). A possible multilingual production might involve a code-switch at the sentence or utterance level that originated at a monolingual point, which then makes its way towards the centre, the 'multilingual' area (marked M), and results in a trilingual switch. A move along the sides of the triangle, the 'bilingual' area, results in a bilingual switch. This illustrative diagram may be viewed as not only multi-layered but also specific for describing, on the one hand, processing, and on the other, competence. Processing can be viewed as the distance and direction away from the monolingual vertex, whereas competence can be considered to be the specific trajectory taken when the different linguistic elements are combined. In the following sections on language mixing and code-switching, a number of examples will illustrate the idea behind this model.

6.4   DEFINING CODE-SWITCHING

Code-switching occurs when speakers alternate between different codes (languages or language varieties) in the course of the same conversation or speech act. It has proved to be a fascinating phenomenon for many. Its study can be approached from a variety of angles and, given the diverse concerns of formal linguists, psycholinguists, sociolinguists, ethnolinguists, philosophers, anthropologists and others, it hardly seems surprising that there is no one generally agreed definition of the term. For example, psycholinguistic perspectives have homed in on the issue of whether syntactic or morphosyntactic constraints on language alternation exist (see Poplack 1980; Sankoff and Poplack 1981; Joshi 1987; Di Sciullo and Williams 1987; Belazi *et al.* 1994; Halmari 1997). A structural focus has been used for the design of production models (Azuma 1991), or as evidence for grammatical theory (MacSwan 2000; Jake *et al.* 2002). Research in the fields of first and second language acquisition has looked at code-switching in terms of its possible relationship with processing and production, so as to gain insights into the cognitive abilities of bilingual speakers and/or language learners. Other second language acquisition researchers look at occurrences of code-switching in classroom and learning practices that involve the use of more than one language (Romaine 1989; Cenoz and Genesee 2001).

  In contrast with the adoption of a syntactic perspective of code-switching (i.e. considering it simply as a product of the grammatical system and not a practice of individual speakers), a *sociocultural* perspective looks at the sociocultural functions and meanings of language use. The study of code-switching from this stance has generated different interpretations and definitions of language alternation and modulation (for a thorough survey, see Nilep 2006). Code-switching has been defined as a unique bilingual speech production when languages or varieties come in contact (Weinreich 1953); as a type of alternation in which two varieties diverge rather than converge (Ferguson 1959; Fishman 1967); and as evidence of social events in terms of participants, setting and topic that 'restrict the selection of linguistic variables' (Gumperz and Hymes 1972: 421). Gumperz (1982: 98) says that 'code-switching signals contextual information equivalent to what in monolingual settings is conveyed through prosody or other syntactic or lexical processes. It generates the presuppositions in terms of which the content of what is said is decoded.' Gumperz's list of code-switching functions inspired many subsequent scholars to refine or propose their own lists of functions (e.g. McClure and McClure 1988; Romaine 1989; Nishimura 1997; Zentella 1997). However, as Auer (1995) reminds us, the functions suggested by such lists are often ill-defined. Code-switching may serve any number of functions in a particular interaction, and a single turn (in the conversation) may have multiple effects. Therefore, any finite list of functions will be more or less arbitrary; consequently, it is preferable to observe actual interaction rather than make theoretical assumptions about the effects of code-switching.

The study of code-switching within sociocultural linguistics may be divided into three main streams. The first is the socio-psychological approach related to Myers-Scotton's markedness model (1993), which states that each language in a multilingual community is associated with particular social roles. In this model, the participant signals understanding of the current situation and, in particular, the relevant role within a context in which, when situations arise where more than one language is involved, speakers may initiate negotiation over relevant social roles.

The second stream concerns the analysis of identity and code choice identified by the observation of behaviour in particular settings. This perspective looks at the place of code-switching, especially in social and historical settings – as, for instance, in Heller's work (1992) and in Rampton's (1995, 1999, 2005) studies on language crossing. In this focus, a type of code-switching behaviour is practised by speakers across boundaries of ethnicity, race or language 'community', typically associated with an ethnic group and used by non-members to accomplish complex functions.

The third view sees code-switching and interaction as grounded in conversational analysis and functional linguistics. The focus here is both on the place of code-switching in the turn and sequence and on the ways that language alternations make broader contextual knowledge relevant to an ongoing discourse. These studies deal with issues such as how code-switching serves to enhance turn selection (Li 1998; Cromdal 2001), soften refusals (Bani-Shoraka 2005; Li 2005), become a resource to accomplish repair (Auer 1995; Sebba and Wooten 1998) or mark responses (Li 1998; Bani-Shoraka 2005). In the same vein are empirical studies on interactional functions that show how switches in language variety make particular elements of situation, speaker identities or background relevant to ongoing talk (e.g. Li 1998, 2005; Gafaranga 2001).

While these studies of code-switching are an integral part of current research, they concern a sociocultural perspective which is slightly different from the one we will describe. Our intention is to look at the phenomenon of code-switching from a socio-psychological and developmental perspective in order to illustrate how its evolution within the individual reflects a unique multilingual ability. One of the most typical linguistic phenomena unique to multilinguals (additional to the ability to produce and comprehend various linguistic systems) is their capacity to combine these systems in a systematic, consistent and non-random manner. This power to draw on their different linguistic systems simultaneously has been the source of controversy regarding multilingual development. There are those who argue that such combinations are evidence for the disadvantage of multilingualism as it results in deficient language productions. Others view such combinations as manifestations of not only the creative aspects of multilingualism, but also the communicative advantage it bestows. The ability to combine linguistic systems is referred to as 'language mixing' – which manifests itself as either code-mixing or code-switching. To gain a better understanding of this multilingual phenomenon, we must first describe how and why multilinguals code-switch or code-mix, and how the code-mixing and code-switching show multilingual processing and competence.

6.5 CODE-SWITCHING AND CODE-MIXING: HOW AND WHY?

The initial definitions of code-switching and code-mixing by Haugen (1956), and later by Gumperz (1982) and Muysken (2000), as the alternate use of two languages have been central to language-contact research for a long time. Largely, the basic definition of code-mixing (CM) refers to the mixing of various linguistic units: morphemes, words, phrases, clauses and sentences, primarily from two participating grammatical systems within a sentence. Code-mixing is *intrasentential* and constrained by grammatical principles, and it may be motivated by socio-psychological factors. Code-switching (CS) concerns the mixing of various linguistic units: words, phrases, clauses and sentences, primarily from two participating grammatical systems across sentence boundaries within a speech event. In other words, CS is *intersentential* and may be subject to discourse principles. It, too, is driven by social and psychological motivations. While this distinction is widely accepted, especially in studies that approach the analysis of these contact phenomena from a structural perspective, the terms have also been used interchangeably. There are some definitions and descriptions that characterise mixes and switches in terms of age, to distinguish between children's and adult's switches and to trace patterns of development.

Poplack (1980) was concerned with the formal structure of switching in bilinguals. She made the initial distinction between code-switching, nonce-borrowing (i.e. ad hoc borrowing), intra- and intersentential switches as being constrained either by the 'equivalent structure constraint' (i.e. the switch can only occur at the boundary where the structure of the two languages is parallel) and/or by the 'free morpheme' constraint (i.e. that a switch can only occur between two free morphemes and cannot occur in combination with a bound morpheme). Since then, there have been studies that show that these constraints are violated in code-switches involving a wide variety of language combinations (Berk-Seligson 1986).

Clyne (1997) looks at both bilingual and trilingual intrasentential switching, and he states that there is no difference between a trilingual and a bilingual switch. A 'trilingual sentence' occurs as a result of the speaker's insertion of an item in language B while uttering a sentence in language A, which in turn may trigger a switch into language C. This view of trilingual code-switching regards the processing of the languages as binary and linear, as described in the previous section, and hence sees the switch as an instantiation of a 'move over', i.e. a shift from the first to the third language via the second one. Clyne also found that, when a third language was involved, the introduction of an item in that language does not produce a switch between the former two languages so long as it is morphologically integrated. Clyne concludes that bilinguals and trilinguals use the same kinds of mechanisms and processes, and that they are more complex when three languages are involved – and that they are also much less likely to occur.

The language use of young trilinguals is often determined by the interactional illocutionary situation (Stavans 1990, 1992). Young trilinguals take their audience into account when making linguistic and non-linguistic choices, and they allow code-switches only when the interlocutor is bi- or trilingual, and not in monolingual interactions. In other words, the trilinguals in this study produced switches between two or three of their languages – depending on the interlocutor – by gauging the '(mono-bi-tri-)lingualism' situation. This ability allows for a variety of possible switching combinations. Nearly 10 per cent of the switches produced by the trilinguals studied constituted elements from three linguistic systems.

In the context of a study of a trilingual child's English–French–Italian conversation with his English-speaking mother, Hoffmann and Widdicombe (1999) propose that the term 'code-switching' can refer to a variety of instances in the child's speech which reflect the use or activation of more than one linguistic system during a single discourse event. They use the term 'coining' for a lexical item borrowed from French and/or Italian and adapted morphologically and/or phonologically to conform to English morphology/phonology. The new coinage would have been incomprehensible to a monolingual English speaker. This study is primarily concerned with formal aspects of code-switching and only marginally with its functional features.

Sometimes the terms code-mixing and code-switching are used as synonyms, to mean intrasentential code-switching. Maschler (1998) defines code-mixing (or a mixed code) as 'using two languages such that a third, new code emerges, in which elements from the two languages are incorporated into a structurally definable pattern' (p. 125). This consideration of code-mixing assumes that, when two code-switched languages generate a third grammaticised code, the outcome has structural characteristics special to that new code.

When characterising code-switching from a functional perspective, the focus is primarily on communicative and pragmatic processes. Linguistic and communicative evidence has been reported in studies of children's switches (Sridhar and Sridhar 1980; Meisel 1994; Vihman 1985; Deuchar and Quay 2000; Döpke 1992) that show no qualitative difference between young children's mixing and adult switching. Other studies have characterised and explained switches in developmental terms, i.e. in terms of emerging competence during the process of acquisition (de Houwer 1990, 2007; Lanza 1997a, b; Stavans 1990, 1992, 2003).

In adult bilinguals, code-switching is mostly associated with the sociolinguistic function of communication, demonstrated as both a formal and functional manipulation of the two languages. This 'unique bilingual' phenomenon is often a result of conversational intentions such as empathy with interlocutors or inclusion in a speech community. Code-switching is attributed to the situation, interlocutor and topic of conversation in such a way that there may be certain topics

that two bilinguals sharing both languages might feel more comfort-
able discussing in one of their languages. For example, two Spanish–
English bilingual linguists trained in English may be more inclined to
discuss linguistics in English but to talk about travelling in Spanish.
When such switches occur, they are systematic, often calculated and
planned language productions that involve various features of the
languages, from the word to the utterance. At the utterance level the
code-switch is more prevalent, for it is at the extended discourse that
the bilingual manipulates his/her languages to suit the interlocutor,
the illocution and the social interaction to sculpt identity, power, ethnicity and other social values. For example, Clyne (2003) reports on a
German–English bilingual in Australia who notices the identity of the
interlocutor and veers to another language, yielding code-switches
that express a different identity by labelling a 'we' code and a 'they'
code (the code-switch is written in italics):

> Manchmal wenn ich deutschsprachige Bekannte treffe, spreche ich
> deutsch, *otherwise I speak only English.*
> Sometimes when I meet German-speaking friends, I speak German,
> *otherwise I speak only English.*
>
> (Clyne 2003; Example 4, p. 160)

Similarly, Clyne shows how the topic brings about a switch in the conversation to delineate the speaker's past life from the present one:

> Ich wollte anfangs bloß zwei Jahre bleiben. Jetzt bin ich schon acht
> Jahre hier. *I think that speaks for itself.*
> I originally only wanted to stay for two years. Now I have been here
> for eight years. *I think that speaks for itself.*
>
> (Clyne 2003, Example 5, p. 160–61)

For infant code-switching, Lanza (1997a, b) demonstrates how, depending on the context of language use, children exhibit pragmatic competence by mixing languages appropriately or by keeping them separate.
She argues that at as early as two years of age, children's code-switching is a specific linguistic behaviour in their developing pragmatic
bilingual competence.

A robust body of studies on adults' code-switching, as well as fewer
studies on children's code-switching, combine qualitative and quantitative, formal and functional explanations of language-contact phenomena. While switching is often associated with a sociolinguistically driven, adult-related, and ethno-communicative focus, mixing
has been described as being developmentally driven, infant/child
related and psycholinguistically motivated. Some argue that actual
mixing patterns of infant bilinguals are formally different from the
code-switching patterns of adult bilinguals; while others claim that

the mixing of very young bilinguals may be the by-product of the young children's linguistic ability (Genesee 1989; Sridhar and Sridhar 1980; King and Fogle 2006; Auer 1998). The definitions differ depending on the unit of analysis, which may be different in terms of the competence or language processing mechanisms and can be drawn purely on sociolinguistic grounds. Nonetheless, code-switching crosses domains (societal, communitarian, individual and relating to language typologies), linguistic elements (phonology, morphology, syntax and semantics) and speaker's competence (as shaped by age, gender, development, education etc.).

6.6 MULTILINGUAL LANGUAGE USE: TRILINGUAL LANGUAGE MIXING AND CODE-SWITCHING

We see code-mixing and code-switching as unique evidence of trilingual competence and processing. We have argued that there is a difference between bilingual and trilingual competence that is more than merely quantitative. There is greater complexity caused by the presence of three linguistic systems, the combinatory choices involved in their use and the interplay of attitudinal, motivational and sociocultural factors. Multilinguals have a bigger linguistic repertoire than monolinguals but essentially the same range of situations in which to use it, as they tend to employ different languages in different situations for different purposes (Cenoz and Genesee 1998). In other words, multilinguals have more specific distributions of functions and uses for each of their languages' forms in the monolingual setting.

Multilinguals, even the very young, are particularly sensitive to the context of communication and responsive to the needs of their interlocutors. They know which language to use and when switching is appropriate. This heightened sensitivity can be seen as an integral part of trilingual (as well as bilingual) competence, or it can be attributed to the multilingual's overall metalinguistic awareness. Bialystok (1991, 1999, 2001; Bialystok and Martin 2004) found differences between monolinguals' and bilinguals' ability to solve problems in three different language domains. In oral language use, bilingual children have heightened metalinguistic awareness because they routinely pay attention to the language(s) being spoken in order to choose which one to use next. Accordingly, bilinguals, unlike monolinguals, have additional demands on their control abilities. Bialystok's framework predicts that balanced bilinguals should perform at least as well as dominant bilinguals on metalinguistic tasks that assess control of linguistic processing, whereas balanced bilinguals may outperform dominant bilinguals on those tasks that test syntactic awareness. Bialystok has recently (2010) claimed that the experience bilingual people have with speaking two languages on a regular basis enhances their cognitive executive control functions across their lifespan. The price bilinguals pay, when compared to monolinguals, is a smaller vocabulary and less rapid access to lexical items, but the benefits outweigh the cost: bilinguals have a range of advantages in the development, efficiency and maintenance of executive functions. Bialystok and Craik (2010) raise some very important questions:

> What about three languages? Is the trilingual advantage even greater? And does the relation between two languages make a difference? That is, does speaking two related languages, such as Spanish and Italian, give a greater (or lesser) advantage than speaking unrelated languages such as English and Chinese? Perhaps most intriguingly, what is the neural basis of the bilingual advantage? Are these performance differences mirrored in functional architecture or structural properties of the brain? Many questions remain for future studies.
>
> (p. 23)

Language awareness in children growing up with more than one language relates not only to awareness of a linguistic construct, as shown by comments on the structural properties of the language, but also to the language as a code or entity, evidenced in naming, sorting and classifying the languages. Although there may be great variability in language awareness across children and also across the child's lifespan, a child who has to deal with three languages may have a greater need to group these in a specific way in order to be able to deal with them effectively compared to a bilingual child. Trilingually raised children develop an awareness of language that differs from that of monolinguals in being interlingually similar to that of bilinguals. However, trilingual language awareness may indeed be significantly different from that of bilinguals because the languages are structured differently, which results in a more complex language input. Such input requires greater discrimination between three languages – and, possibly, also an underlying control of the cognitive foundation of binary thinking, leading to a more complex analysis and classification which is constantly revised.

We believe that trilinguals demonstrate an even greater ability than bilinguals in analysing and controlling their languages. Following

Bialystok's argument, developing trilingual awareness and control is manifested in the children's gradual labelling of their language systems – namely, recognising language as an entity – as illustrated by the younger subject (M) in the study by Stavans (1990) and reported in Stavans and Swisher (2006):

M (2;3) Reference to the Hebrew spoken by the mother:
> **ima**   says …
> mom   says …
> 'Mom speaks like …'
> Reference to the Spanish spoken by the father:
> **aba**   says …
> dad   says …
> 'Dad speaks like …'

M (2;6) Reference to Hebrew:
> **ima**'-s   language
> mom'-s- ENG POSS language
> 'Mom's language'
> Reference to Spanish:
> **aba**'-s language
> dad'-s- ENG POSS language
> 'Dad's language'

M (3;2) Reference to Hebrew:
> **ima** speaks Hebrew
> 'Mom speaks Hebrew'
> Reference to Spanish:
> **aba** speaks Spanish
> 'Dad speaks Spanish'
> Reference to English:
> 'At day-care we speak English'

The gradual awareness of the communicative systems M has at her disposal within an interval of eleven months shows that initially languages are perceived as a unique behaviour attributed to a specific person (in this case the mother or the father). These two (out of the three) languages were the most frequent and useful ones for communication at home. The languages then become personalised by the verb 'says'. Three months later, M already labels the languages as 'language', i.e. not as a personal trait but, rather, as a communication system used by the mother or the father. Finally, M makes a clear statement where the language is a usable and non-private system which is spoken in different settings (day-care, not person) and by different people (parents).

Similarly, structural language awareness by an older trilingual child (Stavans 1990; Stavans and Hoffmann 2007) is evident in the following exchange where E (6;2) engaged in a discussion with his mother on the formal aspects of pluralisation in English and later

on a noun gender issue in the different languages. The child had just
begun attending first grade.

(NOTE: Transcriptions follow English – regular font; **Hebrew** – bold.)

E: **Ima,**   do you know how we do manys in English?
     mom [HEB],   do you know how we do many-s PL[ENG] in English?

Mother: **Le-ma**   **ata**   **mitkaven?**
     to-what   you-1-M-SG mean-PRS-1-SG-M
     'What do you mean?'

E: Well, when you have one book and you want to say many book you put
     /s/ at the end and you make it book-s.

Here the child is clearly making explicit a pluralisation rule which up
to this point had been used and practised in all three languages without comment. Schooling has raised the structural linguistic awareness in English, which becomes an important issue in E's trilingual
processing. The structural language awareness filters into the other
languages and also into their structure, as evidenced by the following
exchange where E and Mother are discussing agreement on the verb
'nafal' (to fall), which must agree with the number and gender of its
noun 'shen' (tooth).

(NOTE: Transcriptions follow English – regular font; **Hebrew** – bold.)

E: **le-xaver**   **shel** me
     to-friend-SG-M of-POSS me [ENG]
     'my friend'

Mother: **nafla**
     fell-PST-3SG-F
     'fell (out)'

E: no **nafla**
     no fell-PST-3SG-F
     'no fell (out)'

Mother: **nafla**   **shen kaxa** **omrim** **be-ivrit**
     fell-PST-3SG-F tooth-F that's-how (we) say-PL-M in-Hebrew
     'fell (out), that is how we say it in Hebrew'

E: **nafla shen**
     fell-PST-3SG-F tooth-F
     '(the) tooth fell (out)'

Mother: **lex**   **le-nagev** **et** **ha-**   **af**
     go-IMP-2SG-M to-wipe-INF PREP the-DEF-ART nose-SG-M
     'go blow (your) nose'

E: yeah, but you said like a girl

Mother: **lo,** **shen**   **be-ivrit**   **omrim** **nafla**
     no, tooth-F in-Hebrew (we) say-PL-M fell-PST-3SG-F
     'no, in Hebrew we say fell (out) for tooth'

     shen be-ivrit **zo**   **mila** **kmo yalda**
     tooth-F in-Hebrew it is-DET-DEF-SG-F word-F like girl

     az **omrim** **shen** **nafla**

so (we)say-PL-M tooth-F fell-PST-3SG-F
'tooth in-Hebrew is (a) word like girl so (we) say tooth fell (out)'

E: Yes, but you said nafla and it sounds like a girl
fell-PST-3SG-F
'yes, but you said fell (out) and it sounds like a girl'

Mother: **naxon, ki shen ze yalda**
right, because tooth-F it-is-DET-DEF-SG-M girl
be-iverit ve-biglal ze tzarix
in-Hebrew and-because of that-DET-INDF-SG have-IMP-SG-M
le-hagid nafla ve-lo nafal
(we) say-pl-m fell-PST-3SG-F and-not fell-PST-3SG-M
'that is right, because tooth in Hebrew is (like a) girl (word) and that is
why we have to say fall (out) like girl and not like boy'

In this example, E is attempting to sort out what Mother is saying about how to use the verb 'fall' in Hebrew. Though Mother is not making the rule explicit, she is modelling by completing the verb in its appropriate form. E, in turn, is not only querying that Hebrew and English differ on the grammatical marking on the verb for gender as well as number, he also carries on a dialogue showing metalinguistic enlightenment with regard to the differences between the languages. There have been several studies (Barnes Alberdi 2002; Hoffmann 1985; Stavans 1990, 1992; Stavans and Swisher 2006; Hoffmann and Stavans 2007, Ivir-Ashworth 2011) on trilingual development in children raised trilingually from birth, which have presented similar examples of different types of language awareness. The different methodology that generated these reports, unlike those conducted in laboratory conditions by Bialystok, provide some initial insights and possible answers to the trilingual questions posed above by Bialystok and Craik (2010).

The trilingual child can access three language systems, but with this choice comes the task of keeping them apart, learning which notions are marked and the formal means by which they are expressed in each language so as to use them appropriately in context. Trilinguals are also able to resort to a language that encodes a salient concept, e.g. a semantic or grammatical one, for special emphasis or a particular function. Equally, having more than one language provides the possibility of an 'escape hatch' in performance, for instance, by being able to avoid temporarily the inflectional complexities of a particular language before they have been mastered, or to exploit them after they have been acquired, as illustrated in the following example of morphosyntactic switches involving verbs in Spanish and English. (Stavans and Swisher 2006).

(NOTE: Transcriptions follow English – regular font; *Spanish* – italics.)

Child:	I am	*vístete* -ing	now
		get dressed -IMP-2SG	
	'I am	getting dressed	now'

Note: The child is wrongly using the imperative verb form instead of the present continuous.

The study of CS in bilingual and trilingual children shows that children can be eclectic in their choice of linguistic items in order to achieve economy and efficiency in their communication with other multilinguals. It reveals that certain language structures or properties of language are more amenable to CS than others, and that the patterns of CS change over time. In other words, while their languages develop, children's trilingual competence builds up, too. Reyes and Ervin-Tripp (2004) trace this development by looking at school-age consecutive bilinguals' borrowing and CS practices, which show that language alternation undergoes a change of pattern – the latter becoming demonstrably more refined as the speakers grow older.

Ivir-Ashworth (2011) describes language contact in the utterances of two trilingual children who grew up with Croatian, English and German. She argues that the children made use of different parts of speech in all three of their languages, and that with time the children mastered all three languages adequately and used them appropriately in a variety of situations. Her findings are similar of those of Stavans (1990). Ashworth also reports on trilingual code-switches in her two subjects.

(NOTE: English – regular font; **Croatian** – bold; *German* – italics.)

EK (3;5):	Anne	*ge***nosila**	teddy**ja**	**od**	Carle.
	Anne	PTM-carry-PST-F-SG	teddy-M-ACC-SG	from	Carla-F-GEN-SG
	'Anne carried Carla's teddy'				
IF (1;7):	My *wollte*	**pisati**.			
	My want-PST-1SG	write			
	'I wanted to write'				

Stavans and Hoffmann (2007) argue that certain forms and functions of code-switches constitute a 'core' of trilingual language behaviour, i.e. some switches are more predominant than others, while yet others are more prone to change; in other words, some structures are more robust and less likely to be switched than others. Consider these code-switching and code-mixing examples produced by a Hebrew–English–Spanish trilingual child.

(NOTE: Transcriptions follow English –regular font; **Hebrew** – bold; *Spanish* – italics.)

> **Ha**-mouse **yoce** **min** **ha**-*hoyito*
> the-mouse exit-PRS-SG-M from the-hole-SG-M
> 'the mouse comes out of the little hole'

or

> *El* frog *está* **mevi**
> the-DEF-ART-SG-M frog is-PR-PROG-2SG bring-PRS-SG-M
> *un* *niño* **be-matana**
> a-INDF-ART boy as-gift
> 'the frog is bringing a child as a gift'

These examples illustrate the artful and complex combinations of the trilingual child's three linguistic systems within the same utterance. These combinations are brought about by incorporating knowledge *of* the languages with knowledge *about* the languages. The organic combinations are clear manifestations of trilingual competence.

On the basis of this kind of trilingual switches, Stavans and Hoffmann (2007) proposed the notion of a developmental competence continuum, arguing, like Auer (1998), that the transition from CS to CM *without* morphosyntax to CM *with* morphosyntax, which Auer labels 'fused lects', is in fact a way of tracing the development of trilingual competence, as in the visual model in Figure 6.5.

The continuum has two parallel scales: degree of multilingual competence and linguistic level of analysis. Language combinations, i.e. mixes and switches, may be analysed along these lines; they reflect the degree or placement along the multilingual competence development scale. Taking this model as a basis for a more comprehensive view of language alternation instances, one can analyse their dynamic nature not only at the performance stage but also at the level of competence. At the time of writing, this proposed model is still in need of both qualitative and quantitative elaboration. The following examples are illustrations of the model proposed above:

(a) A lexico-phonetic switch such as *gardina* may be phonemically parsed either as containing elements from all three languages or only from two. In the latter case it is not possible to trace the 'junction' of the switch to one or another language as clearly as in other cases. (NOTE: Transcriptions follow English – regular font; **Hebrew** – bold; *Spanish* – italics.)

> *el* *niño* *y* *el* *perro*
> the-DEF-ART-SG-M boy and the-DEF-ART-SG-M dog-SG-M

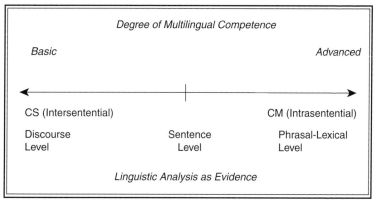

Figure 6.5 A model of developing trilingual competence

buscando	*el*	*sapo en el ...*
search-3PL-PRS-PROG	the-DEF-ART-SG-M	frog in the-DEF-ART-SG-M
en el		**gardina**
in the-DEF-ART-SG-M		garden (Trilingual CS, see explanation below)

Gardina is a phono-morphological code-switch at the syllabic level where there are morphemes chosen and used as a result of phonological and phonemic influences, as illustrated in Table 6.1.

A similar phenomenon is manifested in the following example, which involves morphophonemic switches in plural formation that draw on two (if not three) languages. Both Spanish and English pluralise by adding /-s/ to the singular form (*pit+s* in English and *hueso+s* in Spanish), whereas in Hebrew attending to both gender and number is necessary (i.e. *garin + im* in Hebrew).

(b) Morphophonemic switches such as the three versions of plural formation in Hebrew and English, as here.
(NOTE: Transcriptions follow English – regular font; **Hebrew** – bold.)

Garin-im   -s   >
pit-PL-M [HEB]   -S-PL[ENG]   (oversimplification)
Gar   -s   >   **garin**
pit-SG-M (should be garin)[HEB]   -S-PL[ENG]   (further iteration)   pit-SG-M

Stavans (1990) reported the following example where M (3;4) has a conversation about the olive pit *garin* in Hebrew with the trilingual mother.
(NOTE: Transcriptions follow English – regular font; **Hebrew** – bold.)

Mother: **tizahari**   **im**   **ha-garinim**
(be) careful-PRS-2SG-M   with   the-DEF-ART-PIT-PL-M
'(you be) careful with the pits'

Table 6.1 *The evolution of the gardina code-switch*

Language	Syllabic parsing	Morphemes	Uptake of child to construct trilingual CS
English	/gar – den/	garden-NOUN-N-SG	GAR-
Spanish	/jar-din/	jardin-NOUN-M-SG	-DIN
Hebrew	/gi-na/	גרעין – NOUN- F-SG	-NA
Trilingual CS	/gar-di-na/	NOUN-SG-F	GAR*DI*NA

M: **Ima**, take out the   **garinim**s
                                 pit-PL-M [HEB] -S-PL[ENG]
         'mom, take out the pits'
Mother: **At**   **roa**   **ḥozeti**   **et**   **kulam**
         you-SG-F   see-PRS-2SG-F   take(out)-PST-1SG   PREP   all-PL
        'You see, I took all of them out'
M: You see, there is only one more   **gar**   to take out.
                                       pit-oversimplified-SG-M /garin/
         'you see, there is only one more pit to take out'
Mother: **Ine**   **ein**   **od**   **garin-im**.
        here   (there is) not   more   pit-M-PL
        'here, there are no more pits'
M: All the   **gar**-s   are out now.
                        *pit-oversimplified-SG-M /garin/+ [ENG]PL
        'all the pits are out now'

(c) Morphosyntactic switches such as in the following example.
(NOTE: Transcriptions follow English – regular font; **Hebrew** – bold;
Spanish – italics.)

i.   *Está*   **mitlabesh**-ing
      is-COP-3SG-PRS   dress(up)-3SG-M-PRS-REFL[HEB]+PROG[ENG]
      'she is getting dressed'
ii.   *Yo*   *también*   *te*   send-*o*   *un*
      I   too   to(you)-2SG   send-INF+PRS-1SG   a-INDF-ART-SG-M
      beso
      kiss
      'I also send you a kiss'
iii.   *Este*   *es*   *el*   black-*ito*
      this-DEF-ART   is-PRS-3SG   the-DEF-ART-SG-M   black(noun)+ diminutive-SG-M
      'this is the little black one'
iv.   **Ha**-burglars   will come
      the-DEF-ART burglars   will come
      'the burglars will come'

Figure 6.6 shows how each of these instances of trilingual switching can be placed at the appropriate point across the continuum proposed earlier.

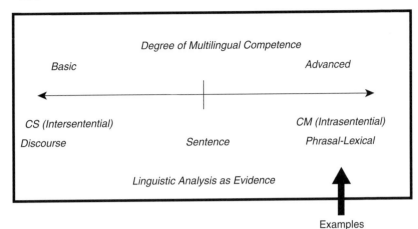

Figure 6.6 Degree of multilingual competence: code-switching and code-mixing

The proposed model establishes a continuum in which code-switches are characterised functionally as carrying important socio-linguistic functions, such as using language for role play, reporting about what someone said or establishing ascription to a speech community. This use of CS is intentional and may create a communicative situation of empathy and inclusion, for instance when used to create comradeship – or, equally, a situation of exclusion or creating 'other-ness'. Although the use of CS may change over time in multilingual children, it is more typical of adults who are deploying communicative forms for social purposes. These types of alternations in CS either occur for purposes of message efficiency or are due to language deficiency. We see the development of trilingual competence in children as a dynamic process of acquiring the three language systems, which includes combining different elements of analysis within and across the languages.

6.7 CONCLUSION

One of the most important points to emerge from the above discussion is that multilingualism is all about choices. Some choices are made by the language users and are driven by knowledge and awareness; others are made by cognitive mechanisms that we have at our disposal when processing the systems. But these mechanisms, too, are ruled by choices. Here we list some of the salient issues concerning multilingual language competence and use:

- Choices are a result of competence in the languages, i.e. the means and modes of language processing, and they reveal awareness of which forms of a language are appropriate for a particular situation, interlocutor or topic, and when; in the end, these forms are an outcome that is unique to multilinguals – code-switching.
- Switching and mixing are often regarded as deficient linguistic behaviour, because they do not adhere fully to monolingual norms. Such judgements can influence social practices and, in particular, language policies.
- Individual multilingualism is diverse and dynamic, not only at its inception, but along its evolution. It changes across the multilingual's lifespan depending on linguistic needs and opportunities driven by social and personal circumstances.
- The dynamic nature of multilingualism is best accounted for by the complementarity principle: at different points in time, multilingual speakers manipulate the different linguistic systems to different degrees, and at other times their competence in the linguistic systems either shifts or equates to that of balanced multilinguals.
- There are methodological difficulties in measuring multilingualism across the wide spectrum of possible types and degrees. Measurements are biased by comparison to a monolingual scale, and this produces a binary measure of 'correct' or 'incorrect' forms in terms of monolingual standards.
- Research in multilingualism tries to account for multilingual language use at the individual level. Multilingual competence is best described by reference to several models of multilingual processing. The outcome can be a unique multilingual production characterised by language alternation and code-switching.
- Multilingual competence establishes important differences between monolinguals on the one hand and bilinguals and trilinguals on the other. For bilinguals or trilinguals it is normal to alternate languages by way of switching, mixing and borrowing. Such practices have been criticised by the monolingual establishment, especially institutions controlling public services and schools.
- Differences exist between monolingual, bilingual and trilingual competence as regards their 'speech modes'. Frequent switching

and borrowing are phenomena at the core of explanatory models of multilingualism that can lead us towards a better understanding – not only of what the multilingual knows and can do (competence), but also of how multilinguals 'do multilingualism' (processing).

- The difference between bilingual and trilingual competence is not merely quantitative. There is more complexity in trilingual speech, caused by the presence of three linguistic systems, the combinatorial choices involved in their use and the interplay of attitudinal, motivational and sociocultural factors.
- Multilinguals have a specific distribution of functions and uses for each of their languages. They are, from an early age, particularly sensitive to the communication context and very responsive to the needs of their interlocutors.

7 Accommodating multilingualism

The world is a mosaic of visions. With each language that disappears, a piece of that mosaic is lost.

François Grosjean

7.1 INTRODUCTION

Multilinguals must (and do) find ways of organising the use of their languages to fulfil their communicative needs and accommodate their social, cultural, economic and psychological needs according to the context in which they find themselves. Multilinguals are guided by basically the same considerations as monolinguals, who make certain linguistic choices and adjust their speech to suit particular situations, interlocutors and topics. However, multilinguals have a broader range of choices, i.e. choice of language in addition to choice of style, register, accent, other dialect features and cultural codes. For instance, the conversation between a multilingual and monolingual will conform not only to the use of a single linguistic system, but also to the appropriate pragmatic codes of the language; and the cultural codes adhered to by that monolingual's speech community. However, when the same multilingual engages in conversation with a bilingual, the communicative needs may change and accommodation might become more complex. In such a situation, the multilingual may speak both of the languages of the bilingual and this may lead to differential use of these languages to express different things; and at the same time, it may cause the alteration and combination of these two languages. If, on the other hand, the same multilingual shares only one of the bilingual's languages, the interaction will resemble that of the interaction with a monolingual but will have an added value of flexibility and empathy to the non-monolingual status that both share. Hence, for the multilingual interacting with another multilingual or a monolingual, language accommodation requires that participants choose the language that is common to all; or, if all participants share the same languages, the choice of appropriate code is likely to be determined by other factors, such as communicative purpose, power, solidarity, inclusion and identity with a certain speech community or group.

This chapter is concerned with issues such as the features or characteristics involved in multilingual language choice; the forces that influence and shape these choices; the strategies necessary to make choices and accommodate to linguistic needs; the differences (if any) between influences such as the individual's motivations and attitudes and those of the family/wider community; and the way in which multilingual accommodation also negotiates beliefs, customs, cultural assumptions and identities.

7.2   ACCOMMODATION AT THE INDIVIDUAL LEVEL

Whenever two people meet, some form of negotiation is implicit. If they want to express solidarity and reduce social distance they tend to seek common features in their behaviour (Lvovich 1997). If speakers wish to express distance towards – or even dislike of – the person they are speaking to, the reverse is true, and differences will be sought. This mechanism also extends to language, and it can be seen to operate in monolingual as well as multilingual contexts when speakers adjust the way they speak.

Giles *et al.* (1991) studied the evaluation of speech in terms of accent and other linguistic features typical of interpersonal communication. Accommodating language varieties not only consists of the different associations that both speakers and listeners make when using their languages, but also their attempt to vary their speech when interacting with others. The central notions in this theoretical model are *convergence*, which tends to have positive underlying associations, and *divergence*, which may be evaluated negatively. When speakers seek to express empathy with their interlocutors they adopt similar speech styles; and they diverge, i.e. speak differently, when they want to emphasise social distance. Subsequent models of speech accommodation have noted the importance of the context of interaction and other motivations, apart from social distance, that may cause speakers to converge or diverge. They have also pointed out that not all participants in a 'speech act' accommodate their speech in similar ways, and that divergence may not necessarily signify an underlying wish to distance oneself from one's interlocutor. Similarly, convergence can carry negative associations if it is perceived as ridiculing some-one's way of talking or in a context where adjusting to someone else's speech is seen as a betrayal of group identity or as taking ownership of something that is not one's own.

Accommodation theorists are interested in the motivations, i.e. the psychological and social factors, that lead individuals to make particular sociolinguistic choices that reflect attitudes towards different linguistic varieties in specific situations. A related area of research interest in multilingual contexts concerns the choice of linguistic patterns in terms of the different languages that individuals or groups of speakers make. According to what considerations do multilingual communities allocate their various languages for particular uses? What kind of choices do members of multilingual communities habitually make, and what causes them to break with their set patterns?

When the focus is on the individual, similar questions can be asked about habitual and spontaneous language choices. A change from the usual pattern can take the form of deciding to use the only – or the stronger – language of one's interlocutor in order to facilitate communication, or to adjust one's speech in such a way as to avoid dialect variants if they are not shared by the person one is speaking to.

In the Nordic countries, especially Norway, Sweden and Denmark, this kind of accommodation can be widely observed and described in terms of 'inter-Scandinavian semi-communication'. Braunmüller (1999: 313) defines this as a form of communication across different diasystems (i.e. languages in Weinreich's (1954) sense), where speakers use their own language without taking recourse to a lingua franca or a pidgin. It does not imply that communication is only partial or that it is somehow impaired. It is successful because speakers have sufficient linguistic knowledge of their own language and linguistic sensitivity to cope with the various partially overlapping varieties.

The Scandinavian languages are similar in that they share many grammatical and lexical features; they vary most noticeably at the phonological level. All three languages have borrowed from other languages, for instance Latin, German, French and English, but they have done so in different ways. Yet there are also many 'false friends' and items with different semantic behaviour that can lead to misunderstanding. Although marked regional dialect differences exist between the three languages, especially noticeable in spoken communication, citizens from the three countries (and to some extent also Icelanders and Swedish-speaking Finns) are able to communicate with each other. Written communication is the easiest form of mutual intelligibility; for oral effective communication linguistic forms that approximate the standard variety of each language need to be chosen. This does not exclude the fact that dialect speakers who find themselves in close proximity to a national border, for instance between Norway and Sweden, can understand each other using their respective regional varieties.

However, a heavily intertwined political and cultural history and typologically similar languages alone do not make for successful communication. The point has been made repeatedly that the most important factor is willingness to understand each other and make linguistic efforts to achieve it. This kind of accommodation requires tolerance and flexibility on the part of both interlocutors, who also have to be prepared to learn, at least passively, some aspects of the other language, such as the most salient morphological and phonological features. Frequent contact between Scandinavians for purposes of economic, political and cultural cooperation and collaboration, as well as travel and leisure, provides both opportunities and motivation.

The Nordic Council has a Language Secretariat that promotes 'Nordisk', the formal variety (which is marked according to a speaker's standard variety and manner of accommodation) used in inter-Scandinavian communication. It has developed a Nordic Language Convention aimed at facilitating understanding between citizens and public institutions in the member states, whilst upholding individual speakers' rights to use their own language with these institutions. Their objective is to promote understanding with minimum need for interpreting services. The Nordic Language Secretariat may be seen as an example of a public institution attempting to foster accommodation. While Scandinavians have not turned into habitual speakers of 'Nordisk' or 'Scandinavian', some of the advice offered may be seen as helpful; but ultimately language accommodation is a personal matter driven by factors that motivate individual speakers.

Code-switching can also be seen as constituting a kind of linguistic adaptation, made more or less consciously by the speaker in the belief that it may make communication easier or more convivial (Lo 1999). Some multilinguals use code-switching to express loyalty to more than one cultural group (Myers-Scotton 1993). This is particularly typical of many immigrant communities for whom code-switching serves as a linguistic practice of membership and inclusion into the multiple social circles in which they move. Myers-Scotton (2006) proposes a theoretical framework for accommodation that she labels a 'markedness model', in which linguistic choices are viewed as a means to the negotiation of self-identity and the desired relationship with others. This model provides a principled procedure whereby both interlocutors judge any linguistic choice made or heard as more or less marked, given the interaction in which it takes place. In other words, there is a continuum ranging from the marked to the unmarked choices for multilingual communication.

The unmarked choices are those that are accepted as appropriate linguistic reflections, in particular those whose use causes no social ripples because they can be seen as an expected choice by all participants (e.g. the unmarked choice used in the USA among Spanish–English bilinguals in the company of their elders is Spanish). Marked choices involve greater accommodation because, unlike unmarked ones, they are not predicted and require more negotiation. Making a marked choice necessitates working out a new set of interlocutors' expectations; it calls for a new situation where the rights and obligations of the speaker-hearer are mediated and set. Marked choices generate negotiation of the speaker's identity in relation to the participants. Code-switching is a common multilingual practice to establish the identity, the affiliation and the relationship (of inclusion or exclusion) of participants.

Myers-Scotton presents several examples of multilingual communication as, for instance, the case of siblings in Nairobi where the rural brother visits the city one who holds a white-collar position in his office; rather than greeting each other in their ethnic language, they use English, which is the language used commonly in higher-level business offices. The choice of English downplays the connection of the two as siblings. It establishes a more formal connection of acquaintance in order for the rural brother not to come across as asking for special allowances to be made while, at the same time, the city brother risks alienating himself from his brother, family and ethnic affiliates.

Multilinguals may use code-switching as a means of establishing solidarity when the use of a particular language would be regarded as marked (that is, the unexpected variety by one speaker towards the other). Code-switching may be a way of establishing social hierarchies between speakers: for instance, an employer may address an employee of the same ethnic group in their common vernacular both to establish solidarity with the employee and as a means to mark segregation from the wider group to which they both belong. According to Myers-Scotton (2006: 163), 'it is important to recognise that [the] speaker (and others) can have multiple goals, and [these] may well be ambiguous'.

Similarly, code-switching – marked or unmarked – is a means to accommodate multilingualism because it may serve to claim a multidimensional persona, i.e. marked choices of code-switching can assert power relations among interlocutors; it may be a locus to establish neutral linguistic platforms, as it were, such as the omnipresence of English in professional jargon. The use of marked code-switching choices may segregate you from the majority (i.e. distinguish you as different or as an outsider), yet, at the same time, from the perspective of the minority-language speaker, it can signal group membership (i.e. be part of the ethnic group or community). The unmarked choice of one person may be a marked choice for another.

Accommodating multilingualism is a complex issue. Seen through Giles' theory of accommodation, the perspective is addressee-driven, whereas the markedness model for accommodation in multilingualism proposed by Myers-Scotton is more speaker-dominant. For multilinguals, but not monolinguals, accommodating different languages, their registers and their uses is a matter of choice and circumstances. The choices open to them are motivated not just cognitively in reception and production, as described in the previous chapter, but also by social and educational issues that accompany language use. Language is the means through which we conduct our social life; it allows us to construct social communities which, in turn, ultimately exist because of it. The centrality of language for humans as social beings lies in its ability to allow a community's past to be shared and transmitted to future generations; it creates a present of cooperation and collaboration, and it opens up the future to planning and maintaining the group's identity. So while one language may serve all these social functions in one community, for the multilingual several communities and options can be open. The need and motivation for these choices and allocations will now be considered.

7.3   LANGUAGE CHOICE AND ACCOMMODATION

Language choice for the multilingual involves at least five different dimensions: speaker, addressee, context or situation, content or topic and purpose. These dimensions correspond to the individual, the contextual and the interactional choices that the multilingual faces. When considering speaker and addressee we make choices based on the participants involved in the conversation. If the bilingual speaker is familiar with the bilingual interlocutors it is likely that this relationship has already been framed in one language, although there is the choice of alternating and using two languages. But if the addressee is unfamiliar, the multilingual will quickly pick up clues such as age, appearance, dress and accent to gauge which language is most appropriate for communication. For instance, in Mali, an African wearing western attire in the capital, Bamako, is likely to be addressed in French or English and not in one of the other languages of Mali.

Language choices driven by individual attitudes or preferences can be a result of contextual considerations that ultimately reflect wider social attitudes as well. When multilinguals are in minority/majority language contexts, they may opt for one or other language to make a particular statement. For instance, among immigrant populations one typically finds – in a situation where either the majority or the minority language could be used – that the older generation choose to use the minority language, whereas the younger members prefer to use the majority language. One such example is seen today in Israel, where people who immigrated as children nearly five decades ago report that they disliked speaking the language of their parents (such as Polish, German, Moroccan or Yemeni Arabic), for it meant at the time that you were not a 'sabra', a genuine locally born Israeli. Today we see this also among the Russian and Ethiopian immigrants. The Russian younger generation prefer to speak Hebrew and regard Russian as the language of the family, even though most of their social circle socialises primarily in Russian. In the Ethiopian case, parents take great pride when their children use Hebrew and do not necessarily find much use or purpose to foster Amharic in their children, even though they (the parents themselves) do not master Hebrew well. Hence, at times and depending on the prestige attached to the languages, the language preferences of older and younger generations may be quite different. Language choices, then, are made by individuals in terms of the context and their perception of the status of each of their languages in the community. For the Russians in Israel, Hebrew may be a language for daily survival purposes, while for the Ethiopian it might be a sign of achievement of upward mobility. The use of a particular language reflects individual identity and projects the image the individual wishes to portray.

The purpose of an interaction affects the language choice one makes, too. A multilingual may change language during an interaction deliberately or subconsciously so as to accommodate the preference of the interlocutor (Okita 2002). The speaker's perception of which language is regarded as more prestigious or more accommodating (whether formal or informal) depends greatly on the interlocutor. For instance, to gain recognition, acceptance or status, a person may deliberately choose the majority language, but that same individual may use the minority language in order to form an affiliation with and gain inclusion into the minority group. This can happen in both formal and informal interactions.

An example from Israel, where English enjoys a high status, may illustrate the point: in newscasts one can often observe the anchorperson inserting an English utterance (not read from the autocue) when interviewing an expert and wishing to seem authoritative or knowledgeable of the subject discussed. This type of language alternation (as discussed in the previous chapter) also has a discursive purpose. For instance, a multilingual may want to discuss some professional issues with another multilingual colleague. Initially she/he may make the statement in one language (supposedly the language used predominantly for professional topics) and then reinforce that statement by paraphrasing it in another language (that is common to both). This is also true in other less formal daily interactions such as conversations, narratives, gossip, where the multilingual may use different languages so as to provide background information to lend strength to the argument. To sum up, the idea of language choice as evidence of accommodating multilingualism contains complex, manifold and interrelated issues concerning the individual and other participants in a communicative act.

There is rarely just one discernible motivation for choosing language X rather than language Y or language Z for a particular speech event. It seems that research can be grouped into explanations of these events in terms of: (a) age – older immigrants choose language X because of competence, identity and status, while younger ones are motivated to use language X to signal identity and ethnicity (but not for reasons of socialisation); (b) dominance as defined by degree and type of multilingualism, stronger and weaker languages and multiculturalism; (c) social inclusion and exclusion, i.e. languages that may represent role models for ethnic inclusion, on one hand, and exclusion from the majority on the other; or (d) the need for maintenance to establish both individual and group identity.

7.4   INCLUSION, IDENTITIES AND NEGOTIATING MULTIPLE IDENTITIES

In the previous section we discussed how multilinguals choose the language on the basis of individual, contextual and interactional forces. We have suggested that these forces operate from within the individual as a reaction to a particular speech event, and that they can be made consciously. Many of these choices are driven by two primal social needs, group inclusion and identity. In dealing with issues of inclusion and identity with regard to multilingualism, one must distinguish between multilingualism that is the result of living in a minority–majority situation that involves either autochthonous or immigrant minorities, multilingualism that is a consequence of contemporary language spread and globalisation, and multilingualism as a lifestyle. The different types of multilingualism are affected differently when it comes to questions of group membership and issues of identity.

Clearly, the choices multilingual individuals make lie within the linguistic repertoire available to them. But what is perhaps more intriguing is the extent to which the multilingual condition contributes to the identity of the multilingual individual, the existence of spheres in which the multilingual functions and the fact that the individual's most compelling issues are at stake. For monolinguals and multilinguals alike, identity is an outcome of the interaction of the inner self and the outer world(s) in which we exist. The Uruguayan poet and writer Eduardo Galeano (1991: 125) wrote:

> *La identidad no es una pieza de museo quietecita en una vitrina, sino la*
> *siempre asombrosa síntesis de las contradicciones nuestras de cada día.*
> (Identity is no museum piece sitting nice and still in a display
> case, but rather the endlessly astonishing synthesis of our daily
> contradictions.)

The migration or accommodation of the self is slower and less abrupt than it is for the physical body. In using their various languages, multilinguals must constantly gauge and reorganise the various subidentities and linguistic systems that enable them to form, project and define themselves. We can argue that, whereas the body of the multilingual remains quite constant, occupying only one place in space at a time, the self can split (and often does) or reside in several spaces (old and new, real and ideal etc.) at the same time. Here we are concerned solely with issues that involve the demarcation, construction and accommodation of languages to the identity of an individual through practices that are upheld by the social group and desired by the individual.

So, for example, with regard to immigrant multilinguals, bridging the worlds of the past and the present (and perhaps the future) imposes certain considerations that are rooted in expectations by both the individual and the outer world. The same is true for an incipient multilingual who grows up with more than one language, and for whom the home and outside language(s) have different emotional and identity features.

There is a considerable body of research on identity, not only from a linguistic perspective but also from sociological, psychological and educational ones. The many broad definitions of what constitutes identity – or even the lack of a definition – are problematic for studies that claim to treat this subject. In fact, identity may be one of those subjects that is so multifaceted, dynamic and particular that creating a clear definition acceptable to all would always fall short for some disciplines and be irrelevant for others.

Identity, for our purpose here, may best be defined by a number of inclusion criteria rather than by a set of characteristics. Consider the individual profile of a female doctor who emigrated to America from Azerbaijan and regards herself as trilingual in English, Azeri and Spanish (which she acquired while spending some years as an intern in Latin America). What is the identity of this multilingual? The answer is rather complex and should be seen as relative to other criteria of inclusion that need to be addressed. She complies with the inclusion criteria of the female group in the same manner as she lacks inclusion in the male group. Within that group she responds to inclusion into the group of professionals, i.e. doctors. But how does multilingual accommodation and group inclusion shape her identity – or, perhaps, is it her identity that shapes the linguistic accommodations which in turn aid group inclusion?

Different paradigms have been proposed to explain language-contact phenomena in multilinguals as a means of defining their identity. Four such theoretical paradigms can serve to illustrate that there may be different perspectives of the complex role of language and identity and how this fact stands at the core of the negotiation of identity in multilinguals.

The *variationist sociolinguistic* paradigm examines the relationship between language and identity, assuming that 'people sound the way you would expect them to sound given the facts about their class, sex, age and region' (Chambers 1995: 100–101). This assumption reduces multilingualism to the expression of the individual's identity instead of constituting a means of creating an identity. The suggestion that identity ought to be regarded as the explanation of multilinguistic phenomena is contested (Pavlenko and Blackledge 2004) on two grounds. First, individuals construct and maintain multiple identities that are created and negotiated through language and are themselves in need of explanation. Here language is seen as an instrument. The second issue contested is to do with the multiple functions of linguistic forms that cannot be linked directly or necessarily to a particular identity without considering the interactional conditions in which they emerge. People may not always sound the way they are expected to, and so what construes identity is not necessarily what is expressed by it.

The *socio-psychological* paradigm theorises language identity, negotiation of identity and language contact according to group membership. Identity in this theoretical framework is viewed as the sum of reflective self images constructed, experienced and communicated by individuals in a given cultural or interactional event. This applies most typically to minorities who perceive their social identity as belonging to an inferior or excluded group and who change their group membership in order to view themselves more positively. This transition or change is an actual negotiation, a transactional interaction process in which multilinguals assert, define and modify their own desired group affiliation and that of others. Such negotiations define identity and affiliation on the basis of culture, ethnicity, gender, role and status relationships, and physical characteristics. Therefore identities, as shaped through interactions and communications, are successful when the individuals feel they are understood, valued, supported and respected by the group members. In a culturally familiar environment the interaction will result in a satisfactory outcome where the individual will feel like part of the group, secure and emotionally safe, while in a non-familiar environment the interaction may cause vulnerability and instability to the identity of the individual as a result of perceived or genuine fear or threat.

The spontaneous acquisition and use of languages 'that are not generally thought to belong to' a particular person or group (Rampton 1995: 280) seems to be common in local negotiations of ethnic, social and linguistic boundaries. These sociolinguistic processes can be termed 'crossing' (Rampton 1995, 2005). Although crossing as a metaphor that connotes 'a step over a heavily fortified and well-guarded linguistic border' (Auer 2003: 74) is disputable, we can relate to it as a general but not necessarily multilingual sociolinguistic phenomenon of negotiation of social boundaries, i.e. across ethnic groups, across cultures, across gender, across religious groups, across age groups – essentially, across any hierarchical or structural social boundary.

In our multilingual context we regard crossing as an additional perspective that goes from the individual to the societal and vice versa. We recognise that the contributions of Hewitt (1986) and Rampton (1995) are important to the understanding of language transgressions within and across groups. Of particular interest is Rampton's (1995,

2005) theoretical and analytic thrust that came with the concept of crossing as related to code-switching, stylisation and double-voicing. The idea that crossing is related to (ethnic) identity and solidarity construction implies that at times speakers use language to negotiate new affiliations or challenge existing ones, rather than in order to fit into one ethnic category and that this results in 'new ethnicities' (p. 297). Speakers can also engage in language crossing so as to negotiate in-group and out-group relations (across ages, but specifically in adolescents as a means to challenge adults' institutionalised settings); or they can use crossing as mocking and joking in processes of stigmatisation and stereotyping; or put crossing at the service of individual networking, specifically with peer groups. Rampton's own complex analysis confirms that crossing is a multifaceted phenomenon that examines form and meaning in locally situated interactions and has a different legitimacy and effect depending on who, where, how, and into which language variety crossing occurs.

The paradigm of *multilingual identities* has also been contested. One contention is that it assumes abstract and rigid categories that do not account for group or individual variability. There is a monolingual and monocultural bias to this paradigm, which conceptualises people as fitting into homogeneous distinct monolingual and monocultural groups. Again, the idea of being in or out of the group, or what could be called strict group inclusion for life, does not allow for the dynamic nature of the needs of individuals to negotiate, change and renegotiate their identity as they move from one group to another at a given point in time, or for belonging to more than one group at the same time. In this sense, the bias can be viewed as a result of the group taking 'ownership' of the individual's identity, or of the individual 'adopting' the identity of the group.

The rigid frame of inclusion poses a serious problem for the multilingual who has immigrated to a new country and culture, for that individual is under pressure to adopt the new language, culture and group identity and abandon the one(s) brought with him or her. The 'melting pot' view, or rather assimilationist approach (Baker 2002: 382) to immigrants' languages, has been overt in some regions of the world at some times in history and covert in others. This sort of societal bilingualism does not allow multilinguals to be members of multiple communities, because they are faced with one of two possibilities: either their culture is thrown in the 'pot' together with all the other different cultures, and the result is a unique mix of contributions made by all groups that enter the pot; or the immigrants give up their cultural heritage and are expected to conform to the dominant national one.

Another contention is the reductionist and static view of culture. This view indexes culture as 'referring to two specific, identifiable, perpetual cultures – a native culture and a host culture' (Syed and Burnett 1999). The paradigm makes allowances for the individual to belong to one or the other culture/group at a given time, suggesting that language users can be or become members of a homogeneous group defined by language, ethnicity and culture. What it fails to account for is the multilayered features that characterise groups, which include socioeconomic status, cultural background, gender and generational gaps that pose additional stratification and blurring of clear-cut homogeneous boundaries. It also fails to explain why some members of an ethnolinguistic group may adhere to their native language while others may learn an out-group language so as to escape affiliation to the original group. For example, for early immigrants from Europe who settled in the 1950s in Israel, Polish and Yiddish were the languages used in many Ashkenazi homes. Although for these immigrants the use of Polish was the first language and the use of Yiddish may have been the 'home' language, upon arrival in Israel, Hebrew became the 'new' language. Many of these immigrants were immersed in intensive Hebrew language programmes, but not all managed to learn the language or actually needed it for daily interactions. Their children, however, were already learning Hebrew at school and Polish was considered a 'shameful' language, as some would testify later. In fact, they felt that it was undesirable and degrading to use or even admit knowledge of Polish, for it was the language that 'smelled of naphthalene [a chemical used in their childhood to protect clothes against moths] like my grandmother's house', as reported by Dganit, a 54-year-old Israeli-born woman, second generation of Holocaust survivors.

Another example is Adriana, who emigrated from Argentina to the USA and lived there for five years before she moved to Israel. She says:

> When I was in Chicago I avoided speaking or being heard speaking
> Spanish with David [her husband] because people were always
> surprised to find out that I am NOT Mexican but Argentinian
> and they would even say it was weird because I do not look like
> a Latina. So I felt that not only was I not Mexican but I was also
> weird because I did not belong to that category, I did not belong to
> the American group and in the eyes of the Mexicans I did not look
> Latina. When I arrived in Israel I met a Cuban family who kept
> telling me that in Israel anyone with a heavy Latin accent in their
> Hebrew is automatically labelled Argentinian. For once I felt proud
> and good. I finally belonged. Not only that I very quickly realised

that Israelis regard a Spanish accent as something good – as opposed
to the Americans who are prejudiced against this accent. My accent,
my identity and my origins were finally recognised and valued.

Unlike Adriana, Jaime – a Mexican immigrant to Israel – says:

… every time people tell me I am from South America or that I
am Argentinian I get annoyed. I always tell them I am from North
America and I am Mexican. What annoys me is that people's
reactions to what I answer are dismissive and they say it is all
the same.

(examples are personal communications (AS), 2008)

The *poststructuralist* paradigm is more ethnographically oriented and
regards identities as fluid and constructed during linguistic interaction. According to this paradigm, language is a site of identity
construction through discourse and ideological affiliations, which
are mainly the product of the macro-social factors that bind identities with language practices, especially in socioeconomic and sociopolitical processes where power and authority are involved. Hence,
language identity is something that changes, that is constantly negotiated, re-evaluated and reshaped, depending on both group-internal
and group-external forces that are not purely linguistic but are manifested through discourse, pronunciation, register, topic, situation,
interlocutor and interlocutionary event.

Pavlenko and Blackledge (2004) discuss this issue and propose the
following – albeit with caveats:

In sum, we view *identities* as social, discursive, and narrative options
offered by a particular society in a specific time and place to which
individuals and groups of individuals appeal in an attempt to self-
name, to self-characterize, and to claim social spaces and social
prerogatives. (p. 19)

This proposed perspective of identities attributes considerable force
to the society as a shaper of identity and, in a way, as the platform
on which the multilingual exhibits a wide variety of features (among
them not only the different languages, but also linguistic registers,
dialects and more) that enable him/her to position himself/herself in
the social group.

What is missing in Pavlenko and Blackledge (2004) is the contribution that individuals make to positioning themselves as members
of a group. For example, a Spanish-speaking professor of linguistics
working in Catalonia is obliged by the statutes of the university to
teach in Catalan, even though the students prefer – and are more
competent in – Spanish. So, the Chilean (Spanish-speaking) professor

places himself as a faculty member of the university by learning and teaching in Catalan, a language for which he may lack natural and personal expression, for it is a foreign language to him. At the same time, he is perceived (and identified by the institution and the students) as a foreigner and is associated with the Latin American community of immigrants in Barcelona.

While language alone does not build identity, identity is not divorced from the contributions language makes to it. Identity feeds on sociopolitical, educational, economic, geographic, cultural, racial, gender and other human and societal characteristics that rely on human qualities of solidarity, dependency, power, charisma and prejudice – and are expressed through language. We argue, then, that identity, group inclusion, multilingualism and language accommodation are all about choices among options. Yet these options must be negotiated to identify, create and establish the multilingual within his or her social context.

Aspects of the negotiation of identities, in particular by linguistic minorities within a larger majority, often involve gender, class, race, ethnicity, sexuality and education. These may contribute to – and to a large extent ensure – the perpetuation of relations of inequality between the majority and minority group; that is, a majority makes sure there is a minority by exercising societal power, and the minority remains a minority so long as it allows such relations of inequality with the majority group to continue. Language is a pivotal element in these relations, for it is through language that human transactions and communications come to fruition. We can therefore say that crucial aspects of the dynamic construction, negotiation and renegotiation of identities in multilingual contexts depend on the beliefs about and practices of language. This does not mean that language is the sole element that shapes our identity, but it certainly is a key tool in negotiating one. In consequence, if a dominant powerful majority in any polity decided that their ideal model of society should be monolingual, monolithic, monotheist and mono-ideological, then it would be setting out in stark terms who is included in / excluded from that construct.

In the past, language has been considered to be the central component of identity. More specifically, language was seen to establish or delimit the boundaries of groups, either as nations or according to geographic regions. More recently, research has focused on recognising the social position, the partiality and the contestability of language uses and beliefs as a result of political and power relations within societies. Thus, negotiating identities becomes not only a linguistic but also a political issue. Language varieties may be regarded as equal in value, but political and popular discourse places superior value on the standard official variety, and this often results in the standardisation and hegemony of a monolingual variety. This hegemonic – not to mention highly political – value makes the language of powerful institutions (such as schools) the dominant language of the group, and members of minorities see it as the superior language. This misattributed superiority also implies that the dominant language has greater moral, aesthetic and intellectual value, all of which devalues the linguistic varieties of the minorities.

Multilinguals must renegotiate their identity in response to hegemonic language ideologies that favour monolingualism, but this process is fraught with uncertainties. What linguistic phenomena are involved? What is the range of identities that are negotiable? From how early on do multilinguals begin negotiating their identities? We can start with this last question as to the early stages of defining frontiers of group inclusion and building identities: children who belong to minority social groups begin negotiating their identity through language use and rights from very early stages in life. Consider the following example from a kindergarten class in Central Israel with children from less privileged families, mostly immigrants from the former Soviet Union, Ethiopia and Yemen. In a public religious kindergarten (range of ages 4;10–5;9), the teacher and the teaching assistant are discussing with a group of children what is needed to make a storybook with Ethiopian tales like the book *Mirkam* they had read (the original conversation was in Hebrew; the translation into English preserves, where relevant, the Hebrew lexical nuances).

1. *Teacher: shows the Mirkam book.*
2. Assistant: Who knows this book?
3. Itzhak: The Ethiopia book.
4. Assistant: What does it have in it?
5. Itzhak: Many stories that happened in Ethiopia many years ago.
6. Israel: Someone told the man and he wrote.
7. Assistant: Who told?
8. Everybody: The Ethiopians.
9. Assistant: Why only the Ethiopians?
10. Chagit: Because they were in Ethiopia.
11. Teacher: The editor was not in Ethiopia. He wanted people to know and remember all these stories that were told, therefore, he wrote. The people from Ethiopia told him and he wrote, now it is written and anyone can read. Let's see what the book looks like.
12. Dina: Pictures.
13. Teacher: One page is written in Hebrew – and here?
14. Rivka: English.
15. Itzhak: No Ethiopian, no Amharic.

16.   Daniel: 'cause the Ethiopians speak Ethiopian, Amharic, and the Ethiopians do not know how to read in Hebrew.
17.   Itzhak: My mum knows how to read in Hebrew.
18.   Rivka: My dad knows too.
19.   Yarden: My mum also knows.
20.   Chagit: How does she know?
21.   Teacher: She learned.
22.   Yarden: What did she learn?
23.   Teacher: To read in Hebrew
24.   Bat-El: My mum knows how to read in Yemenite.
25.   Shoshana and Osher: My mum is also Yemenite.
26.   Osher: My dad knows how to read the Torah.
       They take some time to look at the book.
27.   Teacher: You know, I read all the stories in this book and noticed that almost all of the stories are suited for older children – school children.
28.   Yarden: What a pity, I thought there were stories that are good for us kids.
       Silence.
29.   Assistant: What do you think; can we make a book like this one? That will suit us and that will be ours?
30.   Simcha: Yes, you need paper = *daf* (in Hebrew there is a distinction between paper = *niyar* the material, and sheet of paper = *daf*).
31.   Teacher: Here's paper (*daf*).
32.   Simcha: No, you need a lot.
33.   Teacher: Here there are lots of papers (*dapim*).
34.   Shoshana: You need to staple them.
35.   Teacher: Here I stapled them … that's it. Now we have stories from Ethiopia.
36.   Avi: No you've got to copy.
37.   Assistant: Copy?
38.   Itzhak: It will be the same.
39.   Avi: You have to copy from the Ethiopian who will tell you.
40.   Daniel: Not to copy, to write.
41.   Simcha: You don't know the stories.
42.   Itzhak: You are white.
43.   Avi: The Ethiopian will tell you and you will write.
44.   Itzhak: For example my mum.
45.   Yarden: I know how to tell stories in Ethiopian.
       (He walks over to the middle of the room and says a few words.)
46.   Rivka: These are just words, they are not a story.
47.   Itzhak: My mum could tell a story.
48.   Yarden: My mum too, my mum too.
49.   Teacher: OK. We will invite them to tell us stories.

From this dialogue, in which identity and language rights are clearly contested and put to the test, we see that children themselves construct and renegotiate their identity within the frontiers of what is allowed by the social group. In that way, the 'white' (i.e. non-Ethiopian, Yeminite or Russian) child (line 42) is banned from the right to tell stories for this particular book dealing with Ethiopian tales because they are not Ethiopian, their parents are not Ethiopian and thus they hold no linguistic or cultural legitimacy to tell Ethiopian tales. At the same time, the Ethiopian child (line 45) who wishes to take up this linguistic and cultural challenge claiming that he is Ethiopian and that he speaks Amharic, is very quickly deprived of that right. He, unlike the Yemenite child or the Russian child, has the cultural but not the linguistic requirements to tell such stories (line 46). Not only that, but Ethiopian tales are to be told by older people – namely parents (lines 47 and 48). In other words, while languages may supply the linguistic means by which identities are constructed and expressed, the use of the linguistic resources also serve to define the individual's identity.

So, what does this negotiation involve? We alluded earlier to the fact that negotiation of identity is a two-way process both within the individual (i.e. 'self' and 'body') in relation to the external social habitat (i.e. power and authority) and from the external social habitat towards the inner self of the individual. This interaction is what stands at the core of negotiation. In such interactions, identities are shaped, negotiated, renegotiated, calibrated and owned in a dynamic and relative manner. This manner of creating identity is closely connected with the position each element or member takes up in relation to the other. Harré (1990) proposes two types of such position, interactive positioning (i.e. one individual positioning the other) and reflective positioning (i.e. positioning oneself).

Positioning processes involve – but are not limited to – race, ethnicity, gender, age, geopolitical and social affiliations, and sexual orientation. Once the individuals take ownership of a position, they see the world from the perspective of the images, metaphors, storylines and concepts they embrace. The Argentine novelist Ana María Shua relates to her multiple and dynamic identities as 'Woman, Argentine, Jew and writer in that order or any other order'. Similarly, for many years in Israel, people who spoke Hebrew with a heavy French accent were automatically regarded as being of Moroccan provenance and they were looked down upon by other ethnic groups. Yet French people who emigrated to the USA were embraced for being francophone and their language enjoyed the privileged status attributed to French in the USA, namely, the language of culture, chic and aristocracy.

Which are the linguistic phenomena involved? Negotiation of identity concerns many aspects of language. This is true for monolingual groups, which may negotiate a certain identity by adjusting register, pronunciation, use of vernacular or exploitation of lexicon, for example. When it comes to multilingual negotiation of identity, in addition to the range of possibilities that apply to the monolingual, the multilingual must also negotiate across languages, and these, of course, come accompanied by cultural cues and nuances. This process of negotiation across and within language groups results in a plethora of ways in which language, dialects and registers are used to appropriate, explore, reproduce or challenge influential and powerful images and stereotypes to which individuals might want to belong. Therefore, in addition to crossing borders within a language group or across language groups, the multilingual linguistic identity is highly influenced by the possible combinations across languages – which gives rise to the familiar phenomenon of code-switching and code-mixing.

There is another question that we raised at the beginning of this section: what is the range of identities that are negotiable? Research has tended to see this range in terms of the equation 'race/ethnicity = culture = language'. This approach has been questioned, and different poststructuralists have proposed alternatives. Some of these view negotiated identities as continuous across these categories, yet more recently the tendency has been to regard them as hybrid and to allow language and culture to intersect them. For example, whereas in the past ethnic identities were viewed as stable and given, today this is no longer the case. Hensel (1996) best illustrates this point in an anthropological study of the subsistence discourse of central Alaskan Yup'ik Eskimos. The study shows that the criterion for inclusion was not genetic heritage (or birthright affiliation), but strategic talk and practices about fishing and hunting. That is to say, people were less concerned with the maintenance of 'Yup'ik Eskimo' identity or the individual's 'non-native' identity, and more with 'native-like' practice within the context of a given activity.

The multilingual juggles aspects of identity such as ethnicity, inclusion and exclusion, power and majority–minority relations and status, most of which are always reflected in the languages available to and used by the individual. The nature of multilingual identity involves not only these aspects of identity, but also the prominence that each variable has at a given point in time, in concrete situations, in interactions with certain individuals and for specific social and communicative purposes and contexts. Identity is a dynamic feature of the multilingual that relies on a continuum that ranges from non-changeable to negotiable core characteristics, as well as the abilities and faculties of each individual. The dynamic nature of identity depends on the flexibility and malleability of combining the appropriate identity-making factors in the right dosage so as to position the individual in different social/ethnic contexts. In these linguistic circles, the person can identify with speakers of the languages that are common to them and empathise with other multilinguals with whom they may have no languages in common. Multilinguals can have multiple identities that are not isolated one from the other. In fact, they are privileged to have a kind of 'kaleidoscopic' identity.

7.5 ACCOMMODATING MULTILINGUALISM AND FAMILY LANGUAGE POLICIES

Accommodating multilingualism is a complex task that can be viewed either as a top-down process whereby states or regions establish a language policy for their citizens to adhere to, or as a bottom-up process in which the individuals accommodate their multilingualism so as to satisfy ideological, practical and existential needs. In fact, the process of accommodating multilingualism crosses all these levels and is nourished and influenced all the way from the global to the individual level. The link between the individual and the societal accommodation of multilingualism occurs within the family unit – a unit inherent to human development in which the individual develops into a social being. Incipient steps into socialisation begin in the family – that is, the unit of people committed to start a nuclear and expanding group, with features governing their routine practices and communication integrated into their choice of a language as means of accommodation (Giles *et al.* 1973). Initially, families must decide which language(s) to use, maintain or forgo. Typically, parents manage the children's language as means to socialisation, so that 'younger children and other novices, through interactions with older and/or more experienced persons, acquire the knowledge and practices that are necessary for them to function as, and be regarded as, competent members of their communities' (Garrett and Baquedano-Lopez 2002: 341).

In the nuclear family the crucial choice in establishing a Family Language Policy (FLP) is determining what language the child or children should speak; at the initial stages of language development this includes deciding what language the child should hear in the home. How are these choices created? What turns a linguistic reality into a parental FLP decision and choice? Decisions of this kind are clearly influenced by various aspects of the sociolinguistic ecology inside and outside the home and by the parents' beliefs about the best strategy to follow. Some of these aspects are internal to the family, whereas others are external to the nuclear unit. To mention just a few, families accommodate multilingualism by agreeing on language practices to be used within the family, i.e. they choose which language or languages are used between parents and children and what the role of each of them should be. Their decisions will be based on considerations of practicality, but may also be influenced by their own preferences, motivations and attitudes, by the presence of other people within the family sphere and by changes in the family's circumstances as well as the linguistic needs and preferences of the growing family.

Internal forces that shape the FLP are most noticeable in multilingual families – especially, but not only, immigrant populations with different heritage languages. In these families, one internal force for determining the FLP is the comfort and naturalness of using the heritage language for expressions of affection and emotion, a particular linguistic practice which is typical in family relations. Another internal force is consideration of other family members and the maintenance of ties with the country of origin, which leads to an FLP practice of accommodating another language yet maintaining cultural heritage and linguistic identity.

There is a natural internal force that drives the accommodation of multilingualism in the family: the adults speak the new language (often a basic version of it) in the home, hoping that this will help the children to adapt more quickly to the new linguistic environment. This internal force expands further when more children or other relatives come under the sociolinguistic pressure of school and peers and bring the new language into the home. Internal factors play an important role in shaping the relationships between family members, their respect for each other and the authority that any one of them may have. Other influences of an ideological nature (e.g. cultural or religious ones) may also impact on the choices parents make regarding which languages should be used at home and, in particular, with the children.

External factors that have an impact on the accommodation of languages as part of the FLP are primarily of two types. The first is driven by societal pressures and geopolitical conditions, and the second by ideology and culture. Drawing a clear separation between these is difficult. Social external factors that influence FLPs are heightened when a family moves from one country to another, from the countryside to the city or from one neighbourhood to another. Such moves are subject to societal external forces that require new choices regarding the languages to be used at home with the children and with the new neighbours, and also about what language is to be maintained in order to keep ties with the previous geographic/cultural environment. These new conditions often result in parents having to make decisions about FLP practices on the basis of attitudes towards and perceptions of the worth of each language in the new context, the values attributed to languages either by the family or by the new social group and the prestige of and prejudices against each language. In addition, there are also external factors driven by cultural and ideological (and sometimes emotional) motivations such as language maintenance, language revitalisation, the need for upward mobility in the western world and trends related to globalisation.

7.6   EFFECTS OF ATTITUDES TOWARDS MULTILINGUALISM ON FLP

The attitudes of communities, teachers, parents and children towards the minority and majority languages and towards multilingualism are reflected in the choices made at family level. Speakers form attitudes towards other speakers who sound different because of their accent, pronunciation, lexical choice or usage of other codes. Sometimes these attitudes become prototypical or stereotypical, and this leads to different social perceptions and behaviour in our communicative practices and socialisation. In many ways, attitudes and language use are closely related, not only within the family but also as a link to the other community circles that impact on inclusion into majority and minority groups. Attitudes towards the languages, their use and being bilingual or multilingual are closely connected to the language maintenance, language loss and ethnolinguistic vitality of the community (Hamers and Blanc 2000).

Studies of language attitudes have traditionally measured speakers with regard to different languages, dialects, registers and accents by comparing these within the same society, both in monolingual studies (Labov 1972) and multilingual ones of the same community, such as cases with two languages like French and English in Quebec (Genesee and Bourhis 1988) or multilingual societies where there is an L_1, L_2 and L_3 like the Basque country (Cenoz 2009; Lasagabaster and Huguet 2007). In a succinct description of language attitude studies, Chin Ng and Wigglesworth (2007) argue that '[these] studies generally examine attitudes from four main perspectives' (p. 107). These perspectives can be summarised as follows: most of the time studies target the educational impact or consequences of language attitudes and the use of language in a bilingual community by minorities as well as the majority. Very few studies have inquired about the effect of attitudes on language use in relation to FLP focusing on issues such as: (i) who is affected by these attitudes? (ii) what exactly do they affect? (iii) who are the agents of the effects of attitudes? and (iv) on whom do such attitudes have an impact? These questions are addressed in the following section.

7.7 THE ESTABLISHMENT AND MAINTENANCE OF FLP: STRATEGIES, PRACTICES AND OUTCOMES

One of the strongest driving forces of FLPs is the urge to maintain the heritage language while learning the new one(s) as a means to make the transition from the 'previous life' into the 'new life'. The maintenance of the heritage language provides a link with the cultural provenance of the parent(s). It may involve the language of both mother and father, each parent bringing a language that is different from that of the majority group, and one parent having a heritage language that is different from the one used by the majority group and the other parent.

Although the complexity of factors that influence the maintenance of languages as an FLP within the nuclear family begins with the linguistic constellation of the parents, it soon comes under the influence of the linguistic spheres within which the family circulates, such as community, country, extended family and friends. It is not until the nuclear family begins to grow that the urgency of decisions regarding maintenance of the heritage language becomes more real (Barron-Hauwaert 2003, 2004; Tokuhama-Espinosa 2001). The issues of maintenance that drive the language policy of the family result in a linguistic contest that is influenced by whose language should be maintained, for whom, for what and why.

Often the external force shaping the FLP is the extended family left behind in the homeland to which the culture and language are still attached. Other forces driving maintenance may also be the older generation, which may be less willing or able to forgo the heritage language. Whether from a distance or in the home, the role played by the extended family may demand serious proactive measures, not only in instituting a maintenance FLP, but also in establishing in the younger generation(s) the need to maintain the parental language(s), even though it may not serve any purpose other than the preservation of home and family ties.

Family language policies are important because they shape children's developmental trajectories, connect in significant ways with children's formal school success and collectively determine the maintenance and future status of minority languages. The different strategies employed by families reflect in their implementation the ideological basis for maintaining the heritage language. It is important to note, however, that not all families follow a clearly formulated FLP – many find that they are constantly readjusting their policy, and they may abandon it altogether. Others never think much about matters of language maintenance, as they are more (or solely) focused on the acquisition of the language of the host country. Nonetheless, studies reporting on families who make heritage language maintenance part of their FLP argue that this maintenance has been successful even beyond the stage at which the children begin to identify with peer groups outside the home and the outside language is brought into the home (Hazen 2002).

Joshua Fishman (1991, 2001) has argued persuasively that the pillar of language maintenance is the intergenerational transmission of the language embedded in his Graded Intergenerational Disruption Scale. The basic premise is that, in order to maintain the heritage language, children must learn this language from their parents, and in turn they will be able to pass it on to their children. Intergenerational transmission is propelled not only by the decision made by the parents, but also by the societal and institutional choices which influence parental decisions regarding their language behaviour with regard to their children.

At the heart of Fishman's work on language maintenance and revitalisation is the characterisation of the extent to which a particular language is endangered and serves as a heuristic device to assist communities and individuals to maintain and even revive a heritage language. Accordingly, heritage languages also grow through transfer of language knowledge from one generation to the next within communities and families. This intergenerational transmission of heritage languages is crucial to the vitality of heritage language communities, as in the case of immigrant communities in which the first generation acquires some of the host language while remaining strongest in the native tongue; the second generation usually becomes bilingual with more developed literacy skills in the host language because it is the language of schooling; and the third generation has a tendency to use the host language predominantly with little or no capability in the heritage language. Fishman advocates that heritage language maintenance and its development must be supported so as to encourage transfer of language from one generation to another.

Intergenerational transmission occurs when the non-dominant language becomes the everyday vehicle of informal spoken interaction among members of all three generations within the family. According to Fishman (1991), intergenerational transmission of language is the most difficult and pivotal task in language revitalisation efforts, because it directly affects other societal policies – specifically, at the level of the community or the nation. Fishman argues that language maintenance is not a global 'total language task', but rather a 'functionally specific process that must be tackled on well-chosen, functionally specific grounds' (1991: 65).

External forces such as globalisation and internationalisation, plus the need for upward mobility, also affect FLPs. Globalisation has shrunk the size of the world through media and technology in such a way that the vast majority of the world population is either a consumer or a producer of technology-geared information. Globalisation has put the need or actual practice of multilingualism at the centre of people's lives irrespective of geographical, economic, political, educational, religious, ethnic, gender or age characterisation. Public stances on bilingualism and multilingualism have varied across time and context. These ideologies of language are also linked to broader societal attitudes, for instance towards particular segments of the population (e.g. immigrants or ethnic minorities) or towards particular parenting styles or practices (Dorian 1998; Woolard 1998; King and Fogle 2006).

Parents seldom plan the linguistic future of their children, but those who do may have choices that are driven by the way in which bilingualism is presented in the public discourses. Grosjean (1982: 169, 173) speaks of childhood bilingualism as 'a planned affair' and of 'planned bilingualism in the family' with reference to parents who make a conscious decision to raise their children bilingually (Barron-Hauwaert 2003, 2004). We propose to supplement this vision with the idea that, as multilingualism is becoming more prevalent, it becomes increasingly important that this 'affair be planned'.

Private planning discourses are construed against the various public discourses available to the parents. As a result of the valorisation of the idea of 'elite bilingualism', parents have come to see bilingualism as an investment in their children's future. This, of course, may take many forms, some of which will be mentioned later in this chapter. However, as two radically different examples from the unpublished data collected for the study of Stavans and Goldzweig (2009) show, when both Ethiopian and Russian parents are asked whether it is important that their child be bilingual in Hebrew and the heritage language they both agree it is important and most valuable. But the Russian parents see it as their main role to foster Russian, whereas the Ethiopian couples consider it more important to foster Hebrew. When asked for reasons they gave answers such as the following:

> There are many reasons why my child must speak, read and write in Russian which go beyond communicating with his grandmother. There are things that when you say them in Russian sound more cultured, educated and intelligent. Besides, the Russian cultural baggage is greater and more sophisticated than the Israeli one, and I want my child to read Tolstoy in Russian and not in a Hebrew translation. The Russian language is rich and sophisticated, not to mention the culture it codes.
>
> (Russian parent Irena interviewed in 2004)

The Ethiopian parent, a nurse by training, began this part of her interview discussing how she learned English when studying biology in Addis Ababa and the fact that she recalls a lot of memorisation with little English or biology learning. She recalls how her parents were appreciative of her learning English, as this was something that would make the family proud. Upon her arrival in Israel and after the birth of her first child, Avnesh (in 2006) said:

> When I came to Israel and my child was born it was clear to me that my child needed to learn Hebrew more than he needed to know Amharic. After all, I could translate what my mother-in-law said to him; true, my Hebrew was poor, but I did my best – and we were determined that the best future for our children was a good mastery of the language of Israel. That is the key to making it here, to go to a good high school, to go to a good job in the army and to have a university education with a real profession. Like all Israeli mothers I want my child to be a lawyer or a doctor or a businessman, and without Hebrew he will not make it. So you see, much as Amharic is my heart language, I force myself to speak Hebrew and we try to do that at home with the kids because that is investing in a better future for them. In a way we have succeeded, my kids speak to each other at home in Hebrew.
>
> (Ethiopian parent Avnesh interviewed in 2006)

In a study carried out by Stavans and Goldzweig in 2009, clear motivations to maintain the heritage language vis-à-vis learning the majority language were found. Each of two cohort immigrant groups, Ethiopians and Russians, were compared. The reasons they gave for learning and keeping their languages were very different. Their reasoning was reflected not only in their attitudes towards the languages, their use and their learning, but also in the way they deployed these languages within their adopted FLP. We argue that sociolinguistic and economic forces affect the most intimate of home interactions, and that the importance of the domestic sphere is regularly underrated

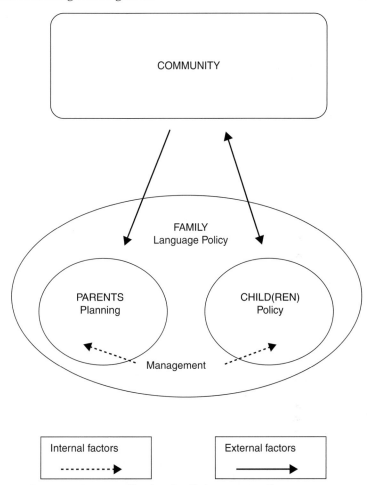

Figure 7.1 Factors affecting family language policy

in discussions of language planning and policy that tend to focus on high-status and highly visible public domains such as the school and the mass media, even though the centrality of these domains to minority-language maintenance or revitalisation is questionable. What is often overlooked is that the FLP is not only a parental project but also the project of the children. Children's role in the linguistic socialisation of adult family members derives from children having greater access than adults to socially valued linguistic resources, itself a result of school assuming socialising functions. The factors affecting FLP are captured in diagrammatic form in Figure 7.1.

This diagram is an attempt to summarise how factors of internal and external pressures influence language accommodation of multilingual families and result in the establishment of planned or unplanned FLPs and practices led by the parents. The community has a direct influence on the FLP. The parents navigate this influence in a planned or unplanned manner through the choices that they make. Their planning and choices then become practices that are managed on a daily basis and imposed on or required from other family members, the children in particular. Children, in turn, have a critical role as the recipients and executors of this planning and policy, and with their responses to the planning of the FLP led by the parents they feed back so as to constantly help to manage and calibrate the policy. The outcome is that the management of the FLP is dynamic, as it is constantly reshaped by feedback and new needs by the parents and the children. The management of the FLP is driven by internal forces such as the need to maintain the heritage language for communication with older generations or for identity purposes and inclusion within a particular ethnic/cultural group. The external forces that configure the FLP come from the community in two flows, through the parents and also through the children. It is therefore the children who provide feedback of external forces to the community, in particular through their socialisation at school and other non-formal socialisation frameworks to which they are exposed and belong.

Issues surrounding FLPs are of great importance, since language socialisation in the home is a determining factor for language maintenance. A dynamic, relational view of language socialisation requires us to attend to children not only as the objects of socialisation, but also as its potential agents. Studies of the acquisition of another language and culture open a window to the interaction between domestic language use and the broader social dynamics of globalisation, modernisation, migration and the emergent identities and social relationships accompanying these processes. All of these feed into ideologies, beliefs, prejudices and practices which are at the core of creating the FLP they desire. According to Spolsky (2009: 431) 'it is common for parents and caretakers to take for granted the authority to manage their children's language', although he also casts doubt as to the actual success or the relative influences fathers and mothers may have, as this success may depend on cultural patterns. What do parents do about managing their children's languages? How do they go about it? In the following we ask how attempts to formulate FLPs can be characterised.

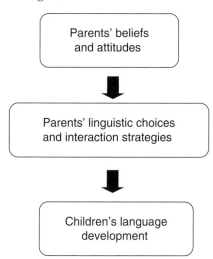

Figure 7.2 Relationship between beliefs, practices and outcomes in childhood multilingualism (based on De Houwer 1999)

In a study on language variation in three families with small children in Antwerp, De Houwer (1999) showed that, whereas there may be distinctions in usage when older children and adults address the younger members of the family, they tend to increase their use of neutral forms and reduce their use of local forms. The younger children's usage depends on who they are addressing. De Houwer's (1999) relationship between beliefs, practices and outcomes in childhood multilingualism is illustrated in Figure 7.2.

In her proposal, De Houwer argues that parents often have reasonably clear ideas about which languages they should use with their children and for what purposes. These ideas are borne from parents' attitudes concerning particular types of interactions, both social and linguistic, such as mixing or use of slang, which influence their own child-directed speech. Also, parents' attitudes towards language learning and bilingualism impact on their interactional strategies, although the degree to which parents see themselves as capable of, and responsible for, shaping their children's language may vary.

The linguistic strategies of families vary widely and are captured in various attempts to set up typologies of multilingual families. Perhaps the most influential one to describe families into which children are born and raised as bilinguals was proposed by Romaine (1985, 1995b). Her typology (see Table 7.1) distinguishes six different

Table 7.1 *Romaine's typology of families raising children bilingually*

Type of family	Strategy	Features	Earlier documented studies exemplifying the strategy			
			Researcher	Mother language	Father language	Community language
1. One person – one language	Each parent speaks their own native language to the child from birth.	Parents: each parent has a different native language but each has some competence in the other's language. Community: the language of one parent is the dominant language of the community.	Ronjat (1913)	German	French	French
			Leopold (1939–49)	English	German	German
			Taeschner (1983)	German	Italian	Italian
2. Non-dominant home language	Both parents speak the non-dominant language to the child and the child is fully exposed to the dominant language only when outside the home.	Parents: have different native languages. Community: the language of one parent is the dominant language of the community.	Fantini (1985)	Spanish	English	English
3. Non-dominant home language without community support	The parents speak their own language (the same) to the child.	Parents: share the same native language. Community: the dominant language is not that of the parents.	Haugen (1953)	Norwegian	Norwegian	English
			Oksaar (1977)	Estonian	Estonian	Swedish/German
			Ruke-Dravina (1967)	Latvian	Latvian	Swedish
			Pavlovich (1920)	Servian	Servian	French

Type	Strategy	Parents / Community	Studies			
4. Double non-dominant home language without community support	Each parent speaks their own (different) language to the child.	Parents: do not share the same native language. Community: the dominant language is different from either of the parents' languages.	Elwert (1959)	English	German	Italian
5. Non-native parents	One of the parents always addresses the child in a language that is not his/her native language.	Parents: share the same native language. Community: the dominant language is the same as that of the parents.	Saunders (1982)	English	English (German)	English
6. Mixed languages	Parents code-switch and mix languages.	Parents: are bilingual. Community: a sector of the community may also be bilingual.	Tabouret-Keller (1962) Ellul (1978)	French/ German/ Maltese/ English	French/ German/ Maltese/ English	French/ German/ Maltese/ English
			Smith (1935) Burling (1959)	English English	English English	Chinese Garo

Based on Romaine (1985, 1995b).

communication strategies that lead to child bilingual, and in one case (Type 4) multilingual, development.

This typology, discussed in Chapter 5 in relation to modes of becoming multilingual, has been used extensively and adapted to trilingual and multilingual contexts (Hoffmann 2001a; Braun and Cline 2010). In other studies (King and Fogle 2006; King and Logan-Terry 2008; Spolsky 2009), however, Romaine's proposed categories have been disregarded, as it is claimed that there are just two main types of strategies for FLP setting, the one-parent-one-language and the home-community ones, a view shared by Piller (2001), who subdivides them into four strategies:

> Strategy 1: 'One person one language' (which includes Romaine's Type 1, Type 4, Type 5) is characterised by contexts in which parents are consistent in their language choice and ensure that the children adhere to the adopted norm. Outcomes can be variable, but the children frequently achieve high levels of competence in both languages.

> Strategy 2: The adoption of 'home language versus community language' (Type 2, Type 3, and Type 4) implies that the family encourages the use of one language at home and the majority one outside the home. However, it often produces an unenforced FLP in contexts where the children, under the influence of peers, deviate from the norm because they do not always accept the use of the home language in the family. As Fantini (1982, 1985) showed, the outcome of a successful implementation of this strategy can be that the bilingual child acquires advanced metalinguistic awareness and a strong interest in languages and cultures.

> Strategy 3: The main feature of 'code-switching and language mixing' (Type 6) is the basic parental acceptance of a mixed code as a means to communicate. Adopting this strategy may represent a conscious choice by parents. If it does, parents adopt the 'play it by ear' style of language policy (Harding and Riley 1986: 85), which in turn can result in considerable mixing of the two languages. Mixing may not be avoided in many multilingual situations (Stavans and Hoffmann 2007; Hoffmann and Stavans 2007; Stavans and Swisher 2006), for instance in conversations on certain topics or in the use of language for affective purposes.

> Strategy 4 is discussed in Grosjean (1982): it means the consecutive (rather than simultaneous) introduction of the

community language(s), i.e. the delay of exposure to this language for a least the first two years.

The typologies and strategies described above represent family language possibilities from which choices must be made. Once parents see what linguistic resources they have at their disposal, define their objectives and decide what FLP to adopt, their child's language development can be set in motion. What is at the core of their FLP is the examination of the methods of implementation of such policy.

The implementation and management of FLPs offers a range of practices to choose from. The most important step is to decide what language to speak at home so as to control its language environment. If the parents are fluent in the language(s) that they wish their children to hear, this strategy can work well; but, as in the case of the Ethiopian parent quoted above, sometimes the refusal to permit any language other than the host language to be spoken in the home may be detrimental to the children if they don't have native-like models on which to base their language acquisition.

Another practice may be to introduce into the household other sources of language interaction in the desired new language; this is typical for monolingual homes or bilingual homes with languages that are not spoken in the community. This can be achieved by the presence of a third party such as a relative from the old country, a caregiver from the new, or neighbours and playmates. A significant input can also be obtained by the constant and active use of technology such as radio, movies, internet and television. Controlling its use in the home may be a form of language management.

A third possible practice is to adhere to a particular language by monitoring the sociolinguistic environment, e.g. insisting that children use a particular language ('did I hear you speaking X?'); or requiring the accommodation of a third party ('you must speak Spanish when Safta [your grandmother] is here; it is rude to speak a language she does not understand!'); or restricting a language to specific activities such as reading a story in language X at bedtime, talking in a specific language about an event that took place in that linguistic environment or setting a language to be used during holiday meals ('we speak Hebrew on Passover because we discuss the story of Passover in Hebrew') etc. These explicit instructions can be reinforced through explanations ('it sounds much better when you say it in Dutch – it sounds more educated'), exercising authority ('why do you speak to *aba* [father] in English, you know he speaks Spanish to you') or simply rejecting the inappropriate use of the alternative

language ('na, na, na, na ... [covers ears] I can't hear you ... if you
want me to hear what you say stop speaking Hebrew to me' or 'I don't
understand English, speak Hebrew').

On the basis of anecdotal evidence we can only guess at the circumstances in which these various methods can be adopted and
what their relative success may be. Piller mentions four underlying
considerations that parents can have for systematically fostering
bilingualism in their child. The first such consideration parents
report on is that they see 'childhood bilingualism as an investment'
(Piller 2001: 71). Their motivations and reasons for educating their
children bilingually are that they see it as good for their children's
future. These parents believe that a small effort on their part (i.e.
to speak their languages to the child) will yield a high return. On
the other hand, if their child will have to learn these languages as
second languages later in life, particularly as part of foreign language learning in school, parents may feel that this kind of learning
demands more effort yet yields lower returns. The desired outcome
for the parents is native-like proficiency in every language. As Heller
(2000: 10) claims: 'what is valued is the careful separation of linguistic practices, being monolingual several times over'. Another
methodological consideration that parents have to address once
they have chosen their strategy is consistency: for multilingualism
to be established successfully, they have to adhere consistently to
the same language practices.

Consistency may be jeopardised in any one of three situations: (a)
when a poor choice of FLP has been made, for instance if one parent
feels excluded because he or she has difficulties participating in the
interactions between the other parent and the child/children; (b) when
one parent does not have the linguistic knowledge and is unwilling or
afraid to admit it to the child or others; and (c) when parents have not
implemented their strategy from the earliest possible time.

Practices, strategies and typologies leading to actual outcomes can
be the product of an established FLP. However, even the best planned
and engineered FLP may be upset by the children themselves, perhaps because they do not appreciate their parents' needs and desires
to foster multilingualism at home. Children make decisions about
the direction of their language development which may or may not
coincide with their parents' plans. The influence of children's emerging competencies on the language habits of other family members
shows that parents and communities are not the only agents of socialisation. A dynamic, relational view of language socialisation requires

us to see children not only as the objects of socialisation, but also as its instigators.

7.8   CONCLUSION

Language accommodation is driven by multilingual language choice, the forces that influence and shape these choices, and the strategies necessary to make choices and adapt to linguistic needs. The most important aspects of language accommodation are the differences (if any) between the motivations and attitudes of the individual and those of the family/wider community, and also the way in which multilingual accommodation negotiates beliefs, customs, cultural assumptions and identities. Here we list some of the most salient issues discussed in this chapter:

- Multilinguals make language choices according to their communicative needs: this may involve choosing different languages according to interlocutor and purpose of interaction.
- Language choices are subject to a number of factors such as power, minority–majority relationships, inclusion and exclusion, ethnic interests, maintenance and adjustability.
- Language choices are influenced by attitudes towards members of the multilingual speech community, and also towards members from outside the multilingual's speech community.
- Individuals use communication to indicate and shape their attitudes towards each other; they do so either by adapting their communicative behaviour to that of their interlocutor or, conversely, by refusing to adapt and thus distancing themselves from the interlocutor's communicative style.
- Adaptation is achieved through choice of language, style and register, together with non-verbal features such as gestures (facial or otherwise) and eye-gaze – all of which are affected by the different socialisation circles and the constant internal need to negotiate a multilingual identity.
- FLPs constitute a pivotal concern for both researchers and minority-language advocates, because they yield insights on minority children's home language acquisition and maintenance and their socialisation.

8 Multilingual education and multilingual literacies

> You can never understand one language until you understand at least two.
>
> Geoffrey Willans

8.1 INTRODUCTION

The centrality and growth of multilingualism worldwide has generated a linguistic reality that has given rise to new educational requirements. Advances in technology and the ever-growing demand for international communication and international mobility have led to the need for people to have command of more than one language. In addition, a greater recognition of minority languages in states that previously promoted monolingualism has produced an increase in multilingualism. Most of the world's languages are minority languages. The need for literacy and communicative skills is changing, and the mobility of people across nations is generating ever more transnational multilingualism. This new multilingualism can jeopardise small languages, but it can also lead to the maintenance of the linguistic uniqueness of the different people who have come into contact with each other. The price of globalisation does not have to be the loss of ethnic individuality, identity or roots; it may bring with it a yearning for recognition of differences and the acceptance of otherness.

Multilingual education has become an urgent concern. It is a dynamic enterprise that involves multiple practices and challenges at various times for different individuals in diverse parts of the world. The importance of multilingual education is uncontested, for it has the role of protecting and maintaining different languages, speech communities, their identities and linguistic longevity. The ecological and sociocultural context of a multilingual world underpins the relationship between languages, and various policy strategies can be used to achieve a harmonious balance between all languages in a given environment (Haugen 1972; Hornberger 2003; Mühlhäusler 2003; Fill and Mühlhäusler 2001; Skutnabb-Kangas *et al.* 2003). This ecology of languages is reflected in multilingual education systems in which multilingualism is no longer a deficit but an asset, as stated, for example, by Baker (2002), who writes about the advantages of multilingualism for communication, culture, cognition, curriculum, cash and career.

8.2 AIMS OF MULTILINGUAL EDUCATION

Multilingual education typically refers to 'first-language-first' education, that is, schooling that is anchored in the mother tongue and later adds other languages. Whereas the multilingual classroom presents ample and creative openings for effective language learning and intercultural understanding, such opportunities are frequently lost. Teachers can easily underestimate the complexities of the multilingual classroom; even if they are aware of them, they may not always know best how to exploit the potential of plurilingual students. Quite often, multilingual education programmes exist in countries where speakers of minority languages or immigrant populations who represent a linguistic minority are regarded as disadvantaged by the mainstream education system. In the following sections we discuss multilingual education from the perspectives of teaching and learning, the role of the languages and of multilingual pupils, and the consequences of multilingual education in terms of literacy.

The definition of multilingual education may be based on different, albeit related, perspectives. Skutnabb-Kangas and McCarty (2008) propose a sociolinguistics-driven definition according to which multilingual education is based on the use of two or more languages rather than the teaching of the formal aspect of these languages. A more sociocultural educational perspective is offered by Cummins (2007, 2009), Baker and García (2007) and May (2007), who suggest that school subjects should be imparted through the medium of two or more languages, which will promote language learning, instead of teaching languages as subject matter.

Cenoz proposes focusing on 'schools and programmes that aim at achieving communicative competence and literacy skills in more than two languages' (Cenoz 2009: 33). In their survey, Coste *et al.* (2009) treat plurilingualism in education with both scepticism and hope. They argue that historically and institutionally the school has not been a place where plurilingualism and pluriculturalism could thrive. Frequently, slogans about the plurality of languages and cultures are nothing but expressions of zealous hopes, unless realistic proposals based on proactive planning and policies that overcome mainstream resistance are progressively put to the test of innovation. Plurilingual individuals generally have contact with foreign languages through school, but the education system plays only a small part in their linguistic competence, for it treats both language and culture as a subject matter. Thus, the school is not necessarily open to all cultures. It is capable of rejection, denying a linguistic and cultural reality that does not conform to national linguistic policy, and it is also capable of disseminating a culture not based on an existing cultural reality. In this sense, the school's contribution to the enhancement of plurilingualism and even pluriculturalism is limited ideologically and practically.

Even when schools assign an important place to language learning, the juxtaposition of separate bodies of knowledge (language by language) prevails over the creation of an integrated plurilingual competence. Languages are taught as decontextualised subject matter. Also, they are often taught following established methodologies and pedagogical approaches in accordance with a strictly structured syllabus. These methodologies treat language as a conglomerate of isolated skills (comprehension, vocabulary, grammar etc.) and abilities rooted simply in its use. Moreover, languages are taught under limited exposure in terms of time, interlocutors, input resources and communicative challenges. Each language is carefully kept separate and expected to coexist in secluded compartments. There is no allowance for transitional systems of interlanguage, mixed systems, forms of code-switching and other occurrences of bilingual speech; moreover, such productions may be considered faulty.

The underlying assumption of the above-mentioned definitions is that the multilingual should attain monolingual competence in each of his or her languages. In consequence, teaching the languages in a multilingual context will always consist of the imparting and the attainment of a certain kind of performance in one or another language, as measured against the monolingual paradigm. This contrasts with the more idealistic aim of educating multilingual children to become true multilinguals. Tucker argues that in quite a few parts of the world there are more bilingual or multilingual children than there are monolingual ones, and that many of them are educated in more than one language at some point in their formal school system. The number of children who are schooled solely in one language is relatively small. This perception has led to a situation where 'innovative language education programmes are often implemented to promote proficiency in international language(s) of wider communication, together with proficiency in national and regional languages. The composite portrait of language education policies and practices throughout the world is exceedingly complex and simultaneously fascinating' (Tucker 1999: 332–33).

The complexity of multilingual education requires an ethos that balances and respects the use of the different languages of the pupils and their communities as a way of life rather than a problem to be solved. Changing perspectives on learners' home languages from 'problem' to 'resource' means that students' multilingual repertoire must be acknowledged and their multilingual competence supported in school. In other words, students from diverse backgrounds are setting a new challenge for our traditionally monolingual school system and policy makers. They are forcing traditionalists to question entrenched ideologies of language and challenging teachers in their everyday classroom to rethink their relationships with language learning and the issue of diversity, whether linguistic, cultural, ethnic or social. The problem of a systematised institutional solution for pluralist societies is that it disregards the risks involved in terms of both learning achievement and loss of linguistic and cultural diversity. Therefore, the diversity of languages, their use, function and societal contribution can provide a compass for successful language teaching.

Safeguarding linguistic diversity today (it is estimated that there are between 6,000 and 7,000 languages in the world) is one of the most urgent challenges facing any multilingual education programme or agenda. This diversity takes the form of uneven interlinguistic forces, for some states are fairly homogeneous linguistically, while other countries and regions display a wealth of linguistic diversity. The distribution of such diversity is overwhelmingly imbalanced, with roughly 70 per cent of all languages of the world found in just twenty states. Multilingual education, whether in modern affluent nations or poorer areas of the world, not only concerns the conservation of all the local languages, but also takes cognisance of the multilingual individual's condition and what the learning outcomes could be. Multilingual education becomes relevant, in particular, in cases where:

(a) there are many individuals for whom multilingualism begins much earlier in life than compulsory education and for whom multilingualism is the L_1;

(b) the language of the formal educational setting (school) is not the same as that of the non-formal setting (home or community);

(c) the attainments of a multilingual are viewed against a monolingual paradigm;

(d) the languages multilinguals have do not serve the same communicative or utilitarian functions in their lives;

(e) a language is taught as subject matter rather than as a vehicle for communication; and

(f) covert agendas drawn up by economic or political forces influence the teaching of language instead of attending to the real needs of the learners.

A desirable multilingual education considers both the teaching that is developed as a consequence of language policy and planning (the macro-level) and the micro-level of multilingualism in education, which is determined by the social networks of the learners. These networks exist within the school boundaries but are not limited to the classroom; they extend beyond the walls of the school into playgrounds, neighbourhood clubs, homes and other socialisation *loci*. Authentic and relevant language is learned in all these networks, which in turn feed into – and are fed by – each other. For example, the Arabic language learned in Israel at school may serve a small set of purposes outside of school and be limited, for a Hebrew-speaking person, to very specific future army service use, while, for that same individual, the English learned at school may expand to more varied socialisation networks. Gregory and Williams (2000) have shown that within the Bangladeshi-British community, the differences in linguistic skills that bilingual children bring to classrooms are the products of a complex and diverse amount of social learning that stems from the cultural environments in which they grow up, which are also dynamic and hybrid.

The relationship between the macro- and micro-level of multilingual education ultimately generates a kaleidoscope of languages. It is therefore too ambitious to expect that attainment of near-native production in all languages will be possible. A clear analysis of why, by whom, when, and for what purpose a given language is learned or acquired may be more realistic.

8.3 TYPES OF MULTILINGUAL EDUCATION

Numerous programmes of bilingual and multilingual education have been developed throughout the world in the past decades, based on various models. Models of multilingual education vary according to the language background of the child at home, in the community and within the national curriculum. Baker (2006), writing about bilingual education, warns that the typologies of this type of education frequently do not address the real-life needs of the bilingual individual. Martin-Jones (2007) reinforces this view as she states that typologies often fail because educational frameworks tend to adopt them in sociolinguistic contexts which are different from those of bilinguals and multilinguals.

According to Baker (2009), the concept of 'bilingual education', which we extrapolate to multilingual education, is ambiguous and generic. He argues that this type of education can refer to one of two situations: either one in which the instruction is carried out in two languages, or one where the pupils in the schools are bilingual. He further suggests (Baker 2006) that there are two versions of bilingual education: a 'strong' version, in which the teaching of some or most of the subjects takes place in two languages, and a 'weak' variety, in which the home language of the students is used to teach content initially and during a transitional period, until the majority language is mastered and introduced in the instructional setting. Under this conceptual framework, multilingual education means practices that take into account the linguistic capital of multilingual children and make scholastic allowances to achieve transitional maintenance. Children shift from minority language to majority language use and undergo cultural assimilation as they acquire the majority language – and, simultaneously, maintain the minority language; or they follow enrichment programmes aimed at developing linguistic diversity by adding a language that they do not already have in their repertoire.

There are also multilingual education practices which are driven by the aims of the school and the policy imposed by the community, and which lead to either additive or subtractive multilingualism (Lambert 1974; Cummins 2000; García 2008; Cenoz 2009; Baker 2009). Such practices are intertwined organically with frameworks that focus on the individual student. Additive multilingual education encourages the use of all languages so as to maintain and enrich the linguistic capital of the pupil. Subtractive multilingual education encourages the prominence of the majority language because the other languages are regarded as hampering academic success.

Socioeconomic and sociolinguistic factors are another pace-setting force in establishing multilingual education, possibly more typically in non-formal education, but they permeate the formal school system.

Such factors are well ingrained in the two types of practices, additive and subtractive multilingual education, because elite and folk bilingualism (Cenoz 2009; Baker 2006) correspond to the sociolinguistic and socioeconomic prestige of the languages in question, their speech community and whether they represent added social value. Elite bilingualism or multilingualism is voluntary and desired, and is driven by the high status the languages hold, whereas folk multilingualism comes about as a necessity for survival and social wellbeing, primarily among minority-language groups such as immigrants, foreign workers and expatriates.

The distinction between the strong and the weak versions of multilingual education rests on the legitimacy, equality and balance accorded to each language within the educational frames. The weak versions of multilingual education encourage mainstreaming but hinder the further development of the home language, usually the minority language. This is typical of schools with special teachers or teaching assistants who help the children acquire the majority language so as to enable them to join the mainstream class as soon as possible. This help often comes at the cost of withdrawing the child from the regular classroom and from a subject class period. The intended outcome of such practices is the achievement of a fluency in the majority language similar to that of monolingual pupils. The drawback is that the actual outcomes often entail lower overall achievement, poor self-esteem, higher rate of drop-outs, deterioration of the home language, derailing of family nucleus communication and a less than satisfactory speed of majority-language acquisition. The negative outcome may be exacerbated by more serious social and emotional factors that extend well beyond the school boundaries. Low self-esteem, loss of confidence and diminished self-image may lead youngsters to detach themselves from the 'old' home language, its heritage and culture. In that sense, then, it is easier to forgo previous learning and literacy skills acquired in the 'old' language and culture. The 'delegitimation' of the child's previous home experiences within the educational framework is not only detrimental to the child, it also affects the parents, extended family and minority-language community. The weak version of multilingual education stresses that it is important for children to function economically, socially and culturally in the majority-language society from as early as possible. It is argued that, if this happens, the desired outcomes will ensure equality in education and employment opportunities, both of which have consequences for the individual and the state. At the same time, the weak version has societal outcomes of majority-language supremacy: the minority language remains subordinate, which can foster social inequality and maintain an underprivileged situation for a section of society.

Researchers such as Baker (2006), Gregory and Williams (2000) and Cummins (2009) regard the weak version of multilingual education as undesirable because it receives no real support from the home, culture and community of the learner. According to these scholars, the strong version of multilingual education yields long-lasting results in producing bilingual, bicultural and biliterate children. Some of the explanations for this preference rest on the fact that most multilingual children come from homes where there is a cultural and linguistic capital, as well as a literacy one, that may differ from the one in school, a capital that serves as a pillar to the building of the child's language and literacy development. Moreover, the contribution of home literacy is complementary to school literacy, not substitutive. It has been shown that the home language and literacy can be markedly different from those of the school, i.e. at home you need not demonstrate knowledge of grammatical rules or be able to write a composition, but at school these are things you must do with your language. Unlike the strong version of multilingual education, the weak version can create a rift between home and school and force the child to give up the home language and with it the heritage capital, in favour of the majority/school language and culture. Weak versions of multilingual education may result in situations where the home is linguistically and scholastically excluded from the child's world, because the home usually loses out. By comparison with school, the home may be considered intellectually inferior or regarded as an undervalued agent that makes little or no contribution to the child's education, especially when it does not conform to the school's standardised practices regarding language and literacy.

Baker (2006) presents a typology of bilingual education, which we have taken as a model for our own typology to represent different education programmes used in multilingual contexts. Baker's typology is specific to the bilingual situation, whereas our adaptation of the typology (see Table 8.1) involves, at least in part, the consideration of different populations, including children who are or are becoming multilingual.

There are many types of programme spread around the world, and in some places there may be more than one of them in operation at a given time. The following are some illustrative examples of our typology. The Nigerian case illustrates the monolingual dominant-language / heritage programme type. In an official document first published in 1977, revised in 1981, entitled *Federal Republic of Nigeria*

Table 8.1 Types of multilingual education programme involving more than two languages

Multilingual education version	Programme type	Description
Non-forms	Mainstream Monolingual dominant-language/heritage	Programmes with foreign language teaching for dominant-language speakers Programmes in which indigenous/minority children learn the mother tongue/ heritage language as a subject, often outside regular school hours in after-school programmes.
	Submersion ('sink-or-swim')	Programmes in which linguistic-minority children with a low-status mother tongue are taught through a foreign/majority/official/dominant language, in classes in which the teacher does not know the minority language; or programmes in which linguistic-majority children are taught through the medium of a foreign (often former colonial) high-status language.
	Segregation	Programmes geared to linguistic-minority children undergoing instruction through their mother tongue in classes with minority children with the same mother tongue, and the dominant language is taught as a second/foreign language.
Weak	Transitional – early-exit	Linguistic-minority children are initially instructed through their mother tongue for a few years; the mother tongue serves as a means to teach the dominant language and scholastic content. Children are transferred to a majority-language class as soon as they have achieved communicative competence in the majority language.
	Transitional – late-exit	Linguistic-minority children are initially instructed through their mother tongue for a few years; the mother tongue serves as a means to acquire the dominant language and academic content. Children may receive some instruction through L_1 during the early elementary school years and sometimes the L_1 is taught as a subject thereafter.

Strong	Maintenance/ shelter	Linguistic-minority children choose voluntarily, among existing alternatives, to be instructed through the medium of their L_1, in classes with minority children of the same L_1, while following a programme in the majority language that is taught as a second or foreign language, all provided by bilingual teachers.
	Dual language/ immersion	Approximately half majority and half minority students in the class who have the same L_1 choose voluntarily to be instructed by a bilingual teacher. These programmes are often carried out either by means of a 90/10% proportion of instruction in the L_1/L_2 or a 50/50% proportion of instruction in L_1/L_2, keeping instruction separate for the majority and minority groups and teaching the language as a subject.
	Plural multilingual	These programmes are special in e.g. European schools with sections for various languages in which each language (mostly students' L_1) is the primary medium of education. The first foreign language is introduced gradually in elementary school, starting in context-embedded subjects (e.g. physical education, arts), followed later by subjects that are decontextualised verbally and intellectually (e.g. history) and concluding with the introduction of instruction in this language in the upper grades of all other subjects. Instruction in a second or foreign language (one of the languages of other sections) is introduced in middle school. Students choose the language in which to take the final exams in each subject. Everyone becomes at least a fluent bilingual or competent trilingual.

National Policy on Education (NPE) Language teaching based on the language policy in Nigeria, it is stipulated that:

(a) in primary school, which lasts six years, each child must study two languages, namely: (i) the mother-tongue (if available for study) or an indigenous language of wider communication in the area of domicile, and (ii) English;

(b) in junior secondary school (JSS), which is of three years' duration, the child must study three languages: (i) and (ii) as above and (iii) any one of the three major indigenous languages of the country, namely, Hausa, Igbo and Yoruba, provided the language chosen is different from the child's mother-tongue; and

(c) in senior secondary school (SSS), which also lasts three years, the child must study two languages: (i) and (ii). (Awobuluyi 1992: http://fafunwafoundation.tripod.com/fafunwafoundation/id8.html)

French and Arabic exist under the policy as language options at both the JSS and SSS levels. The Nigerian National Policy on Education is an illustration of how multilingualism can be catered for within a school system when there are several languages in use. However, the provision in the Nigerian National Policy on Education that every Nigerian child should be encouraged to learn one of the country's major languages in addition to his or her own has not been fully implemented, in part because the minority speakers regard this recommendation as an imposition (Oyetade 2003).

There are other multilingual contexts in which the teaching of languages makes provision for each age level, each language, each skill and the desired outcome of language proficiency. Several African countries are (much like Nigeria) examples of intended multilingual systems. Most of these systems were started after the countries gained independence and the minority/indigenous/ethnic languages were introduced into education side by side or sequentially with the colonisers' languages. Such is the case in Algeria, Burkina Faso, Burundi, Chad, Democratic Republic of the Congo, Côte d'Ivoire, Eritrea, Gabon, Guinea-Bissau, Madagascar, Mali, Mozambique and Senegal. Every one of these countries has made provision, mostly on an experimental basis, to introduce minority/indigenous languages to coexist with a colonial language such as French, English, Dutch or Portuguese (Albaugh 2005). The complexity and fluidity of multilingual education models in Africa is best captured by Albaugh's summary of the changes in emphasis on languages taught in the school systems at three points in time: roughly, policies established at independence, interim and current time (see Table 8.2).

Table 8.2 *Language use in education in Africa*

Country	Independence/1960	1990	2010
Algeria	0	1.8	1.8
Angola	0	0	4
Benin	0	0	3
Botswana	6	7.2	6
Burkina Faso	0	0	4.8
Burundi	9	9	9
Cameroon	0	0	3
Cape Verde	0	0	0
Central African Republic	0	0	0
Chad	0	1.8	3
Comoros	0	0	0
Congo, Dem. Rep.	5.4	5.4	5.4
Congo, Rep.	0	0	0
Côte d'Ivoire	0	0	3
Djibouti	0	0	5
Equatorial Guinea	0	0	0
Eritrea	10	N/A	10
Ethiopia	4	4	9
Gabon	0	0	3
Gambia	0	0	0
Ghana	0	7.2	3.6
Guinea	0	0	5
Guinea-Bissau	0	3	0
Kenya	0	7.2	6
Lesotho	9	9	9
Liberia	0	0	0
Madagascar	0	9	9
Malawi	7.2	5.4	4.8
Mali	0	3	6
Mauritania	1.5	3	1.8
Mauritius	0	0	0
Mozambique	0	0	5
Namibia	9	9	6
Niger	0	4	5
Nigeria	9	9	9
Rwanda	9	9	9
Sao Tome e Principe	0	0	0
Senegal	0	0	5
Seychelles	0	9	9
Sierra Leone	3.6	4.8	4.8
Somalia	1.8	9	6
South Africa	10	7.5	6
Sudan	1.5	2	4
Swaziland	0	9	7.5
Tanzania	4.5	6	6

Table 8.2 (*cont.*)

Country	Independence/1960	1990	2010
Togo	0	0	0
Uganda	5.4	6	6
Zambia	5.4	0	4
Zimbabwe	4.5	5.4	4.8

From Appendix A of Albaugh (2014). The numbers represent Albaugh's ranking of the policy on a scale from 'most foreign (0–2)' to 'most local (9–10)' for the medium of instruction, and a distinction is made between (i) one or several languages used in education and (ii) the extent to which the policy has penetrated the education system: 'experimental (3–4)', 'expanded (5–6)', or 'generalised (7–8)'.

What emerges from this report is that, while non-profit or other philanthropic organisations provide for alternative policies which are inclusive and multilingual, such policies are usually put into practice for experimentation, and expansion is seldom achieved – and generalisation even less frequently. In countries such as Eritrea, where linguistic disputes have been extreme, it is rare for such alternative policies to yield a multilingual educational policy supported by the local authorities. Eritrea is an example of the strong version of multilingual education, as compared to most other countries in Africa, where the weak or Baker's 'non-form' versions of multilingual education programmes are prevalent.

Some multilingual programmes were encouraged in Europe after the foundation of the EU, as in Luxembourg or the European Schools (Hoffmann 1998). In these cases, three languages are used as both subjects and vehicular languages where there are linguistic minorities, and there may even be instruction available through non-formal education in a fourth language. The European Schools cater for children whose home language is not the majority language of the host community where the school is located. These schools aim to develop a pluralist identity and to prepare pupils for life in linguistically and culturally heterogeneous societies, including the country of origin of the family. This implies the pursuit of additive multilingualism, with high levels of functional proficiency and literacy in at least two languages, the child's home language and one of the school's working languages. Dual immersion programmes are those where a third language is introduced to bilingual children, such as in the case of the Basque Country (Cenoz 2009; Lasagabaster and Huguet 2007). Here, the education system supports three types of school: one in which the predominant language of instruction is Basque, another where it is Spanish, and a mixed type where both Spanish and Basque are learned. In all schools, the teaching of the foreign language begins at the age of 4 (as of 2000). English has a predominant position in this system, and, as a result of the considerable support it has received in the last decades inside the EU, and owing to its role as a lingua franca, English is without any doubt the most widespread foreign language in the Basque Country school system.

Another strong version of multilingual education is the maintenance/shelter type that characterises the Finnish language policy. As a country whose main national language is hardly spoken outside its borders, Finland has long recognised the importance of foreign language learning. The official language education policy, which has been in place in Finland for the last thirty years, emphasises the importance of offering a wide range of languages at school so that the whole of the educated population has a command of Finnish, Swedish and English, and a sizable proportion also has knowledge of German, Russian or French (Joensuu 2007). With a large Finnish-speaking majority and legislated allowances for free choice of L_1 instruction (i.e. Finnish or Swedish), a large number of Finnish-speaking and Swedish-speaking people have become at least bilingual, if not trilingual (Sjöholm 2004). This language education policy has been in place for some time. In recent years there has been a dramatic transformation in the languages taught at Finnish schools in that English has gained ground at the expense of German and other foreign languages.

Of a different nature are the 'non-form' types of monolingual dominant-language/heritage programmes, especially where ethnic minorities develop alternative language instruction in supplementary non-formal systems. Such minorities are social enclaves within a majority. In some cases, they represent advanced generations of immigrants who are already local people (e.g. Jewish communities outside Israel, Pakistanis in London). Within those frames, trilingualism is fostered through formal schooling in countries where legislation has accommodated these ethnic needs and in those where such communities are numerically and economically well represented and can self-cater to sustain this option.

Some characteristics of one programme may resemble those of a different one, and both types may produce the same results. Each may be adapted at various points in time and according to differing needs. These types of programme were developed in response to particular educational ideologies or educational linguistic policies with a view to mainstreaming, standardising, unifying and providing equal opportunities for achievement.

8.4   GLOBALISATION, MULTILINGUAL EDUCATION POLICIES AND OUTCOMES

The common aim of multilingual education in many parts of the world is to cater for everyday needs (Dutcher and Tucker 1994). Some, but not all, of these multilingual education programmes try to provide students with multiple language proficiencies and access to multilingual academic content material (Tucker 1999). The reality in many classrooms today, however, is that the linguistic needs of bilingual/multilingual children are not met. The reason is that educational systems throughout the world have been slow to question the very essence of language education. In Europe, for example, the main agenda of European institutions remains the acquisition of the languages of schooling (rather than those of minority communities), the teaching of 'foreign' languages and the development of a European identity.

The changing linguistic world order presents new challenges to nations with populations which are culturally and linguistically diverse. In a globalised world, multilingual education is pivotal for the linguistic heterogeneity of a country or region (Tucker 1999). In fact, while globalisation may impose the need to mainstream (i.e. ensure access to) the majority language, it also generates an immediate need for multicultural and multilingual education as an instrument by which all children are educated to coexist harmoniously and to develop intercultural skills (Trueba 1990). The quest for quality education today is inextricably bound up with the impact of such globalisation (UNESCO 2001, Resolution 12) and it is aimed at catering for the economic and political needs that have brought new kinds of multilingualism to places such as Europe, Asia, Africa and parts of the Americas (Lüdi 2003; Sasaki 2000). In Chapter 4 it was argued that Asia, Africa and the Americas have always been much more multilingual than Europe, where adherence to the single or dominant national language ideology has done much to accelerate the demise of indigenous minority languages. But there is now a new kind of multilingualism, one that involves English.

The need for multilingual education goes beyond world trends in the economy and the geopolitics of regions. It permeates countries, nations, societies and communities. The idea that it can contribute to a betterment of the current condition of many individuals is beginning to gain traction. There are many examples of the principles promoting multilingualism and their successful application in multilingual education programmes around the world (Pufahl *et al.* 2001; Tucker 1999; Hoffmann and Ytsma 2004), but ultimately multilingualism can be successful only if there is respect for multiplicity, and 'respect for the different' in a society (Pattanayak 1990: viii–xii). In other words, multilingual education must consider: (a) that multilingualism is already the norm in our schools; (b) what 'foreign' language learning entails; (c) what language learning should be; and (d) whether the role of the language of instruction is in need of revision. The challenges lie in determining which languages should be vehicular languages and which ought to be taught as subjects, in order to achieve a greater hegemonic role in education (Hélot and Ó Laoire 2011: xiii; Hélot 1988). Spolsky has argued that language policy at a national level in general, and at the educational level in particular, only comes after comprehensive planning if the people participate in the decision-making process. In this context, he has suggested that there are many sources of pressure affecting societal language planning, such as: family, religion, ethnicity, politics, economy, culture, mass media, and legal and military institutions (Spolsky 1978).

Baker (2009) says that a multilingual education typology such as the one described in the previous section highlights the components around which school systems may differ in carrying out language education needs. These components are shaped by either covert or overt language policies formulated through aims and strategies. School components such as the linguistic background of the child, the balance of language proficiency of children and their linguistic proficiency in the classroom, the position of languages in the curriculum, the availability of teachers, curricular and extra-curricular resources, the declared or intended aims of multilingualism and the economic and social value of multilingual education for the wider community – all contribute to shaping the type of multilingual education and the programme or programmes to be fostered in the school.

It has been argued that the most effective multilingual education programmes are those which conform to the strong version of multilingualism, because they promote several languages concurrently and not one at the expense of the other. Although this claim has been validated by some research, for instance in North America, some contentions have surfaced in the shape of methodological criticism – specifically with regard to the populations that have been studied. It is said that, by and large, the subjects (whether pupils or parents) who opt to engage in multilingual education are already in favour of it and therefore are not a neutral group. Nonetheless, one should ask not only whether these forms of multilingual education are effective as compared to monolingual education or other weak forms of multilingual education, but also what factors ensure the effectiveness of these multilingual education programmes. More specifically, what measures contribute to successful multilingual education in schools and classrooms and result in multilingual, multiliterate and multicultural children? Baker (2009: 145–47) suggests that strategies for bilingual education should have the following attributes:

(a) a shared vision, mission and ideology among staff and planners;
(b) school leadership that fosters multilingual education for staff, community leaders and families;
(c) professional training and development for staff;
(d) enhancement of multilingual and multiliteracy development across the ages and subject matters;
(e) comprehensive assessment for multilinguals (not based on monolingual models);
(f) a supportive environment that makes allowances for all languages and cultures and allocates special places to the parents, as well as the home language and culture, within the classroom and the curriculum;
(g) allow for code-switched and code-mixed discourse as a unique discourse in multilingual education.

In an increasingly globalised world, there are many advantages to multilingual education, especially in the strong forms, from infancy to adulthood. According to Baker (2009), these advantages can be: continuity of heritage, processes of language maintenance and revitalisation, preservation of cultural capital, development of informed citizenship, national educational achievement levels, social and economic inclusion, the expansion of socialisation and social networks and the establishment of an ethnic identity characterising the ethnic group as distinct and self-determined. These positive points provide a supportive environment for children in multilingual education, whether they are part of a minority or majority group. Baker favours multilingual education in the strong version because, being centred on the child and the community, it brings more benefits to both than mainstream educational frameworks. However, the question still remains as to whether minority children who are in the mainstream educational system are invariably deprived culturally, linguistically and cognitively. The answer to this is still very much debated.

Studies usually focus either on programmes that primarily maintain heritage languages and only secondarily foster a second or a foreign language, or on multilingual education programmes that concentrate on teaching a second/foreign language and ignore other languages known by the learner. This dichotomous perspective of the relationship of the languages within a multilingual educational framework does not account for the hybrid element that becomes an important part of it – namely, that multilingualism may be the first language of an individual. The pattern of growing up multilingually from birth was discussed in Chapter 7 as a widespread result of globalisation and mobility. Many children are exposed to more than one language in the environment even if not in the form of child-directed speech (Stavans and Hoffmann 2007; Grosjean 2010). In many ways, multilingual education constrained by 'hard boundaries' (Cenoz 2009: 235) cannot yield the best results because in most cases these boundaries are maintained by school practices, curricular design, assessment constraints and perhaps practical limitations like:

- one teacher – one language (i.e. each teacher handles one language);
- one classroom – one language (i.e. the spaces for each language are separated physically);
- one discourse – one language (i.e. only the target language can be used to discuss/learn specific domains or disciplines, e.g. English used in computer science classes, whereas history may be taught in the first language);
- one language – one end achievement goal (i.e. intended outcomes in any language should be native-like levels of performance, that is to say, the aim should be native or native-like performance in each language);
- one curriculum and assessment – one language (i.e. each language has a separate language policy, planning and evaluation).

These constraints, which result from establishing hard boundaries for each language, create a divisive line in multilingual education in that languages are learned as single entities and, if they happen to coexist in the educational system, they are kept apart. Assessing language proficiency and competence and matching them to a monolingual model has been criticised by prominent psycholinguists (discussed in Chapter 6), as, for example, Grosjean (1992, 2008, 2010), who have long argued that the multilingual's linguistic repertoire is different from that of monolinguals. For the multilingual, the language-contact situation is not accidental, nor is it detrimental, as it can be a resourceful linguistic device for different purposes. Ferguson (2003) shows that in strong forms of multilingual education, where content is introduced in another language (say, mathematics), the use of more than one language is not only prevalent across a wide range of educational settings, but it seems to arise naturally, for instance as a pragmatic response when pupils and teachers have insufficient control of the required languages. Jessner (2006) claims that curricular languages are still treated as self-contained independent entities, and that teachers do not allow any code-switching or reference to a learner's other languages. However, Lin (1996) claims that code-switching in Hong Kong classrooms does serve as an important pedagogical and social resource, for example to indicate the beginning of a class, or for more intimate/informal interaction with a student, or for purposes of discipline. Therefore, multilingual education ought to value pupils' multilingual competences and make use of them in all relevant contexts.

8.5 LITERACY: DEVELOPMENT, SOCIAL PRACTICE AND CONSEQUENCES

Before we can proceed to discuss literacy in the context of multilinguals, it will be useful to address three issues that are pivotal to the evolution of this concept: (i) why literacy was initially treated as merely the ability to read and write; (ii) how the understanding of literacy has changed to encompass other language and communication skills; and (iii) how literacy is viewed today as a social practice.

Historically, the term 'literacy' was contrasted with 'illiteracy'. These terms have been used to describe a person's ability or inability to read and write in a given language. Writing has been with us for at least five millennia (Hannon and Bird 2004), with the discovery of earliest records in Mesopotamia being followed by evidence from China and America. The development of writing went hand in hand with other social and human developments, such as the invention of writing materials, printing on an industrial scale and, more recently, cybernetic media. Throughout history, literacy was the privilege of some, yet the need for reading and writing was always an essential part of human development. When concerned with children, literacy is automatically associated with practices of how to teach a child to read and write; when it relates to adults, it brings to mind the idea of overcoming illiteracy and all its concomitant disadvantages. Different views have been put forward on the ways literacy is acquired and how adult literacy should be understood. A great deal of work also remains to be done in terms of research into multilingual literacy (the literacy of the multilingual individual), multiliteracies (the different literacies that the individual masters in one or several languages) and multiple literacies (the literacies multilinguals have at their disposal when using their languages separately and together).

Literacy is an enhancer of cultural, cognitive and scientific development. However, a literacy practice that may be valued in the western world may not be relevant for the non-western world. In some cultures, the oral narrative tradition is more central than the written one; in others, the functional literacy (the competence required to conduct oneself in daily life) of one individual may be radically different from that of another. Even within that same individual, the functional literacy in one aspect of life may be radically different from that in another.

New paradigms have been developed that see literacy practices as embedded in social and cultural contexts that are sociologically and ethnographically driven. The 'New Literacy Studies' (NLS) (Gee 1991, 2000, 2001; Street 1996; Lankshear 1999) are concerned with the nature of literacy, and they focus not so much on acquisition of skills but rather on what it means to think of literacy as a social practice (Street 1984). Since the late 1970s, the study of this topic has moved away from the traditional perspective to a more sociocultural one, looking at literacy (Barton and Hamilton 1998; Purcell-Gates 1995, 2007; Street 1984) as a mediating factor in people's lives that reflects social practices (Brandt and Clinton 2002) and shifts power relationships. But literacy and literacy education have been and continue to be contested subjects. Barton and Hamilton (2000) see literacy as embedded in social and cultural contexts and, therefore, not as a unitary set of neutral and transportable skills: in other words, literacy can mean different things to different people at different times (Baynham 1995; Luke and Freebody 1997). If one takes this view, academic literacy is one of many literacies to consider (Gee 1996; the New London Group 1996), alongside functional literacy, personal literacy, transactional literacy and cultural literacy. Instead of identifying competence in academic literacy as a set of 'basics' that students can acquire, this view considers the social nature of literacy in terms of ideologies, power relations, values and identities (Luke 1994; Street 2002).

What transpires from these developments is that people have (or are exposed to) distinct or multiple literacies, and that each of these involves different social practices, socialisation needs and identities. It is therefore necessary to make a distinction between 'autonomous' and 'ideological' models of literacy (Street 1984) and between 'literacy events' and 'literacy practices' (Street 1988). The 'autonomous' model of literacy, with its response to those social practices that are dictated by a school system, assumes that literacy affects social and cognitive practices independently of other factors. Introducing literacy to 'illiterate' people enhances their cognitive skills, it is argued, and improves their economic prospects by making them upwardly mobile and economically productive, irrespective of the initial conditions responsible for their illiteracy. This model assumes that there is one literacy that fits all.

The alternative 'ideological' model of literacy is culturally sensitive and accounts for literacy practices that vary from one context to another. Here, literacy is about knowledge – the ways in which people address reading and writing are part of social practices, such as those of a job market or in a particular educational context. The effects of learning or performing will be context-dependent (Gee 1991; Besnier and Street 1994). Promoting plurilingualism means more than offering many languages in the classroom, community or home. In the educational system it means:

> take[ing] into account and build[ing] further on the diversity of languages and literacy practices that children and youth bring to school. This means going beyond acceptance or tolerance to cultivation of children's diverse languages … as teaching languages.
> (García et al. 2007: 14)

The tension between languages and what they represent creates a relationship of greater or lesser power for one language over the other and this values or underestimates the cultural capital for speakers in general and for ruling majorities in particular (Hélot and Ó Laoire 2011: xxii).

A different, ethnographic, approach to literacy adopts a wider perspective by moving from text to context. It makes the distinction between 'literacy events' (Heath 1983) and 'literacy practices' (Scribner and Cole 1981; Street 1984): the former constitutes a social action surrounding a text in which the writing matters for the way people interact; the latter is the more abstract concept of the literacy practice, usually treated as the socially regulated, recurrent and patterned things that people do with literacy as well as the cultural significance they ascribe to those actions. These concepts are an important contribution to the analytic frames needed to explain social participation and literacy learning, especially as a form of socialisation. For instance, it is a common practice for parents to read a bedtime story to their children (especially in western privileged populations). This reading is important, as it is regarded as a literacy practice, i.e. an activity that may be repeated every night. This reading by the parent will become a literacy event if, and only if, the parent and the child engage in a conversation that goes beyond the 'here and now' of the book or the story at hand. It is literacy events that expose the child to different genres, registers, cultures and situations.

8.6 DEVELOPING LITERACY IN MULTILINGUALS: MULTILITERACY AND MULTIPLE LITERACIES

In today's world, multiliteracy is becoming a necessity, no longer a commodity, because advances in technology and multimedia are changing the way we communicate. The printed text in the public space combines written words and images in public notices, billboards and other visual signs, and it combines with the spoken word on the internet, television and in films. All these means of communication require the ability to understand quite complex language, as can be observed while travelling through the world, particularly where the printed text serves not only as the medium but also as the message itself. For example, in Figures 8.1 and 8.2, signs in public spaces make up a linguistic landscape that reflects the cultural and social practices of the place and its people.

Both signs are meant as warnings in areas frequented by tourists, and both post the message in English first. In England (Figure 8.2) this is appropriate, but in Kerala, India (Figure 8.1), it would have been more appropriate for Tamil (Kerala's first language) to come first. The local authorities chose to give priority to India's second national language, presumably so that non-speakers of Tamil could understand the message. In addition, the sign in India is bilingual, bi-textual and bi-alphabetic. The sign in England puts the same message in six languages, and the order in which they are listed suggests that the people who erected the notice know who is likely to read it and what their linguistic background is.

Figure 8.3 is a sign on the sidewalk in downtown Mopti in Mali, Africa, where there is an internet service. This sign is in French, the official language. There are thirty-two languages listed for Mali, but a large part of the population uses Bambara as its mother tongue and as a secondary language employed to communicate nationwide. The regional language of Mopti is Malinke. However, the knowledge of

Figure 8.1 Public sign in Kerala, India

Figure 8.2 Public sign in Cambridge, UK

mathematical literacy (numeracy) that is deemed necessary here is specified – namely, that one hour is 60 minutes and that the cost, 750F, is the same. To mention the time as 'one hour' or 'sixty minutes' is a clarification deemed advisable, perhaps because of different conventions in one or several of the local languages. The separation between the numerical and alphabetical notational systems is not consistent as the numeral 1 could have been replaced by a quantifier.

In the example illustrated in Figure 8.4, it is quite likely that the reader will be able to detect that this is a label (which is predominantly green in colour) for a product called 'Cnaan' and that this product has to do with something that is natural, environmentally

Figure 8.3 Shop sign in Mopti, Mali

friendly or perhaps organic (the colour of the advertisement supplies further information which will not be discussed here but might be considered in a wider scheme of multiliteracy). The words 'parabens' and 'paraffin' and the initials 'SLS' refer to chemicals of sorts that in this context, aided by the word 'FREE', seem to emphasise the 'naturalness' of the product. For some readers, the word Cnaan may mean a geographic region (namely, Israel today), and so the diacritic signs under the letters /,/ and /,/ and /./ can be interpreted as the graphemic representation of the vowels that would be used together with the Hebrew consonants which write out the word 'Cnaan'. For a 'Hebrew-Latinised' multilingual reader this advert is attractive, as the graphophonemics will be known to him or her. This label may well be puzzling or less appealing for a monolingual/monoliterate individual, whether English- or Hebrew-speaking.

The above examples illustrate different forms of multilingual literacy. The last one (Figure 8.4) draws on a multilingual individual's ability to master different literacies, whereas Figure 8.2 addresses

Figure 8.4 Israeli product label (permission granted by CNAAN Made by Nature Headquarters)

the privileged monolingual (one who can travel). Figure 8.1 seems to comply with language legislation and language policy in Kerala (signs must be bilingual), as it presents a regional and lingua franca choice. In Figure 8.3 readers may be monolinguals or multilinguals: although the sign itself is monolingual, it is used in a multilingual context.

However, there's more to the examples than meets the eye. They assume an ability not only to decode different alphabetical systems, but also to draw on the context and the space in which the messages are embedded. But why is the multiliterate multilingual able to interpret such signs?

The notion of literacy in monolingual as well as multilingual contexts has been controversial in at least three areas of inquiry, which overlap yet represent different approaches. The studies carried out have produced different results in relation to the acquisition and consequences of literacy and its accompanying social practices. Literacy involves the ability to read, write and respond to texts in ways that mediate cultural lives. Unfortunately, literacy research, with respect to both monolinguals and multilinguals, has in the past failed to consider the cultural aspects of how and why people in different social and linguistic communities engage with written texts, as well as the social interactions surrounding such practices. Purcell-Gates *et al.* (2011: 22) argue that 'language and literacy practices are profoundly sociocultural in nature'. Children enter the process of literacy development as active participants in routine language and practices that are embedded in their homes and cultural communities in patterned ways of organising everyday life (Pollock 2008). Acquiring literacy allows for the expansion of cultural resources in ways of being, doing, thinking and acting, as well as reading and writing in one or more languages.

Historically, 'literacy' was conceptualised as the means to overcome 'illiteracy' by teaching people how to read. Reading was the main focus of research, and attention to cognition was pivotal to claims relating to the outcomes of literacy for people. Sociocultural approaches – as well as adult learning theories – launched a plethora of studies that looked into what constitutes literacy and how it affects human socialisation and communication. The major trends of these studies were identified in the work of Snow *et al.* (1998) with regard to the treatment of literacy as a decontextualised learning process, in the seminal contribution of Scribner and Cole (1978), who link the cognitive processes to the social practices involved in literacy events, and in the work of Street (1991), who placed the teaching of literacy within broader social and political contexts that account for the variety of language backgrounds and styles, instead of just following proposed 'templates'. More recently, the work done by Cope and Kalantzis (2000) and Gee (1992) has placed literacy in a semiotic context of visual and gestural modes and modalities of expression, focusing more on 'multiliteracy and multimodality'; studies by Martin-Jones and Jones (2000) and Gregory (1996, 2001; Gregory and Williams 2000) are in the same line. These authors advocate contextualising literacy, not just in formal educational frameworks, but also in those which are non-formal, such as the home and cultural or religious centres. The different approaches of these studies emphasise the distinction between 'multiple literacies', 'multiliteracies' and literacy in multilingual and multicultural settings.

Are multiple literacies the same as multiliteracies? Do they refer to the same or different levels of analysis when looking at literacies of multilinguals in multilingual contexts? These are some of the questions posited by Martin-Jones and Jones (2000: 5):

> Focusing on the plurality of literacies means recognising the diversity of reading and writing practices and the different genres, styles and types of texts associated with various activities, domains or social identities ... In multilingual contexts, different languages, language varieties and scripts add other dimensions to the diversity and complexity of literacies.

Street (2000) claims that these terms – multiple literacies and multiliteracies – are not interchangeable and, further, that both are in 'danger of reification' (p. 19) if their context and practice are not considered. He acknowledges his own early contribution to the coinage of 'multiple literacies' when the notion was that there was just one literacy which had effects on other elements involved in policy making, teaching, assessment and so on. But Street is concerned with today's use of 'multiple', which assumes that, just as there is a single literacy associated with a single culture and a single language, there are also multiple literacies associated with many languages and cultures.

This issue goes back to the previously discussed perception of plurilingual/literate/cultural individuals as being the sum total of the single language/literacy/culture. Street's 'multiple literacy' was associated with culture; but the New London Group (a team of ten academics who met in 1996 to discuss how literacy pedagogy might address rapid change in literacy due to globalisation, technology and increasing cultural and social diversity) introduced the notion of 'multiliteracy' to refer to the multiple literacies associated with different modes of communication, including visual literacy, computer literacy and other semiotic systems. Street's criticism of the term 'multiliteracy' is that it concerns the 'how' (i.e. modes of communication), whereas 'multiple literacy' relates to the 'what' (i.e. cultural/social drivers of communication). Accordingly, if we choose 'multiliteracy' (the how) we end up shaping meaning by the means of communication and not by the social practices underlying them. For example, the use of emoticons on the mobile phone replaces written expressions of affection and reduces the use of the linguistic repertoire.

Street seems to suggest that multiliteracy is closely related to the concept of 'literacy events', which are specific observable occasions that involve reading and/or writing, such as checking a timetable, following a recipe, browsing through a magazine, reading signs on the road, looking up a phone number in the directory or making a grocery list. Unlike 'literacy events' (a concept that derived from the idea of 'speech event'), 'literacy practices' are interwoven into Street's multiple literacies concept. The notion of literacy practices encompasses literacy events and links them to broader social and cultural patterns. For instance, when studying literacy patterns in Ethiopian immigrant families, Stavans et al. (2009) found that, while there may be many indicators of literacy events in the home, there are very few literacy practices of the type that the Israeli educational system values or expects from families. Ethiopian parents, instead of reading books (some cannot read in either their native language or in Hebrew) tend to tell stories which are highly culture-bound, with moral messages resembling the fable genre. In western child-rearing practices, storybook reading is deemed a desired, valued and prototypical literacy event which becomes a literacy practice, and academic literacy is expected to develop towards an adult literacy both in spoken and written modes of language. For the Ethiopian parent, storytelling is an integral part of the teaching of moral values: beyond being a pleasant literacy event, it is actually a social and educational literacy practice. Similar findings were reported by Gregory (1998, 2001; Gregory and Williams 2000) regarding Bangladeshi–English immigrant children to the UK.

Defining literacy as much more than just the ability to read and write and embedding this ability into literacy practices interwoven with social, cultural, political and economic factors activated in social interactions poses an additional challenge when considering that literacy events are no longer confined by boundaries or geographical borders. Literacy in one language has been transposed to the more complex situation of multilingualism in which the concepts of 'biliteracy' or 'multiliteracy' have replaced the notion of 'literacy' in the monolingual sense.

There are several definitions of 'biliteracy' that could apply to 'multiliteracy', often drawn from the monolingual paradigm. Definitions of 'multiliteracies' rely on a separation between the linguistic systems underlying literacy practices, because they are often definitions that have been formulated on the basis of the educational framework of 'literacy'. Examples are Goodman *et al.* (1979) and Fishman (1980), who regard biliteracy as the mastery of reading and writing in two languages; or Reyes (2001: 98) who extends it to:

> mastery of the fundamentals of speaking, reading and writing …
> in two linguistic systems. It also includes constructing meaning by
> making relevant cultural and linguistic connections with print and
> the learners' own lived experiences [and] the interaction [of the two
> linguistic systems].

Hornberger interprets biliteracy as 'the use of two or more languages in and around writing … encompassing not only events but actors, interactions, practices, activities, programmes, situations, societies, sites, worlds' (2003: xiii, 2000: 362). In the course of three decades, the concept of 'literacy' has changed from a purely pragmatic and educational enterprise related to the teaching of reading (and consequently writing) to the recognition that literacy events involve much more than the techniques of encoding and decoding written language (Olson 1977). The refined concept of 'multiliteracy' has been endorsed by scholars to the extent that having multiliteracies does not only mean having many literacies but rather making different spaces for literacies and combining these literacies in diverse linguistic systems. The multilingual individual who achieves high multiliterate ability is able to meet multi-communicative needs that emerge with technological advancement. It is precisely this multiliteracy that will enable users of more than one language to decode and encode – as well as attribute meaning to – the signs in the notices discussed above (e.g. a Hebrew–English bilingual and Figure 8.4).

The complexity of 'multiliteracy' has generated further distinctions, such as the one proposed with the term 'pluriliteracies' by García *et al.* (2007), who suggest that:

> pluriliteracies ... describe the complex language practices and values
> of speakers in multilingual communities ... practices and values
> that are not equivalent or even homologous in different languages,
> but are integrated, variable, flexible, and changing ... [pluriliteracy]
> requires the integration of unevenly developed competences in a
> variety of languages, dialects and registers, as well as the valuing of
> linguistic tolerance. (p. 208)

More specifically, taking such complexity to the educational setting, there is a need for school managers, administrators and teachers to consider the various dimensions of the multilingual classroom. Such consideration may lead to abandoning traditional approaches to language teaching, critically rethinking the relationship between language teaching and language learning and forging new pedagogies.

What this plethora of definitions seems to indicate is that there are different types and different degrees of literacies, not only among monolinguals but especially among multilingual and multicultural populations. In fact, the reality of multilingual individuals (children and adults alike) develops in families, homes and communities, not only in schools, whenever people confront different scripts in functionally different ways. The reality of these multilinguals is embedded in attitudes, values and beliefs regarding literacy practices that are associated with certain individuals, identities or social situations. In this sense, a Russian immigrant father who is, together with his wife and daughter, participating in a workshop on emergent literacy will be 'reading' a children's story to his daughter from a Hebrew-scripted book but in spoken Russian. That is, he will be turning pages from right to left (as is done in Hebrew) and will be pointing to the pictures from right to left as the Hebrew sequencing will require, but he will 'read/tell' the story in Russian while he is 'pretending to read' (an appropriate activity for an incipient literacy engagement of the pre-school child). Similarly, the Arabic used for Qur'an reading among Bangladeshi–English children in London will be required exclusively for prayers and religious usage rather than daily communicative exchanges with Arabic speakers (Gregory and Williams 2000).

Bridging the gap between theory and practice in terms of multilingual literacies is not a trivial pursuit. Research findings are often based on studies that are biased because of the status of one language in relation to the other (the first language as opposed to the second or foreign language) and because they are driven by standards and competencies dictated according to monolingual paradigms and the utility value of the respective languages.

Since the terms 'multiliteracies' and 'multiple literacies' were primarily developed in the context of 'monoliteracies', it seems that the respective definitions become less than satisfactory when applied to multilingual contexts (Belcher and Connor 2001). 'Multi' versus 'multiple' as defined in the literature is concerned with different aspects of literacy in one language group, namely the modality of literacy or the practices. However, when we have one or more language/literacy groups with cultures that may vary, converge or clash, such definitions have to be reconsidered. Martin-Jones and Jones (2000) discuss both multiple literacies and multiliteracies in the context of multilinguals, and they give four reasons for this: (a) multilinguals have two or more spoken and written languages or language varieties in their communicative repertoire; (b) their repertoires have a multiplicity and complexity of communicative goals and purposes; (c) repertoires may vary among individuals in terms of degrees of expertise across languages and literacies; and (d) multilinguals benefit from the multiple linguistic and literacy systems available to them because they can draw from – and combine – the different codes, forms and signs. In this sense, multilingual literacies are rich and flexible, consist of different spoken and written forms, can be combined and exploited for efficiency and clarity, and are constantly calibrating, reaffirming and redefining themselves within the individual's repertoires across a lifespan and as part of a wider social circle within the cultural borders.

The study of multilingual literacies provides new insights into the vulnerability and flexibility of the conceptual frames provided by the New London Group's literacy studies described above. In fact, in a world that capitalises on multilingualism and literacy across languages in terms of writing, speaking and other visual communication, multilingual literacies can introduce new and different frameworks, such as mixed-code literacies (Auer 1990; Mor-Sommerfeld 2002) or transliteracies, in which the local and internal literacy is reshaped because it is seen to go beyond the linguistic or literacy repertoire boundaries, as suggested by Brandt and Clinton (2002) in reaction to the autonomous and ideological models proposed by Street. Similarly, Hélot and Ó Laoire (2011: xix) show that it is of crucial importance to develop multilingual literacy practices from the start of schooling, not only for multilingual learners but also for monolinguals. The use of books that are translated or published in two languages provides practical opportunities for reading and writing activities that are central to a better understanding of basic notions such as language contact, transfer, code-switching and the simultaneous use of two languages. Implementing multiliteracies and multiple literacies in the multilingual classroom as the norm means acknowledging diversity and changing identities in migration contexts, recognising the potential of the multilingual classroom ecology in language education, transcending the traditional sociocultural barriers in the implementation of a multilingual curriculum, defending the positioning of teachers' policies, exploiting students' metalinguistic awareness at the pedagogical level and redefining power relations in the case of minority languages in the language constellation.

8.7 MODELS OF MULTILITERACY: FROM THEORY TO PRACTICE

Several studies have looked at classrooms where the languages of multilingual learners are heard, legitimated and used for instruction (Menken *et al.* 2011; O'Rourke 2011; Ngomo 2011). In these studies it is shown that students' multilingualism is valued, and that it is negotiated in the classroom by incorporating a variety of multilingual activities focusing on languages and by creating a valuable space for all languages. Some contributions are centred on language policy. They conceptualise the use of different languages for instruction as a process in which a variety of societal actors endeavour to achieve authoritative contextualisation (Silverstein and Urban 1996; Stavans and Narkiss 2004) by actively engaging in the planning, interpretation, modification and/or (selective) implementation of policy in accordance with existing institutional practices, external pressures and individual preferences. It is interesting to see how language affiliations and experiences with languages can either influence behaviour or be used as a discursive resource to justify such behaviour.

One of the models for multilingual language policy and planning, proposed by Hornberger (1989, 1990, 2003) and Hornberger and Skilton-Sylvester (2000), views 'biliteracy' as a continuum. Hornberger considers the educational system to be the link between language policy and language ecology expressed in 'continua of biliteracy' which are 'a comprehensive, ecological model I have proposed as a way to situate research, teaching, and language planning in multilingual settings' (Hornberger 1990: 213; Hornberger and Skilton-Sylvester 2000). The very notion of bi-(or multi-)literacy assumes that one 'language and literacy' develops in relation to each one or more language(s) and literacies (language evolution). The model situates biliteracy development, whether in the individual, classroom, community or society, in relation to the contexts, media and content through which it develops (i.e. the language environment); and it provides a heuristic method of addressing the unequal balance of power across languages and literacies (i.e. for both studying and counteracting language endangerment) (Hornberger 2002: 37).

Hornberger's model accounts for the various languages and cultures in terms of registers, uses, abilities, typologies, scripts, modalities, modes etc. The model is an analytical framework for the complexity of multilingual literacy and consists of a scalar value across four dimensions: (i) the context of biliteracy (micro–macro, oral–literate, multilingual–monolingual); (ii) the individual's development of biliteracy (reception–production; oral–written; L_1–L_2); (iii) the medium of biliteracy (simultaneous or successive exposure, dissimilar–similar structures, divergent–convergent scripts); and (iv) the content of biliteracy (minority–majority; vernacular–literary; contextualised–decontextualised). Although the scalar system places each pair of elements of each dimension as polar, Hornberger (2007: 277) claims they 'represent the infinity and fluidity of movement along each of the continua' which through integration along and across the elements provide a positive transfer across literacies. The implementation of such a model relies on variables like social or group power; monolingual versus multilingual society; languages that have different structures, scripts and literacies; schools in which the languages of the community are taught; and the needs and opportunities to receive and produce texts in different languages.

Cenoz (2009), drawing on Hornberger's biliteracy continua model, proposed what she calls 'the continua of multilingual education'. This model provides a descriptive framework to characterise multilingual education situations. Like Hornberger, Cenoz suggests looking at the model as continuous rather than discrete points consisting of four variables: (i) subject (the different languages taught as subject matter, languages used to teach other subjects, or incipience and intensity of language instruction); (ii) language of instruction (using the languages for instruction, or integrating the languages into the syllabus and curriculum planning); (iii) teacher (language proficiency of the teacher, or specific training to teach in multilingual contexts) and (iv) school (the use beyond the classroom of the languages used for communication in the school, plus information transmission and formal events).

These variables have to do with linguistic factors concerning the typological proximity of the languages and with historical language-contact situations that had a propensity for mixing and switching in a multilingual context. Such variables relate also to sociolinguistic factors divided into two broad categories, the micro and the macro. The micro-sociolinguistic variables (as defined in Cenoz's model) are the direct reference to the individual student and the social networks in the inner and the outer socialisation circle, such as parents, siblings, friends, relatives, community members. The macro-sociolinguistic variables are defined as the number of speakers of each language, the national and international status of the language and its speakers, and its presence in the media or within the linguistic landscape. These sociolinguistic, linguistic and educational variables are dealt with along a continuum of a 'more' or 'less' multilingual education context, which reflects the interaction between the school and the community/society in which it operates.

Similarly, García *et al.* (2007) adapt Hornberger's model from biliteracy to pluriliteracies. This adaptation incorporates the literacy continua and emphasises also 'literacy practices in sociocultural contexts, the hybridity of literacy practices afforded by new technologies and the increasing interrelation of semiotic systems' (p. 215). Accordingly, in a pluriliteracy model, when two languages are used to read and write, the social contexts play an important role because both languages interact and are imbued with the cultural contexts and social purposes of their use. Therefore, deriving meaning from print and script varieties is also dependent on the social contexts in which they occur. The social contexts impose regulated and patterned literacy activities that recur and assign cultural significance to certain social events. For instance, obituary announcements in print, in the media and cyberspace (within and across a given culture and language) are very different in their forms, and their function is driven by cultural codes, linguistic constraints and social situations.

García *et al.* (2007) draw up a pluriliteracy model based on three conceptual frames: the one developed by New Literacy Studies (the New London Group); the concept of 'hybridity' (e.g. discourse, boundaries, sociolinguistic perspectives); and semiotics. Following the premises of the New London Group, this model of pluriliteracy moves away from the polarised/dichotomous pairing of the native and other languages as separate and autonomous entities. Instead, it encourages the use of interrelated, flexible and equivalent linguistic systems. In other words, the pluriliteracy of an individual is not the sum total of his/her monoliteracy in each language or in each cultural practice. It is, rather, the ability to 'capitalise' on the conversions, intersections and overlaps of the interconnected literacies that generate a new pluriliteracy which has 'the potential for transformation and change, precisely because of the dynamism and flexibility of integrated hybrid practices' (García *et al.* 2007: 216). The hybrid practices interweave the linguistic codes and the literacy needs in the multilingual classroom, where ample opportunities arise for mergers between individual, home and community literacy practices. Last is the semiotic aspect that typifies pluriliteracies as a new space that is not only marked by national, geographical or ethnic boundaries, but has become the arena of economic and social capital of a large number of members in the globalised world (Heller 1999). The merger of languages, dialects, registers, scripts and other visual and iconic semiotic systems is the basis for these upcoming pluriliteracies. One example is Europe's strenuous efforts to develop pluriliteracy for its citizens' practices and needs. For instance, the centrality of education in the EU focuses not only on training for proficiency in several languages, but also on valuing and accepting pluriliteracies and plurilingualism among its population, for example in the form of the European Language Portfolio (2001): the ELP is a document in which those who are learning or have learned a language – whether at school or away from school – can record (and reflect on) their language learning and cultural experiences.

To sum up, multiliteracy incorporates basic concepts from literacy and multilingualism. The paradigms we have discussed reflect different approaches to and perspectives of the complexity of multiliteracy. Hornberger proposes a model focused primarily on literacy and bilingualism in which her emphasis moves from the individual's learning (in particular learning a second or foreign language) to the societal issues that exert power and impact on the literacy needs and practices of such an individual in a multilingual context. The 'biliteracy continua' model centres on literacy and the individual's production and use of the languages under personal, cognitive, cultural and social constraints. Cenoz builds on Hornberger's 'biliteracy continua' model to deal with multilingual education as the product of an educational system driven by agents and consumers of education, policy makers and deliverers, planning and execution, social and individual demands, and national and political aspirations. Cenoz's 'continua of multilingual education' steers the educational environment/establishment towards the individual's multilingualism (and consequently multiliteracy), as illustrated by the educational system developed in the Basque Country. While both models take into account the individual and the societal factors leading to multilingualism, they are fully anchored in the formal educational framework and what it has offered historically and canonically in its practices – mostly L_1 and L_{other}. The model of pluriliteracies conveyed by García's 'biliteracy continua' is an extension of the individual and societal models of Hornberger and Cenoz, and it is aligned to global and sociolinguistic forces that are imposing new world literacy orders.

8.8 CONCLUSION

The main concerns of this chapter have been two important issues, education and literacy. Both have important implications in multilingual contexts, and these have led to a variety of practices. Here we list some of the most salient issues that we discussed with regard to literacy and multilingualism:

- People transfer, preserve and maintain their languages to sustain their cultures and to differentiate between them. Cultures give character to communities across generations and provide a framework of belonging.
- Multiliteracy in multilingual contexts builds cultural groups by bringing peoples together, but it can also cause divisions because of the diverse ways in which multiliteracy and multilingualism affect human thought and cognition.
- Rapid changes in geopolitical situations in the world have created the need for multilingual education as a dynamic enterprise.
- The need for multilingual education is increasingly recognised by policy makers; in consequence, new models and types of multilingual education programmes are being developed.
- Literacy plays a central role in the enhancement and maintenance of culture and knowledge. In this process, it is important that the educational systems foster multilingualism and multiliteracy.
- Growing numbers of children and adults are exposed to multiple literacy events that relate to different identities, social practices and socialisation needs. Mapping out social and communicative situations draws on the known literacy events and practices at a given time and space and contributes to the introduction of novel literacy events and practices.
- Analytical models of multiliteracy proposed by Hornberger, Cenoz and García contribute to our understanding of the importance of multiliteracy in advanced and advancing societies. These models agree in the perception that the variability inherent in

multilingualism needs to be accepted by individuals, institutions and societies.

- Multilingual education systems should look on multilingualism and multiliteracy not as deficits but as assets that contribute to the development of communication, culture, cognition and economic growth.

Glossary

Accommodation The process by which speakers adjust their way of speaking, either consciously or unconsciously, and attune it to that of their interlocutor(s).

Acculturation The process whereby a person adjusts to and/or acquires a new culture. It tends to include learning the language of that culture.

Additive multilingualism The process of adding one or more languages to an individual's linguistic repertoire in an enriching fashion and without any detrimental effects on the subject's first language(s).

Assimilation A process whereby individuals or groups of minority-language speakers adopt the language and culture of another group, usually the linguistic majority. It is often accompanied by a loss of their own language and culture.

Attrition The process whereby an individual gradually loses competence in a language either as a result of lack of contact with that language, as in the case of immigrants or refugees, or because of some impairment.

Balanced bilingualism/balanced multilingualism A situation where an individual is roughly equally competent in his/her two or more languages; also referred to as **ambilingualism** and **equilingualism**.

Base language The language which provides the morphosyntactic framework of an utterance that also contains code-mixed and code-switched items; also referred to as **matrix language**. See **embedded language**.

Bilingualism A situation where an individual uses two languages, or the presence of two languages in a community normally used by sizeable numbers of its speakers; sometimes used when more than two codes are involved (**multilingualism**). See **trilingualism**.

Bilingual/multilingual education A general term used to refer to education programmes that involve the use of two or more languages. Students may be monolingual or bilingual/multilingual when they start this form of education, and the programmes can have a variety of aims, e.g. linguistic and cultural enrichment, language maintenance or language revival.

Bilinguality/multilinguality The psychological state of the individual who has access to and competence in two or more languages for social communication.

Bilingual/multilingual literacy The ability of a bilingual/multilingual individual or community to read and/or write with understanding, i.e. to make decontextualised use of more than one language, especially in written mode. Like **bilingualism/multilingualism**, bilingual/multilingual literacy is seen as greater than the sum total of single language literacies.

Borrowing Borrowing occurs when a vocabulary item from one language enters the vocabulary of another, either temporarily or permanently. A borrowed item is known as a **borrowing** or a **loan word (= loanword)**.

Code (linguistic code) An accepted system of linguistic symbols and rules used by speakers for communication, i.e. a language or language variety; **to encode** and **to decode** are used for composing and interpreting the message. See **codification**.

Code alternation A generic term for the communication strategy used by bilinguals/multilinguals consisting of the alternate use of two or more languages in the same utterance or in conversation with other bilinguals/multilinguals. See **code-switching** and **code-mixing**.

Code-mixing A communication strategy used by bilinguals/multilinguals whereby linguistic elements from one language (L_A) are transferred into another (L_B) without being linguistically adapted to conform to the phonetic or morphological conventions of language L_B. An item so used is known as a **mix**.

Code-switching A communication strategy used by bilinguals/multilinguals whereby speakers alternate between languages in the course of conversations with other bilinguals/multilinguals. An item so used is known as a **switch**. Switches may involve different amounts of speech and can occur within an utterance (**intrasentential switching**) or at the end of one utterance and the start of the next (**intersentential switching**).

Codification The establishment of standardised norms of a linguistic code through the publication of grammars, dictionaries, spelling rules and style manuals.

Cognition The mental process that relates to the ability of the human mind to perceive, learn, think and make judgements.

Community language A language used by the speakers of a specific group, usually a linguistic minority; also called **heritage language**.

Complementarity principle A principle of language competence bilinguals/multilinguals usually acquire and use their languages for different purposes, in distinct domains of life, with a variety of people. Different situations of their life require different languages.

Convergence Linguistic accommodation to attune to the speech of one's interlocutor(s) in order to accentuate similarities, express solidarity or decrease social distance. See **divergence**.

Corpus planning The activities of language planners aimed at standardising a particular language system (for instance, its grammar or spelling system) or at elaborating or modernising its vocabulary. See **status planning**.

Creole A creole is normally a pidgin that has become the first language of a new generation of speakers. The process of **creolisation** is characterised by an expansion of linguistic forms and functions. See **pidgin**.

Crossing A speaker's use of some forms of a language variety associated with a social group or a language group that the speaker does not normally subscribe to. It is a type of code-switching described as typically practised by some inner-city groups of young people.

Diglossia A situation in which two forms of the same language coexist in a complementary relationship in a society, with each having distinct functions.

Divergence The opposite of linguistic **convergence**: speakers accentuate the differences between their speech styles and those of their interlocutor(s); the result is usually an increase in social distance.

Domain A term used to refer to a social sphere of activities that represent a combination of specific setting, times and role relationships such as, among others, 'family' and 'employment'.

Dominant bilingualism/multilingualism A situation in which individuals have greater proficiency in one of their languages and use it more often than their other languages.

Dominant language The language of a socially powerful and influential group; it is usually also the language in which the bilingual/multilingual is most competent.

Embedded language The items of language that are inserted in utterances in another language; such insertions are instances of **code-switching** or **code-mixing**.

Ethnolinguistics The study of the interrelationship between language and other aspects of culture.

Exogamy The practice of marrying outside a specific ethnic or social group.

Exogenous language A language that is not spoken as a native language within a specific speech community but only as an official or administrative language within that community.

First language(s) The language or languages that an individual first acquires in early childhood. See **mother tongue**.

Foreign language A language that is normally learnt as a second or subsequent language in an educational or formal context and is not used by most speakers in the learner's community.

Heritage language see **community language**.

Immersion (programme) A type of bilingual education in which learners are taught through the medium of a language that is not their first language. In **total immersion** programmes, learners are taught exclusively through the medium of their non-primary language; in **partial immersion** programmes, they are taught partly through the medium of their primary language and partly in a language that is different from their native tongue.

Incipient bilingualism/multilingualism A situation where individuals are at an early stage of becoming bilingual/multilingual, i.e. one or both (or all) of their languages are not yet fully developed.

Interdependence A relationship between two or more linguistic systems or psychological mechanisms in which neither can function without reference to the other.

Interference A situation in which a language feature or pattern from one language, usually the first language, is mistakenly used for a dissimilar target language feature or pattern; also referred to as **negative transfer**.

Interlanguage The version of a language produced at successive stages by a second or foreign language learner while acquiring mastery of the target language.

Interlocutor The person one is engaged with in a conversation. The term implies interaction and reciprocity in the communicative event.

International language A language of wider communication used beyond the national boundaries of a linguistic community, often for specific communicative purposes.

Intersentential code-switch A change from one language to another (and sometimes back again) in which the switch occurs at clause or sentence boundaries, i.e. outside the clause or sentence; also called **extrasentential code-switch**.

Intrasentential code-switch A change from one language to another (and often back again) in which the switch occurs within a clause or sentence.

Language awareness A general term referring to the understanding and appreciation an individual has of what language is, how it works and how it is used in society.

Language change The process whereby natural languages evolve over time on all linguistic levels (pronunciation, grammar, lexis) and in their patterns of usage.

Language choice The selection a bilingual/multilingual makes among his or her available languages or language varieties, for use in particular situations, contexts and domains.

Language competence/linguistic competence The knowledge that the speaker-listener has of his/her language and the ability to produce correct sentences and recognise ungrammatical ones.

Language contact The coexistence of two or more languages in a geographical area or in a speech community, usually involving some degree of bilingualism or multilingualism on the part of some individuals or throughout the speech community.

Language dominance The situation where one language is the stronger or preferred code of a bilingual/multilingual speaker.

Language loss There is language loss when a language ceases to be used by a speech community because it has been (or is being) replaced by another.

Language loyalty The purposeful maintenance and retention of a language that is perceived to be under threat from encroachment of another language.

Language maintenance The preservation and continued use of a language, usually a minority language, in contexts where there is pressure on speakers to shift towards a more dominant code.

Language planning Activities aimed at influencing and modifying the language behaviour of a speech community and developing, promoting, supporting or protecting languages within that community.

Language shift The process whereby a speech community ceases to maintain its native language in the face of competition from another more dominant language.

Language spread The process by which the uses of a language or the number of users of a language increase, usually as a result of political expansion of a dominant group who impose their language either directly on other speech communities, or indirectly via the prestige of the expanding group's speakers, their culture, technology or economic dominance.

Lingua franca A language used as a common means of communication between speakers whose native languages are mutually unintelligible.

Linguistic majority, see **majority language**.

Linguistic minority, see **minority language**.

Linguistic pluralism, see **pluralism**.

Linguistic repertoire, see **repertoire**.

Linguistic variety, see **variety**.

Literacy The ability of an individual or community to read or write with understanding, i.e. to make decontextualised use of language, especially in written mode. See **bilingual/multilingual literacy**.

Literacy event This expression describes an event in which the reading or production of a written text takes place within a specific context. It is typically associated with achieving a particular goal such as, for example, reading public notices and published information, or with carrying out specific tasks such as letter-writing or storytelling.

Literacy practices This expression is used to emphasise that reading and writing are activities that take place in specific social and cultural contexts. Such practices are of a social nature and are used with children as a means of socialisation.

Loan word A word that has been borrowed from one language and introduced into another.

Majority language A language used by a socioeconomically more dominant group which may also be numerically stronger than other linguistic groups within the same geographical area; also called **dominant language**. See **minority language**.

Marked form In language description an **unmarked form** usually is the base form of a linguistic item and is seen as more neutral than the **marked form**, which typically shows the presence of additional characteristics such as number, gender, derived verbal forms etc.

Matrix language, see **base language**.

Metalinguistic (awareness) A language user's awareness of language and his or her ability to think and talk about language. See **language awareness**.

Minority language A language used by a socially subordinate group or a language that has been designated as culturally inferior in relation to another language in the community (the **dominant language**. See also **majority language**.

Monolingual The person who habitually uses only one **code** for all his or her linguistic needs.

Mother tongue A general term for the language an individual acquires and uses from birth, i.e. the usual language of the home and the community; similar (and similarly general) terms are **native language** and **primary language**. See **first language**.

Multilingualism A situation where a person has competence in more than one language, can use each of his or her languages in appropriate contexts and is able to alternate between languages; or the simultaneous presence in a community of more than two languages normally used by sizable numbers of its speakers. See **bilingualism** and **trilingualism**.

Multilingual literacy, see **bilingual/multilingual literacy**.

Multiliteracy Multiple forms of literacy associated with different channels or modalities such as, for instance, computer literacy, mathematical literacy (numeracy) and visual literacy.

National language A language that is associated with a particular country where it is formally recognised as a component or a symbol of national identity.

Native-like Native-like (linguistic) competence or proficiency refers to the ability to use a non-native language at a level which equals or approximates the linguistic competence of educated native speakers. See **language competence**.

Native language See **mother tongue**.

Native speaker A general term used to refer to someone who is a speaker of a language acquired from birth, rather than having learnt it later in his or her life.

Official language A language which has recognised status and is used for legal, administrative and political communication within a given political territory.

Passive bilingualism/multilingualism A situation in which an individual understands another language/other languages in its spoken and/or written form but does not use it/them actively for spoken or written communication; also called **receptive bilingualism/ multilingualism**.

Personality principle A principle of language legislation and language policy which implies that all citizens of a given state have access to government services in their own language.

Pidgin A new and initially simple linguistic variety that arises out of language contact between speakers of two or more languages who do not share a common code. It is characterised by a simplified grammatical structure and reduced vocabulary. It is not the native language of anyone but may become a more stable and complex variety used as a **lingua franca** and eventually develop into a **creole**.

Pluralism (linguistic pluralism) A situation in which people from different ethnic or linguistic communities, cultures, religions or similar groups live together in a society that accepts their differences and does not insist on linguistic and cultural conformity to majority norms.

Plurilingualism A situation where a person has competence in more than one language, can use each of his or her languages in appropriate contexts and is able to alternate between languages; often used as a synonym of **multilingualism**.

Preferred language The language a bilingual/multilingual chooses from among his or her linguistic repertoire to use in given situations.

Productive bilingualism/multilingualism A situation in which individuals understand and make active use of two or more languages in their spoken and/or written form. Also called **active bilingualism/multilingualism**.

Register Variation in language, especially in lexis and style, according to the context in and purpose for which the language is used.

Repertoire (linguistic/language repertoire) The range of languages or language varieties that is available to the bilingual/multilingual speaker to use in particular situations and with different interlocutors.

Second language The language that is acquired or learnt by an individual after his or her first language has been acquired. It also refers to a non-native language that is used by a speech community alongside its native language.

Semilingualism A situation in which an individual possesses insufficient knowledge in any of his or her languages, including his/her first language(s).

Simultaneous bilingualism/multilingualism A situation in which an individual acquires two or more languages at the same time as their first language, i.e. from birth.

Speech community A regionally or socially defined group of speakers who share the same language, use it habitually and adhere to shared sociolinguistic norms. Also called **linguistic community** or **language community**.

Standard language A relatively uniform language variety which: (i) does not show (or shows minimal) regional or social variation; (ii) is used officially with a wide range of communicative functions in both spoken and written form; and (iii) has been accorded special status, which causes many people to consider it socioculturally superior to other varieties of the same language.

Standardisation The process by which a standard language is developed: it involves the establishment of descriptive linguistic norms (including the orthography) and the promotion and acceptance of these norms by the speech community.

Status planning The activities of language planners aimed at changing the use and function of a linguistic variety within a speech community. See **corpus planning**.

Submersion A type of education in which the child is schooled in a language that is not his or her mother tongue.

Subtractive bilingualism/multilingualism A situation in which a person's acquisition of a second or subsequent language is achieved at the expense of some loss in aptitude already acquired in their first language.

Successive bilingualism/multilingualism A situation in which a bilingual's or multilingual's subsequent language(s) is/are added after the first language has been established, either fully or partially; also called **consecutive bilingualism/multilingualism**.

Territorial bilingualism/multilingualism A situation in which two or more languages are used within the same given territory.

Territorial monolingualism A situation in which only one language is used in a given territory.

Territoriality principle A principle in language legislation and language policy which divides bilingual/multilingual states into distinct, largely monolingual areas.

Transfer The effect or influence of one language, often the learner's first language, on his or her production of a second or subsequent language.

Trilingualism/trilingual A situation where a person has competence in three languages, can use each of them in appropriate contexts and is able to alternate between the three; trilingualism can also be used to refer to the simultaneous presence in a community of three languages normally used by sizable numbers of its speakers. The reference to this situation is often subsumed when the term multilingualism is used. See **bilingualism** and **multilingualism**.

Variety A general term for a linguistic system used by a given group of speakers or in specified social contexts; often used as a hyponym of 'language' or an alternative to 'dialect'.

Vernacular The indigenous language or dialect of a speech community, often associated with the spoken, non-standard variety of a particular ethnic, social or geographical group.

References

Albaugh, Ericka A. 2005. *The colonial image reversed: advocates of multilingual education in Africa*. PhD dissertation, Duke University.
  2014. *State-building and multilingual education in Africa*. New York: Cambridge University Press.
Alcock, Antony 2000. *A history of the protection of regional cultural minorities in Europe: from the edict of the nantes to the present day*. London: Macmillan.
Anderson, Ben 1983. *Imagined communities*. London: Verso.
Angerer, Barbara 2010. *Individuelle und institutionelle Zweisprachigkeit: das besondere Spannungsfeld in Südtirol*. Master's thesis, University of Geneva. Online: archive ouverte UNIGE http://archive-ouverte.unige.ch.
Aronin, Larissa and Ó Laoire, Muiris 2004. 'Exploring multilingualism in cultural contexts: towards a notion of multilinguality', in Hoffmann and Ytsma (eds.), 11–29.
Aronin, Larissa and Toubkin, Lynne 2002. 'Language interference and language learning techniques transfer in L_2 and L_3 immersion programmes', *Journal of Bilingual Education and Bilingualism*, 5 (5): 267–78.
ASTAT (eds.) 2004. *Südtiroler Sprachbarometer 2004, Sprachgebrauch und Sprachidentität in Südtirol*. Bozen: La Bodonina.
Auer, Peter 1990. 'A discussion paper on code alternation', in European Science Foundation (ed.) *Network on Code-Switching and Language Contact. Papers for the workshop on concepts, methodology and data, Basel, 12–13 January*, 69–89.
  1995. 'The pragmatics of code-switching: a sequential approach', in Lesley Milroy and Pieter Muysken (eds.) *One speaker, two languages: cross-disciplinary perspectives on code-switching*. Cambridge University Press, 115–35.
  1998. 'From code-switching via language mixing to fused lects: toward a dynamic typology of bilingual speech', *InLiSt No. 6 Interaction and Linguistic Structures*.
  2003. 'Crossing the language border into Turkish? Uses of Turkish by non-Turks in Germany', in L. Mondada and S. Pekarek (eds.) *Plurilinguisme–Mehrsprachigkeit–Plurilingualism: Festschrift für Georges Lüdi*. Tübingen: Francke, 73–93.

Auer, Peter and Li, Wei (eds.) 2009. *Handbook of multilingualism and multilingual communication*. Berlin: Mouton de Gruyter.

Awobuluyi, Oladele 1992. 'Language education in Nigeria: theory, policy and practice', *Fafunwa Foundation Internet Journal of Education*, 1–7. Retrieved 8th November 2011 from http://fafunwafoundation.tripod.com/fafunwafoundation/id8.html.

Azuma, Shoji 1991. *Processing and intra-sentential code-switching*. Doctoral dissertation, University of Texas, Austin.

Baetens Beardsmore, Hugo 1986. *Bilingualism: basic principles* (Vol. 1). Clevedon: Multilingual Matters.

Baker, Colin 2002. 'Bilingual education', in Robert Kaplan (ed.) *The Oxford handbook of applied linguistics*. New York: Oxford University Press, 294–305.

   2006. *Foundations of bilingual education and bilingualism* (4th edn). New York: Multilingual Matters.

   2009. 'Becoming bilingual through bilingual education', in Auer and Wei (eds.), 131–53.

Baker, Colin and García, Ofelia 2007. *Bilingual education: an introductory reader*. Clevedon: Multilingual Matters.

Baker, Colin and Jones, Sylvia Prys 1998. *Encyclopedia of bilingual education and bilingualism*. Clevedon: Multilingual Matters.

Bamgbose, Ayo 2000. 'Introduction', *International Journal of the Sociology of Language*, Sociolinguistics in West Africa, 141: 1–8.

Bani-Shoraka, Helena 2005. *Language choice and code-switching in the Azerbaijani community in Tehran: a conversation analytic approach to bilingual practices*. Uppsala, Sweden: Acta Universitatis Upsaliensis.

Barbour, Stephen and Stevenson, Patrick 1990. *Variation in German: a critical approach to German sociolinguistics*. Cambridge University Press.

Barnes Alberdi, Julia 1997. 'Early trilingualism: Basque, English and Spanish', paper given at 1st International Symposium on Bilingualism, April 1997, University of Newcastle upon Tyne, UK.

   1999. 'The acquisition of English, Basque and Spanish in a trilingual child 1.11–3.08', paper given at 2nd International Symposium on Bilingualism, April 1999, University of Newcastle upon Tyne, UK.

   2002. *The acquisition of questions in English by a trilingual child*. Unpublished PhD dissertation, University of the Basque Country.

Barnes, J. 2006. *Early trilingualism: a focus on questions*. Clevedon: Multilingual Matters.

   2011. 'The influence of child-directed speech in early trilingualism', *International Journal of Multilingualism*, 8 (1): 42–62.

Barron-Hauwaert, Suzanne 2000. 'Issues surrounding trilingual families: children with simultaneous exposure to three languages', *Zeitschrift für interkulturellen Fremdsprachenunterricht: Didaktik und Methodik im Bereich Deutsch als Fremdsprache*, 5: 1. www.ualberta.ca/~german/ejournal/barron.

2003. 'Trilingualism: a study of children growing up with three languages', in T. Tokuhama-Espinosa (ed.) *The multilingual mind: issues discussed by, for, and about people living with many languages*. Westport, CT: Praeger, 129–50.

2004. *Language strategies for bilingual families*. Clevedon: Multilingual Matters.

Barton, David and Hamilton, Mary 1998. *Local literacies: reading and writing in one community*. London: Routledge.

2000. 'Literacy practices', in *Situated literacies: reading and writing in context*. London: Routledge, 7–15.

Bates, Elizabeth and MacWhinney, Brian 1989. 'Functionalism and the competition model', in B. MacWhinney and E. Bates (eds.) *The crosslinguistic study of sentence processing*. New York: Cambridge University Press.

Baynham, Mike 1995. *Literacy practices: investigating literacy in social contexts*. London: Longman.

Belazi, Hedi M., Rubin, Edward J. and Toribio, Almeida Jacqueline 1994. 'Code switching and X-Bar theory: the functional head constraint', *Linguistic Inquiry*, 25 (2): 221–37.

Belcher, Diane and Connor, Ulla (eds.) 2001. *Reflections on multiliterate lives*. Clevedon: Multilingual Matters.

Ben-Rafael, Eliezer 1994. *Language, identity and social division: the case of Israel*. Oxford: Clarendon Press.

Benson, Carol 2003. 'Trilingualism in Guinea-Bissau and the question of instructional language', in Hoffmann and Ytsma (eds.), 166–84.

Berk-Seligson, Susan 1986. 'Linguistic constraints on intra-sentenial code-switching: a study of Spanish/Hebrew bilingualism', *Language in Society*, 15 (3): 313–48.

Besnier, Niko and Street, Brian 1994. 'Aspects of literacy', in T. Ingold (ed.) *Encyclopedia of Anthropology: human, culture and social life*, London: Routledge, 527–62.

Bialystok, Ellen 1991. 'Letters, sounds, and symbols: changes in children's understanding of written language', *Applied Psycholinguistics*, 12: 75–89.

1999. 'Cognitive complexity and attentional control in the bilingual mind', *Child Development*, 70: 636–44.

2001. *Bilingualism in development: language, literacy, and cognition*. New York: Cambridge University Press.

Bialystok, Ellen and Craik, F. 2010. 'Cognitive and linguistic processing in the bilingual mind', *Current Directions in Psychological Science*, 19 (1): 19–23.

Bialystok, Ellen and Martin, Marilyn 2004. 'Attention and inhibition in bilingual children: evidence from the dimensional change card sort task', *Developmental Science*, 7: 325–39.

Bialystok, Ellen and Shapero, D. 2005. 'Ambiguous benefits: the effect of bilingualism on reversing ambiguous figures', *Developmental Science*, 8: 595–604.

Bialystok, Ellen, Craik, F. and Luk, G. 2008. 'Cognitive control and lexical access in younger and older bilinguals', *Journal of Experimental Psychology: learning, memory, and cognition*, 34 (4): 859–73.

Blackledge, Adrian 2000. 'Monolingual ideologies in multilingual states: language, hegemony and social justice in western liberal democracies', *Estudios de Sociolingüística*, 1 (2): 25–45.

Blackledge, Adrian and Creese, Angela 2010. *Multilingualism: a critical perspective*. London: Continuum.

Bloomfield, Leonard 1935. *Language*. London: Allen & Unwin.

Brandt, Deborah and Clinton, Katie 2002. 'Limits of the local: expanding perspectives on literacy as a social practice', *Journal of Literacy Research*, 34 (3): 337–56.

Braun, Andreas and Cline, Tony 2010. 'Trilingual families in mainly monolingual societies: working towards a typology', *International Journal of Multilingualism*, 7 (2): 110–27.

Braunmüller, Kurt 1999. *Die skandinavischen Sprachen im Überblick*, 2. Auflage. Tübingen: Francke.

Brincat, John 1991. *Malta 870–1054. Al-Himyari's Account*. Quoted in http://my-malta.com/interesting/MalteseLanguage.html.

Brutt-Griffler, Janina 2002. *World English: a study of its development*. Clevedon: Multilingual Matters.

Canetti, Elias 1977. *Die gerettete Zunge: Geschichte einer Jugend*. Munich: Carl Hanser.

Cenoz, Jasone 2003a. 'The additive effect of bilingualism on third language acquisition: a review', *The International Journal of Bilingualism*, 7 (1): 71–87.

  2003b. 'Teaching English as a third language: the effect of attitudes and motivation', in Hoffmann and Ytsma (eds.), 202–18.

  2009. *Towards multilingual education: Basque educational research in international perspective*. Clevedon: Multilingual Matters.

Cenoz, Jasone and Genesee, Fred (eds.) 1998. *Beyond bilingualism: multilingualism and multilingual education*. Clevedon: Multilingual Matters.

Cenoz, Jasone and Genesee, Fred (eds.) 2001. *Trends in bilingual acquisition* (Vol. 1). Amsterdam: John Benjamins.

Cenoz, Jasone and Jessner, Ulrike (eds.) 2000. *English in Europe: the acquisition of a third language*. Clevedon: Multilingual Matters.

Cenoz, J., Hufeisen, B. and Jessner, U. (eds.) 2001. *Crosslinguistic influence in third language acquisition: psycholinguistic perspectives*. Clevedon: Multilingual Matters.

Cenoz, J., Hufeisen, B. and Jessner, U. (eds.) 2003. *The multilingual lexicon*. Dordrecht: Kluwer.

Cerrón-Palomino, Rodolfo 1989. 'Language policy in Peru: a historical overview', *International Journal of the Sociology of Language*, 77: 11–31.

Chambers, Helen 1995. 'Acquisition of lexical and pronunciation variants', *Proceedings of the International Congress of Dialectologists*, 4, (ed. Wolfgang Viereck). Stuttgart: Franz Steiner Verlag, 3–19.

Chevalier, Sarah 2011. *Trilingual language acquisition: contextual factors influencing active trilingualism in early childhood*. Unpublished habilitation thesis, Univeristy of Zurich.

Chin, Ng Bee and Wigglesworth, Gillian 2007. *Bilingualism: an advanced resource book*. London: Routledge.

Clyne, Michael 1997. 'Some of the things trilinguals do', *International Journal of Bilingualism*, 1 (2): 95–116.

   2003. *Dynamics of language contact: English and immigrant languages*. Cambridge University Press.

Cooper, Robert L. 1982. *Language spread: studies in diffusion and social change*. Bloomington, IN: Indiana University Press.

Cope, Bill and Kalantzis, Mary 2000. *Multiliteracies: literacy learning and the design of social futures*. London: Routledge.

Coronel-Molina, Serafín 1999. 'Functional domains of the Quechua language in Peru: issues of status planning', *International Journal of Bilingual Education and Bilingualism*, 2 (3): 166–80.

Coste, Daniel, Moore, Danièle and Zarate, Geneviève 2009. *Plurilingual and pluricultural competence*. Strasbourg, France: Council of Europe.

Cremona, Joseph 1994. 'The survival of Arabic in Malta', in W. Davies, M. Parry and R. A. M. Temple (eds.) *Changing voices of Europe: social and political changes and their linguistic repercussions, past, present and future*. Festschrift for Glanville Price, University of Wales Press, 280–294.

Cromdal, Jakob 2001. 'Overlap in bilingual play: some implications of code-switching for overlap resolution, *Research on Language and Social Interaction*, 34 (4): 421–51.

Cummins, Jim 2000. 'Putting language proficiency in its place: responding to critiques of the conversational / academic language distinction', in Cenoz and Jessner (eds.), 54–83.

   2001. *Negotiating identities: education for empowerment in a diverse society* (2nd edn). Los Angeles, CA: California Association for Bilingual Education.

   2007. 'Foreword', in M. Carder, *Bilingualism in international schools: a model for enriching language education*. Clevedon: Multilingual Matters, viii–xi.

   2009. 'Pedagogies of choice: challenging coercive relations of power in classrooms and communities', *International Journal of Bilingual Education and Bilingualism*, 12: 261–72.

Cunningham-Andersson, Ulla and Andersson, Stephan 1999. *Growing up with two languages: a practical guide*. London: Routledge.

Dakubu, M. E. Kropp 2000. 'Multiple bilingualisms and urban transitions: coming to Accra', *International Journal of the Sociology of Language*, Sociolinguistics in West Africa, 141: 9–26.

Dalby, Andrew 1998. *Dictionary of languages*. London: Bloomsbury.

Daoud, Mohammed 2001. 'The language situation in Tunisia', *Current Issues in Language Planning*, 2 (1): 1–52.

De Bot, Kes 1992. 'A bilingual production model: Levelt's "speaking" model adapted', *Applied Linguistics*, 13 (1): 1–24.

De Houwer, Annick 1990. *The acquisition of two languages from birth: a case study*. Cambridge University Press.

1999. 'Two or more languages in early childhood: some general points and practical recommendations'. Eric Digest. In http://askeeric.org/plweb-cgi/obtain.pl.

2007. 'Parental language input patterns and children's bilingual use', *Applied Psycholinguistics*, 28: 411–66.

Deuchar, Margaret and Quay, Suzanne 2000. *Bilingual acquisition: theoretical implications of a case study*. Oxford University Press.

Di Sciullo, Anne-Marie and Williams, Edwin 1987. *On the definition of word* (Vol. 14). Cambridge, MA: MIT Press.

Döpke, Susanne 1992. *One parent – one language: an interactional approach*. Amsterdam: John Benjamins.

Dorian, Nancy 1998. 'Western language ideologies and small-language prospects', in L. A. Grenoble and L. J. Whaley (eds.) *Endangered languages: current issues and future prospects*. Cambridge University Press, 3–21.

Dua, Hans 1993. 'The national language and the ex-colonial language as rivals: the case of India', *International Political Science Review*, 14 (3): 293–308.

Dutcher, Nadine and Tucker, Richard 1994. *The use of first and second languages in education: a review of educational experience*. Washington, DC: World Bank, East Asia and the Pacific Region, Country Department III.

Edwards, John 1977. 'Ethnic identity and bilingual education', in H. Giles (ed.) *Language, ethnicity and intergroup relations*. London: Academic Press, 253–82.

1985. *Language, society and identity*. Oxford: Basil Blackwell.

2001. *Multilingualism and multiculturalism in Canada*, in Extra and Gorter (eds.), 315–32.

Edwards, Malcolm and Dewaele, Jean-Marc 2007. 'Trilingual conversations: a window into multicompetence?' *The International Journal of Bilingualism*, 11 (2): 221–41.

Edwards, Viv 2001. 'Community languages in the United Kingdom', in Extra and Gorter (eds.), 243–60.

2004. *Multilingualism in the English-speaking world*. Oxford: Blackwell.

Egger, Kurt 2001. *Sprachlandschaft im Wandel. Südtirol auf dem Weg zur Mehrsprachigkeit*. Bozen: Verlagsanstalt Athesia.

Egger, Kurt and Lardschneider McLean, Margareth 2001. *Dreisprachig werden in Gröden: eine Studie zum Spracherwerb in der frühen Kindheit*. Bozen: Institut Pedagogich Ladin.

Eichinger, Ludwig 2002. 'South Tyrol: German and Italian in a changing world', *Journal of Multilingual and Multicultural Development*, 23 (1 and 2): 137–49.

Elwert, Wolfgang 1973. 'Das zweisprachige Individuum: ein Selbstzeugnis', in *Studien zu den romanischen Sprachen*, Band IV (1–81), Wiesbaden: Franz Steiner Verlag.

European Language Portfolio (ELP) 2001. *Modern languages: learning, teaching, assessment: a common European framework of reference.* Strasbourg: Council of Europe and Cambridge University Press.

Extra, Guus and Gorter, Durk 2001. *The other languages of Europe.* Clevedon: Multilingual Matters.

Extra, Guus and Yagmur, Kutlay 2004. *Urban multilingualism in Europe: immigrant minority languages at home and school.* Clevedon: Multilingual Matters.

Fantini, Alvino E. 1982. *La adquisición del lenguaje en un niño bilingüe.* Barcelona: Herder.

   1985. *Language acquisition of a bilingual child: a sociolinguistic perspective.* Clevedon: Multilingual Matters.

Fasold, Ralph 1984. *The sociolinguistics of society.* Oxford: Basil Blackwell.

Federal Ministry of Information 1977. *Federal Republic of Nigeria National Policy on Education.* Lagos: Federal Ministry of Information.

Ferguson, Charles A. 1959. 'Diglossia', *Word*, 15: 325–40.

Ferguson, G. 2003. 'Classroom code-switching in postcolonial contexts: functions, attitudes and policies'. *AILA Review*, 16: 38–51.

Fill, Alwin and Mühlhäusler, Peter (eds.) 2001. *The ecolinguistic reader: language, ecology and environment.* London: Continuum.

Fishman, Joshua A. 1967. 'Bilingualism with and without diglossia; diglossia with and without bilingualism', *Journal of Social Issues*, 23 (2): 29–38.

   1980. 'Ethnocultural dimensions in the acquisition and retention of biliteracy', *Basic Writing*, 3 (1): 48–61.

   1989. 'Language and nationalism: Part II', in J. A. Fishman (ed.) *Language and ethnicity in minority sociolinguistic perspective.* Clevedon: Multilingual Matters, 269–367.

   1991. *Language and ethnicity.* Amsterdam and Philadelphia: J. Benjamin.

   1992. 'Sociology of English as an additional language', in B. B. Kachru (ed.), 19–26.

Fishman, Joshua A. (ed.) 2001. *Can threatened languages be saved? Reversing language shift, revisited: A 21st Century Perspective.* Clevedon: Multilingual Matters.

Flynn, S., Foley, C. and Vinnitskaya, I. 2004. 'The cumulative-enhancement model of language acquisition: comparing adults' and children's patterns of development in first, second and third language acquisition of relative clauses', *International Journal of Multilingualism*, 1 (1): 3–16.

Gafaranga, Joseph 2001. 'Linguistic identities in talk-in-interaction: order in bilingual conversation', *Journal of Pragmatics*, 33 (12): 1901–25.

Galeano, Eduardo 1991. *The book of embraces.* Trans. Cedric Belfrage. New York: Norton.

Gallagher, C. F. 1966. 'Language and identity', in L. C. Brown (ed.) *State and society in independent North Africa*. Washington DC: Middle East Institute, 73–96.

García, Ofelia 1997. 'New York's multilingualism: world languages and their role in a US city', in O. García and J. Fishman (eds.) *The multilingual apple: languages in New York City*. Berlin: Mouton de Gruyter, 3–50.

2008. 'Multilingual language awareness and teacher education', in J. Cenoz and N. Hornberger (eds.) *Encyclopedia of language and education* (2nd edn, Vol. 6: Knowledge about language). Berlin: Springer, 385–400.

García, Ofelia and Fishman, Joshua A. (eds.) 2002. *Multilingual apple: languages in New York* (2nd edn). Berlin: Mouton de Gruyter.

García, Ofelia, Bartlett, Lesley and Kleifgen, Jo Anne 2007. 'From biliteracy to pluriliteracies', in P. Auer and Li Wei (eds.) *Handbook of Applied Linguistics*. (Vol. 5: Multilingualism). Berlin: Mouton de Gruyter, 207–28.

Garland, Stanley 2007. *The bilingual spectrum*. Orlando, FL: Guirnalda Publishing.

Garrett, P. and Baquedano-Lopez, P. 2002. 'Language socialisation: reproduction and continuity, transformation and change', *Annual Review of Anthropology*, 31: 339–61.

Gee, James Paul 1991. *Social linguistics: ideology in discourses*. London: Falmer Press.

1992. *The social mind: language, ideology, and social practice*. New York: Bergin & Garvey.

1996. *Social linguistics and literacies: ideology in discourses* (2nd edn). London: Falmer Press.

2000. 'New people in new worlds: networks, the new capitalism and schools', in B. Cope and M. Kalantzis (eds.) *Multiliteracies: literacy learning and the design of social futures*, 43–68.

2001. 'Progressivism, critique, and socially situated minds', in C. Dudley-Marling and C. Edelsky (eds.) *The fate of progressive language policies and practices*. Urbana, IL: NCTE, 31–58.

Genesee, Fred 1989. 'Early bilingual development: one language or two?', *Journal of Child Language*, 16: 161–79.

Genesee, Fred and Bourhis, Richard Y. 1988. 'Evaluative reactions to language choice strategies: the role of sociocultural factors', *Language and Communication*, 8: 229–50.

Genesee, Fred and Nicoladis, Elena 2007. 'Bilingual acquisition', in E. Hoff and M. Shatz (eds.) *Handbook of language development*. Oxford: Blackwell, 324–42.

Giles, H., Coupland, N. and Coupland, J. 1991. 'Accommodation theory: communication, context, and consequence', in H. Giles, J. Coupland and N. Coupland (eds.) *Contexts of accommodation: developments in applied sociolinguistics*. Cambridge University Press, 1–68.

Giles, H., Taylor, D. M. and Bourhis, R. Y. 1973. 'Dimensions of Welsh identity', *European Journal of Social Psychology*, 7: 29–39.

Gonzalez, Andrew 1998. 'The language planning situation in the Philippines', *Journal of Multilingual and Multicultural Development*, 19 (5): 487–525.

Goodman, K., Goodman, Y., and Flores, B. 1979. *Reading in the bilingual classroom: literacy and biliteracy*. Rosslyn, VA: National Clearinghouse for Bilingual Education.

Graddol, David 2006. *English next*. British Council.

Green, David 1986. 'Control, activation and resource: a framework and a model for the control of speech in bilinguals', *Brain and Language*, 27: 210–23.

Gregory, Eve 1996. 'Learning from the community: a family literacy project with Bangladeshi origin children in London', in S. Wolfendale and K. Topping (eds.) *Family involvement in literacy: effective partnerships in education*. London: Cassell.

1998. 'Siblings as mediators of literacy in linguistic minority communities', *Language and Education*, 12 (1): 33–54.

2001. 'Sisters and brothers as language and literacy teachers: synergy between siblings playing and working together', *Journal of Early Childhood Literacy*, 1 (3): 301–22.

Gregory, Eve and Williams, Ann 2000. *City literacies: learning to read across generations and cultures*. London: Routledge.

Grosjean, François 1982. *Life with two languages: an introduction to bilingualism*. Cambridge, MA: Harvard University Press.

1992. 'Another view of bilingualism', *Advances in Psychology*, 83: 51–62.

1997. 'The bilingual individual', *Interpreting*, 2 (1/2): 163–87.

1998. 'Studying bilinguals: methodological and conceptual issues', *Bilingualism: Language and Cognition*, 11 (2): 131–49.

2001. 'The bilingual's language modes', in J. Nicol (ed.) *One mind, two languages: bilingual language processing*. Oxford: Blackwell, 1–22.

2008. *Studying bilinguals*. Oxford University Press.

2010. *Bilingual: life and reality*. Cambridge, MA: Harvard University Press.

Gumperz, John J. 1982. *Discourse strategies*. Cambridge University Press.

Gumperz, John J. and Hymes, Dell H. (eds.) 1972. *Directions in sociolinguistics: the ethnography of communication*. New York: Holt, Rinehart and Winston.

Haarmann, Harald 1980. *Multilingualismus*. Tübingen: Narr.

1992. 'Measures to increase the importance of Russian within and outside the Soviet Union – a case of covert language-spread policy', *International Journal of the Sociology of Language*, 95: 109–29.

Halmari, Helen 1997. *Government and codeswitching: explaining American Finnish* (Vol. 12). Amsterdam: John Benjamins.

Hamers, Josiane F. and Blanc, Michel H. A. 1989. *Bilingualism and bilinguality*. Cambridge University Press.

2000. *Bilinguality and bilingualism*. Cambridge University Press.

Hannon, Peter and Bird, Viv 2004. 'Family literacy in England: theory, practice, research, and policy', in B. H. Wasik (ed.) *Handbook of family literacy*. Mahwah, NJ: Lawrence Erlbaum, 23–39.

Harding, Edith and Riley, Philip 1986. *The bilingual family: a handbook for parents*. Cambridge University Press.

Harré, Rom 1990. 'Some narrative conventions of scientific discourse', in C. Nash (ed.) *Narrative in culture: the uses of storytelling in the sciences, philosophy, and literature*. London: Routledge.

Haugen, Einar 1956. *Bilingualism in the Americas*. Alabama: American Dialect Society.

1972. *The ecology of language*. Stanford University Press.

Hazen, Kirk 2002. 'Identity and language variation in a rural community', *Language*, 78 (2): 240–57.

Heath, Shirley B. 1983. *Ways with words: language, life and work in communities and classrooms*. Cambridge University Press.

Held, David, McGrew, Anthony, Goldblatt, David and Perraton Jonathan 1999. *Global transformations*. Cambridge: Polity Press.

Heller, Monica 1992. 'The politics of codeswitching and language choice', in Carol Eastman (ed.) *Codeswitching*. Clevedon: Multilingual Matters, 123–42.

1999. *Linguistic minorities and modernity: a sociolinguistic ethnography*. London: Longman.

2000. 'Bilingualism and identity in the post-modern world', *Estudios de sociolinguistica*, 1 (2): 9–24.

2006. *Linguistic minorities and modernity: a sociolinguistic ethnography*. London: Bloomsbury.

Hélot, Christine 1988. 'Bringing up children in English, French and Irish: two case studies', *Language, Culture and Curriculum*, 1 (3): 281–87.

Hélot, Christine and Ó Laoire, Muiris (eds.) 2011. *Language policy for the multilingual classroom: pedagogy of the possible*. Brighton: Multilingual Matters.

Hensel, Chase 1996. *Telling our selves: ethnicity and discourse in Southwestern Alaska*. New York: Oxford University Press.

Herdina, Philip and Jessner, Ulrike 2002. *A dynamic model of multilingualism: perspectives of change in psycholinguistics*. Clevedon: Multilingual Matters.

Hewitt, Roger 1986. *White talk, black talk: inter-racial friendship and communication amongst adolescents*. Cambridge University Press.

Hoffmann, Charlotte 1985. 'Language acquisition in two trilingual children', *Journal for Multilingual and Multicultural Development*, 6 (6): 479–95.

1991. *An introduction to bilingualism*. London: Longman.

1994. 'Language loss and language recovery: the case of the *Russlanddeutsche*', in M. M. Parry, W. V. Davies and R. A. M. Temple (eds.) *The changing voices of Europe: social and political changes and their linguistic repercussions, past, present and future*. Cardiff: University of Wales Press, 311–324.

1998. 'Luxembourg and the European Schools', in F. Genesee and J. Cenoz (eds.) *Beyond bilingualism: multilingualism and multilingual education*. Clevedon: Multilingual Matters, 143–74.

2001a. 'The status of trilingualism in bilingualism studies', in J. Cenoz, B. Hufeisen and U. Jessner (eds.) *Looking beyond second language acquisition: studies in tri- and multilingualism*. Tübingen: Stauffenburg Verlag, 13–25.

2001b. 'Balancing language planning and language rights: Catalonia's uneasy juggling act', *International Journal of Multilingual and Multicultural Development*, 21 (5): 425–41.

Hoffmann, Charlotte and Stavans, Anat 2007. 'The evolution of trilingual code-switching from infancy to school age: the shaping of trilingual competence through dynamic language dominance', *International Journal of Bilingualism*, 11 (1): 55–72.

Hoffmann, Charlotte and Widdicombe, Sue 1999. 'Code-switching and language dominance in the trilingual child', *AILE, Proceedings of 8th EUROSLA Conference Paris*, Vol. 1, Special Issue: 51–61.

Hoffmann, Charlotte and Ytsma, Jehannes (eds.) 2004. *Trilingualism in family, school and community*. Clevedon: Multilingual Matters.

Hornberger, Nancy H. 1989. 'Continua of biliteracy', *Review of Educational Research*, 59 (3): 271–96.

1990. 'Creating successful learning contexts for bilingual literacy', *Teachers College Record*, 92 (2): 212–29.

2000. 'Bilingual education policy and practice in the Andes: ideological paradox and intercultural possibility', *Anthropology and Education Quarterly*, 31 (2): 1–30.

2002. 'Multilingual language policies and the continua of biliteracy: an ecological approach', *Language Policy*, 1 (1): 27–51.

2003. *Continua of biliteracy: an ecological framework for educational policy, research, and practice in multilingual settings*. Tonawanda, NY: Multilingual Matters.

2007. 'Biliteracy, transnationalism, multimodality, and identity: trajectories across time and space', *Linguistics and Education*, 8 (3–4): 325–34.

Hornberger, Nancy H. and King, Kendall A. 2001. 'Reversing Quechua language shift in South America', in J. Fishman (ed.) *Can threatened languages be saved?*, 166–94.

Hornberger, Nancy H. and Skilton-Sylvester, Ellen 2000. 'Revisiting the continua of biliteracy: international and critical perspectives', *Language and Education: An International Journal*, 14 (2): 96–122.

Huber, Danielle 2001. 'Communication in multilingual style', *The Bilingual Family Newsletter*, 18 (2): 3–4.

Hufeisen, Britta 1998. 'L3-Stand der Forschung – was bleibt zu tun? [L3-State of the art – what needs to be done?]', in B. Hufeisen and

B. Lindemann (eds.) L₃-L₃ *und ihre zwischensprachliche Interaktion: Zu individueller Mehrsprachigkeit und gesteuertem Lernen* [L₂-L₃ and their crosslinguistic interaction: about individual multilingualism and instructed learning]. Tübingen: Stauffenburg, 169–83.

Ivir-Ashworth, Ksenija Corinna 2011. *The nature of two trilingual children's utterances: growing up with Croatian, English and German.* Unpublished doctoral thesis, University of East Anglia.

Jake, Janice L., Myers-Scotton, Carol and Gross, Steven 2002. 'Making a minimalist approach to codeswitching work: adding the matrix language', *Bilingualism: Language and Cognition*, 5 (1): 69–91.

Jessner, Ulrike 2006. *Linguistic awareness in multilinguals: English as a third language.* Edinburgh University Press.

2008. 'A DST model of multilingualism and the role of metalinguistic awareness', *The Modern Language Journal*, 92 (2): 270–83.

Joensuu, Chris Hall 2007. 'Recent developments in Finnish language education policy: a survey with particular reference to German', *German as a Foreign Language Journal*, 3: 1–24.

Joshi, Aravind K. 1987. 'An introduction to tree adjoining grammars', *Mathematics of Language*, 1: 87–115.

Kachru, Braj B. (ed.) 1992. *The other tongue: English across cultures.* Urbana/Chicago: University of Illinois Press.

Kazzazi, Kerstin 2011. 'Ich brauche mix-cough: cross-linguistic influence involving German, English and Farsi', *International Journal of Multilingualism*, 8 (1): 63–79.

Kefi, R. 2000. 'Quel avenir pour le français?', *Jeune Afrique*, 2036: 30–32.

King, Kendall A. and Fogle, Lyn W. 2006. 'Bilingual parenting as good parenting: parents' perspectives on family language policy for additive bilingualism', *International Journal of Bilingual Education and Bilingualism*, 9 (6): 695–712.

King, Kendall A. and Logan-Terry, Aubrey 2008. 'Additive bilingualism through family language policy: ideologies, strategies and interactional outcomes', *Calidoscópio*, 6: 5–19.

Kirkpatrick, Andy 2007. *World Englishes: implications of international communication and English language teaching.* Cambridge University Press.

Koplewitz, Immanuel 1992. 'Arabic in Israel: the sociolinguistic situation of Israel's Arab minority', *International Journal of the Sociology of Language*, 98: 29–66.

Kreindler, Isabelle 1982. 'The changing status of Russian in the Soviet Union', *International Journal of the Sociology of Language*, 33: 7–39.

Labov, William 1972. *Language in the inner city.* Philadelphia: University of Pennsylvania Press.

Lamarre, Patricia 2003. 'Growing up trilingual in Montreal: perceptions of college students', in Robert Bayley and Sandra R. Schecter, *Language socialisation in bilingual and multilingual societies.* Clevedon: Multilingual Matters, 62–80.

Lamarre, Patricia and Dagenais, Diane 2004. 'Language practices of trilingual youth in two Canadian cities', in Charlotte Hoffmann and Jehannes Ytsma (eds.) *Trilingualism in family, school and community*. Clevedon: Multilingual Matters, 53–74.

Lambert, Richard D. 1995. 'Language policy: an overview', Paper read at the International Symposium on Language Policy. 20 December, Bar-Ilan University, Israel.

Lambert, Wallace E. 1974. *Culture and language as factors in learning and education*, paper presented at the 8th TESOL Conference, Washington State College.

Lankshear, Colin 1999. 'Literacy studies in education', in M. Peters (ed.) *After the disciplines*. Westport, CT: Greenwood Press.

Lanthaler, Franz 2006. 'Die Vielschichtigkeit des Deutschen in Südtirol – und wie wir damit umgehen', in A. Abel, M. Stuflesser and M. Putz (eds.) *Mehrsprachigkeit in Europa: Erfahrungen, Bedürfnisse, gute Praxis*. Bozen: EURAC Research.

Lanza, Elizabeth 1997a. 'Language contact in bilingual two-year-olds and code-switching: language encounters of a different kind?', *International Journal of Bilingualism*, 1 (2): 135–62.

 1997b. *Language mixing in infant bilingualism: a sociolinguistic perspective*. Oxford University Press.

 2001. 'Bilingual first language acquisition: a discourse perspective on language contact in parent-child interaction', in J. Cenoz and F. Genesee (eds.) *Trends in bilingual acquisition*. Amsterdam: John Benjamins, 201–29.

Lasagabaster, Davied and Huguet, Ángel 2007. *Multilingualism in European bilingual contexts. language use and attitudes*. Clevedon: Multilingual Matters.

Levelt, Willem J. M. 1989. *Speaking*. Cambridge, MA: MIT Press.

Li, Wei 1998. 'The "why" and "how" questions in the analysis of conversational code-switching', in Peter Auer (ed.) *Code-switching in conversation: language, interaction and identity*. London: Routledge, 156–76.

 2005. '"How can you tell?" Toward a common sense explanation of conversational code-switching', *Journal of Pragmatics*, 37 (3): 375–89.

Lin, Angel M. Y. 1996. 'Bilingualism or linguistic segregation? Symbolic domination, resistance and code-switching in Hong Kong schools', *Linguistics and Education*, 8: 49–84.

Lo, Adrienne 1999. 'Codeswitching, speech community membership and the construction of ethnic identity', *Journal of Sociolinguistics*, 3 (4): 461–79.

Lüdi, Georges 2003. 'Code-switching and unbalanced bilingualism', in J. Dewaele, A. Housen and Li Wei (eds.) *Bilingualism: beyond basic principles*. Clevedon: Multilingual Matters, 174–88.

Luke, Allan 1994. *The social construction of literacy in the primary school*. Melbourne: Macmillan Education.

Luke, Allan and Freebody, Peter 1997. 'The social practices of reading', in S. Muspratt, A. Luke and P. Freebody (eds.) *Constructing Critical Literacies*. Creskill, NJ: Hampton Press, 185–225.

Lvovich, Natasha 1997. *The multilingual self: an inquiry into language learning.* Mahwah, NJ: Lawrence Erlbaum.

Mackay, Ronald 1978. 'Identifying the nature of the learner's needs', in R. Mackay and A. Mountford (eds.) *English for Specific Purposes*. London: Longman, 21–37.

MacSwan, Jeff 2000. 'The architecture of the bilingual language faculty: evidence from intrasentential code switching', *Bilingualism: Language and Cognition*, 3 (1): 37–54.

MacWhinney, Brian 2001. 'The Competition Model: the input, the context, and the brain', in P. Robinson (ed.) *Cognition and second language instruction*. New York: Cambridge University Press, 69–90.

2007. 'The TalkBank Project', in J. C. Beal, K. P. Corrigan and H. L. Moisl (eds.) *Creating and digitizing language corpora: synchronic databases* (Vol. 1). Houndmills: Palgrave Macmillan, 163–80.

Maneva, Blagovesta 2004. '"Maman, je suis polyglotte!": a case study of multilingual language acquisition from 0–5 years', *International Journal of Multilingualism*, 1 (2): 109–22, http://dx.doi.org/10.1080/14790710408668182.

Mar-Molinero, Clare 2000. *The politics of language in the Spanish-speaking world*. London: Routledge.

Mariátegui, J. C. 1973. *Siete ensayos de interpretación de la realidad peruana*. Lima: Biblioteca Peruane.

Marley, Dawn 2004. 'Language attitudes in Morocco following recent changes in language policy', *Language Policy*, 3: 25–46.

Martin-Jones, Marilyn 2007. 'Bilingualism, education and the regulation of access to language resources: changing research perspectives', in M. Heller (ed.) *Bilingualism: a social approach*. Houndmills, Basingstoke: Palgrave Macmillan, 161–82.

Martin-Jones, Marilyn and Jones, Kathryn (eds.) 2000. *Multilingual literacies: comparative perspectives on research and practice*. Amsterdam: John Benjamins.

Maschler, Yael 1998. 'On the transition from code-switching to a mixed code', in P. Auer (ed.) *Code-switching in conversation: languages, interaction and identity*. London: Routledge, 125–49.

May, Stephen 2007. 'Sustaining effective literacy practices over time in secondary schools: school organisational and change issues', *Language and Education*, 21 (5): 387–405.

2012. 'Language rights: promoting civic multilingualism', in M. Martin-Jones, A. Blackledge and A. Creese (eds.) *Handbook of multilingualism*. London: Routledge, 131–42.

Mayer, Felix 2000. 'Sprachpolitik in Südtirol: Fragmentierung vs. Globalisierung', in W. Wilss (ed.) *Weltgesellschaft, Weltverkehrssprache, Weltkultur*. Tübingen: Stauffenburg, 96–111.

McArthur, Tom 1998. *The English languages*. Cambridge University Press.

McClure, Erica and McClure, Malcolm 1988. 'Macro- and micro-sociolinguistic dimensions of code-switching in Vingard (Romania)', in Monica Heller (ed.) *Codeswitching: anthropological and sociolinguistic perspectives*. Berlin: Walter de Gruyter, 25–51.

McNamara, Jim 1967. 'The bilingual's linguistic performance: a psychological overview', *Journal of Social Issues*, 23: 58–77.

McRae, Kenneth 1983. *Conflict and compromise in multilingual societies. Switzerland*. Waterloo, Ontario: Wilfried Laurier University Press.

Meisel, Jürgen (ed.) 1990. *Two first languages: early grammatical development in bilingual children*. Dordrecht: Floris.

Meisel, Jürgen 1994. 'Code-switching in young bilingual children: the acquisition of grammatical constraints', *Studies in Second Language Acquisition*, 16: 413–39.

2001. 'The simultaneous acquisition of two first languages: early differentiation and subsequent development of grammars', in J. Cenoz and F. Genesee (eds.) *Trends in bilingual acquisition*. Amsterdam: John Benjamins, 11–41.

Menken, K., Funk, A. and Kleyn, T. 2011. 'Teachers at the epicenter: engagement and resistance in a biliteracy programme for "long-term English language learners" in the United States', in Hélot and Ó Laoire (eds.), 79–104.

Mesthrie, Rajend and Bhatt, Rakesh 2008. *World Englishes: the study of new linguistic varieties*. Cambridge University Press.

Mikes, Melanie 1990. 'Some issues of lexical development in early bi- and trilinguals', in G. Conti-Ramsden and C. Snow (eds.) *Children's Language*. Hillsdale, NJ: Lawrence Erlbaum, 103–20.

Mirkam-Sipurim, M'pi 2001. *Yotzei Etiopia (textured stories told by Ethiopian emigrants)*, Tel-Aviv: Center for Educational Technology (CET).

Montanari, Simona 2009a. 'Pragmatic differentiation in early trilingual development', *Journal of Child Language*, 36: 597–627, http://dx.doi.org/10.1017/S0305000908009112.

2009b. 'Multi-word combinations and the emergence of differentiated ordering patterns in early trilingual development', *Bilingualism: Language and Cognition*, 12 (4): 503–19, http://dx.doi.org/10.1017/S1366728909990265.

2010. 'Translation equivalents and the emergence of multiple lexicons in early trilingual development', *First Language*, 30 (1): 102–25, http://dx.doi.org/10.1177/0142723709350528.

2011. 'Phonological differentiation before age two in a Tagalog–Spanish–English trilingual child', *International Journal of Multilingualism*, 8 (1): 5–21, http://dx.doi.org/10.1080/14790711003671846.

2013. 'Productive trilingualism in infancy: what makes it possible?', *World Journal of English Language*, 3 (1): 62.

Moore, Leslie 1999. 'Secondary language socialisation in a multilingual context: incongruence between community and classroom practice', *AILE, Proceedings of 8th EUROSLA Conference Paris*, Vol. 1, Special Issue: 143–53.

Morales, H. L. 2008. *Enciclopedia del español en los Estados Unidos: anuario del Instituto Ceivantes.* Madrid: Santillana, 127.

Mor-Sommerfeld, A. 2002. 'Language mosaic: developing literacy in a second-new language: a new perspective', *Reading, Literacy and Language*, 36 (3): 99–105.

Mühlhäusler, Peter 2003. *Language of environment – environment of language: a course in ecolinguistics.* London: Battlebridge.

Murrell, Martin 1966. 'Pragmatic differentiation in early trilingual development', *Studia Linguistica*, 20: 9–35.

Muysken, Peter 2000. *Bilingual speech: a typology of code-mixing.* Cambridge University Press.

Myers-Scotton, Carol 1993. *Social motivations for codeswitching: evidence from Africa.* Oxford: Clarendon Press.

    2006. *Multiple voices: an introduction to bilingualism.* Malden, MA: Blackwell.

Myhill, John 1999. Identity, territoriality and minority language survival', *Journal of Multilingual and Multicultural Development*, 20 (1): 34–50.

Navracsics, Judith 1998. *The acquisition of Hungarian by trilingual children.* Unpublished doctoral thesis, Janus Pannonius University of Pécs, Hungary.

New London Group 1996. 'A pedagogy of multiliteracies: designing social futures', *Harvard Educational Review*, 66 (1): 60–92.

Newmark, Peter 1996.'Looking at English words in translation', in Gunilla M. Anderman and Margaret Rogers (eds.) *Words, words, words: the translator and the language learner.* Clevedon: Multilingual Matters, 56–68.

Newton, Gerald 1996. *Luxembourg and Lëtzebuergesch: language and communication at the crossroads of Europe.* Oxford: Clarendon Press.

Ngomo, P. 2011. 'Exploring new pedagogical approaches in the context of multilingual Cameroon', in Hélot and Ó Laoire (eds.), 126–46.

Nilep, Chad 2006. '"Code switching" in sociocultural linguistics', *Colorado Research in Linguistics*, 19 (1).

Nishimura, Miwa 1997. *Japanese/English code-switching: syntax and pragmatics.* New York: Peter Lang.

O'Rourke, B. 2011. 'Negotiating multilingualism in an Irish primary school context', in Hélot and Ó Laoire (eds.), 105–25.

Okita, Toshie 2002. *Invisible work: bilingualism, language choice and childrearing in intermarried families.* Amsterdam: John Benjamins.

Oksaar, Els 1977. 'On becoming trilingual', in C. Molony (ed.) *Deutsch im Kontakt mit anderen Sprachen.* Kronberg: Scriptor Verlag, 296–306.

1983. 'Multilingualism and multiculturalism from the linguist's point of view', in T. Hush and S. Opper (eds.) *Multicultural and multilingual education in immigrant countries*. Oxford/NewYork: Pergamon Press, 17–38.

Olshtain, Elite, Stavans, Anat and Kotik-Friedgut, Bella 2003. 'The development of first language attrition and second language acquisition in Russian-speaking immigrants to Israel', Final Report, The Israeli Science Academy, October 2003.

Olson, D. R. 1977. 'From utterance to text: the bias of language in speech and writing', *Harvard Educational Review*, 47: 257–81.

Oyetade, O. S. 2003. 'Language planning in a multi-ethnic state: the majority/minority dichotomy in Nigeria', *Nordic Journal of African Studies*, 12 (1): 106.

Pattanayak, Debi P. (ed.) 1990. *Multilingualism in India*. Clevedon: Multilingual Matters.

Pavlenko, Aneta and Blackledge, Adrian (eds.) 2004. *Negotiation of identities in multilingual contexts*. Clevedon: Multilingual Matters.

Perecman, Ellen 1989. 'Language processing in the bilingual: evidence from language mixing', in K. Hyltenstam and L. Obler (eds.) *Bilingualism across the lifespan*. Cambridge University Press, 227–44.

Phillipson, Robert 1992. *Linguistic imperialism*. Oxford University Press.

Piller, Ingrid 2001. 'Private language planning: the best of both worlds?' *Estudios de Sociolingüística*, 2: 61–80.

Pollock, Mica 2008. 'From shallow to deep: toward a thorough cultural analysis of school achievement patterns', *Anthropology and Education Quarterly*, 39: 369–80.

Poplack, Shana 1980. 'Sometimes I'll start a sentence in English y termino en español: toward a typology of code-switching', in J. Amastae and L. Elías-Olivares (eds.) *Spanish in the United States: sociolinguistic aspects*. Cambridge University Press, 230–63.

Pufahl, Ingrid, Rhodes, Nancy C. and Christian, Donna 2001. 'What we can learn from foreign language teaching in other countries', ERIC Clearinghouse on Languages and Linguistics, Washington, DC: http://purl.access.gpo.gov/GPO/LPS26158.

Purcell-Gates, Victoria 1995. *Other people's words: the cycle of low literacy*. Cambridge, MA: Harvard University Press.

Purcell-Gates, Victoria (ed.) 2007. *Cultural practices of literacy: complicating the complex*. Mahwah, NJ: Lawrence Erlbaum.

Purcell-Gates, V., Melzi, G., Najafi, B. and Orellana, M. F. 2011. 'Building literacy instruction from children's sociocultural worlds', *Child Development Perspectives*, 5 (1): 22–27.

Quay, Suzanne 2001. 'Managing linguistic boundaries in early trilingual development', in J. Cenoz and F. Genesee (eds.) *Trends in bilingual acquisition*. Amsterdam: John Benjamins, 149–99.

2008. 'Dinner conversations with a trilingual two-year-old: language socialization in a multilingual context', *First Language*, 28 (1): 5–33, http://dx.doi.org/10.1177/0142723707083557.

2011a. 'Introduction: data-driven insights from trilingual children in the making', *International Journal of Multilingualism*, 8 (1): 1–4, http://dx.doi.org/10.1080/14790711003671838.

2011b. 'Trilingual toddlers at daycare centers: the role of caregivers and peers in language development', *International Journal of Multilingualism*, 8 (1): 22–41, http://dx.doi.org/10.1080/14790711003671853.

Rajagopalan, Kanavillil 2004. 'Language politics in Latin America', in K. Rajagopalan (ed.) *Applied Linguistics in Latin America*, AILA Review 18. Amsterdam: John Benjamins, 76–93.

Rampton, Ben 1995. *Crossing: language and ethnicity among adolescents*. London: Longman.

1999. 'Styling the other: introduction', *Journal of Sociolinguistics*, 3: 421–27.

2005. *Crossing: language and ethnicity among adolescents* (2nd edn). Manchester: St Jerome.

Reyes, Iliana and Ervin-Tripp, Susan 2004. 'Code-switching and borrowing: discourse strategies in the developing bilingual children's interactions', *Proceedings from the Second International Symposium on Bilingualism* held in October 2002, University of Vigo (Spain), 319–31.

Reyes, María de la Luz 2001. 'Unleashing possibilities: biliteracy in the primary grades', in M. L. Reyes and J. J. Halcón (eds.) *The best for our children: critical perspectives on literacy for Latino students*. New York: Teachers College Press, 96–121.

Reyes, María de la Luz and Halcón, John J. (eds.) 2001. *The best for our children: critical perspectives on literacy for Latino students*. New York: Teachers College Press.

Romaine, Suzanne 1985. 'Syntactic variation and the acquisition of strategies of relativisation in the language of Edinburgh schoolchildren', in Sven Jacobson (ed.) *Papers from the Third Scandinavian Symposium on Syntactic Variation*. Stockholm: Almqvist and Wiksell International, 19–33.

1989. *Bilingualism*. Oxford: Blackwell.

1995a. *Bilingualism* (2nd edn). Oxford: Blackwell.

1995b. 'Sociolinguistics', in J. Blommaert, J.-O. Östman and J. Verscheuren (eds.) *Handbook of pragmatics*. Amsterdam: John Benjamins, 489–95.

2004. 'The bilingual and multilingual community', in T. Bathia and W. C. Ritchie (eds.) *The handbook of bilingualism*. Oxford: Blackwell, 385–406.

Rubín, Joan 1968. *National bilingualism in Paraguay*. The Hague: Mouton.

Sankoff, David and Poplack, Shana 1981. 'A formal grammar for code-switching', *Research on Language & Social Interaction*, 14 (1): 3–45.

Sasaki, Miyuki 2000. 'Toward an empirical model of EFL writing processes: an exploratory study', *Journal of Second Language Writing*, 9: 259–91.

Schmal, John P. 2008. *Indigenous Mexico: an introduction to Mexico's remarkable diversity*. www.somosprimos.com/schmal/IndigenousMexico.pdf.

Schneider, Edgar W. 2007. *Postcolonial English: varieties around the world.* Cambridge University Press.

2010. *English around the world: an introduction.* Cambridge University Press.

Scribner, Sylvia and Cole, Michael 1978. Literacy without schooling: testing for intellectual effects. *Harvard Educational Review*, 29 (2): 448–61.

Scribner, Sylvia 1981. *The psychology of literacy.* Cambridge, MA: Harvard University Press.

Sebba, Mark and Wooten, Tony 1998. 'We, they and identity: sequential versus identity-related explanation in code-switching', in Peter Auer (ed.) *Code-switching in conversation: language, interaction and identity.* London: Routledge, 262–86.

Seidelhofer, B. 2003. 'The shape of things to come? Some basic questions about English as a lingua franca', in K. Knapp and C. Meierkord (eds.) *Lingua Franca Communication.* Frankfurt/Main: Peter Lang, 269–302.

Silverstein, Michael and Urban, Greg 1996. 'The natural history of discourse', in M. Silverstein and G. Urban (eds.) *Natural histories of discourse.* University of Chicago Press.

Sjöholm, Kaj 2004. 'English as a third language in bilingual Finland: basic communication or academic language?', in Hoffmann and Ytsma (eds.), 219–38.

Skutnabb-Kangas, Tove 1981. *Bilingualism or not: the education of minorities.* Clevedon: Multilingual Matters.

2000. *Linguistic genocide in education – or worldwide diversity and human rights?.* London: Routledge.

Skutnabb-Kangas, Tove and McCarty, Teresa 2008. 'Clarification, ideological/epistemological underpinnings and implications of some concepts in bilingual education', in J. Cummins and N. H. Hornberger *Encyclopedia of language and education* (2nd edn, Vol. 5: Bilingual Education). New York: Springer, 3–17.

Skutnabb-Kangas, Tove and Phillipson, Robert 1989. '"Mother tongue": the theoretical and sociopolitical construction of a concept', in U. Ammon (ed.) *Status and function of language and language variety.* New York: Walter de Gruyter, 450–77.

Skutnabb-Kangas, Tove, Maffi, Luisa and Harmon, David 2003. *Sharing a world of difference: the earth's linguistic, cultural, and biological diversity.* Paris: UNESCO.

Skutnabb-Kangas, Tove, Phillipson, Robert and Rannut, Mart 1995. *Linguistic human rights: overcoming linguistic discrimination.* Berlin/New York: Mouton De Gruyter.

Snow, Catherine E., Burns, M. Susan and Griffin, Peg 1998. *Preventing reading difficulties in young children.* Committee on the Prevention of Reading Difficulties in Young Children. Washington, DC: National Academy Press.

Spolsky, Bernard 1978. 'Language testing: art or science', in G. Nickel (ed.) *Language testing*. Stuttgart: Hochschulverlag, 216–25.

2009. *Language management*. Cambridge University Press.

Spolsky, Bernhard and Shohamy, Elana 1999. *The languages of Israel: policy, ideology and practice*. Clevedon: Multilingual Matters.

Sridhar, S. N. and Sridhar, Kamal K. 1980. 'The syntax and psycholinguistics of bilingual code-mixing', *Canadian Journal of Psychology*, 34: 407–16.

Stavans, Anat 1990. *Codeswitching in children acquiring English, Spanish and Hebrew: a case study*. Unpublished PhD dissertation, University of Pittsburgh.

1992. 'Sociolinguistic factors affecting code-switches produced by trilingual children', *Language, Culture and Curriculum*, 5 (1): 41–53.

2001. 'Trilingual narratives: relating events in three languages', in L. V. S. Stromqvist (ed.) *Narrative development in a multilingual context*. Amsterdam: John Benjamins, 340–72.

2003. 'Bilinguals as narrators: a comparison of bilingual and monolingual Hebrew and English narratives', *Narrative Inquiry*, 1 (1): 151–91.

2005. 'Advantages and benefits trilingualism', in I. Kupferberg and E. Olshtain (eds.) *Discourse in education: educational events as a field of research*. Tel Aviv: Mofet, 418–49 [in Hebrew].

Stavans, A. and Goldzweig, G. 2009. 'Insights on learning Hebrew as L$_2$ by Ethiopian and Russian immigrants in Israel: "must" or "have"', *Iyunim Besafa Vehevra* [Studies in Language and Society], 1 (2): 59–85.

Stavans, Anat and Hoffmann, Charlotte 2007. 'From code-switching via code-mixing to trilingual competence', in A. Stavans and I. Kupferberg (eds.) *Studies in language and language education*. Jerusalem: The Magnes Press, 147–84.

Stavans, Anat and Muchnik, Malka 2008. 'Language production in trilingual children', *Sociolinguistic Studies*, 1 (3): 483–511.

Stavans, Anat and Narkiss, Doron 2004. 'Creating and implementing a language policy in the Israeli educational system', in Hoffmann and Ytsma (eds.), 139–65.

Stavans, Anat and Swisher, M.V. 2006. 'Language switching as a window on trilingual acquisition', *International Journal of Multilingualism*, 3 (3): 193–220.

Stavans, A., Olshtain, E. and Goldzweig, G. 2009. 'Parental perceptions of children's literacy and bilingualism: the case of Ethiopian immigrants in Israel', *Journal of Multilingual and Multicultural Development*, 30 (2): 111–26.

Stewart, William A. 1968. 'A sociolinguistic typology for describing national multilingualism', in J. A. Fishman (ed.) *Readings in the sociology of language*. The Hague: Mouton, 531–45.

Street, Brian V. 1984. *Literacy in theory and practice*. Cambridge University Press.

1988. 'Literacy practices and literacy myths', in R. Saljo (ed.) *The written word: studies in literate thought and action*. Berlin: Springer Verlag, 59–72.

1996. 'Academic literacies', in D. Baker, C. Fox, and J. Clay (eds.) *Challenging ways of knowing: literacies, numeracies and sciences*. Brighton: Falmer Press, 101–34.

2000. 'Literacy events and literacy practices', in Martin-Jones and Jones (eds.), 17–29.

2002. 'Academic literacies and the 'New Orders': implications for research and practice', Paper presented to the NCTE Conference, New York, 22–24 February.

Street, J. C. and Street, Brian V. 1991. 'The schooling of literacy', in D. Barton and R. Ivanic (eds.) *Writing in the community*. London: Sage, 143–66.

Syed, Z. and Burnett, A. 1999. 'Acculturation, identity, and language: implications for language minority education', in Kathryn A. Davis (ed.) *Foreign language teaching and language minority education* (Technical Report No. 19). University of Hawai'i at Mānoa, Second Language Teaching and Curriculum Center.

Taeschner, Traute 1983. *The sun is feminine: a study on language acquisition in childhood*. Berlin/Heidelberg: Springer Verlag.

Thomason, Sarah G. 2001. *Language contact: an introduction*. Edinburgh University Press.

Tokuhama-Espinosa, Tracey 2001. *Raising multilingual children: foreign language acquisition and children*. Westport, CT: Bergin & Garvey.

Trueba, Henry T. 1990. *Cultural conflict and adaptation: the case of Hmong children in American society*. Bristol, PA: Falmer Press.

Tucker, Richard G. 1999. 'A global perspective on bilingualism and bilingual education', Digest EDO-fl-99-04 US Department of Education, Office of Educational Research and Improvement, National Library of Education.

Turell, M. Teresa (ed.) 2001. *Multilingualism in Spain: sociolinguistic and psycholinguistic aspects of linguistic minority groups* (Vol. 115). Clevedon: Multilingual Matters.

Vaish, Viniti 2005. 'A peripherist view of English as a language of decolonization in post-colonial India', *Language Policy*, 4: 187–206.

Verschick, Anna 1999. 'Some aspects of the multilingualism of Estonian Jews', *International Journal of the Sociology of Language*, 139: 49–67.

Vihman, Marilyn M. 1985. 'Language differentiation by the bilingual infant', *Journal of Child Language*, 12: 297–324.

Von Gleich, Uta 1994. 'Language spread policy: the case of Quechua in the Andean republics of Bolivia, Ecuador and Peru', *International Journal of the Sociology of Language*, 107: 77–113.

Wang, Xiao-lei 2008. *Growing up with three languages: birth to eleven*. Bristol: Multilingual Matters.

Wardhaugh, Ralph 1987. *Languages in competition*. Oxford: Basil Blackwell.

2002. *An introduction to sociolinguistics* (4th edn). Oxford: Blackwell.

Weinreich, Uriel 1953. *Languages in contact: findings and problems*. The Hague: Mouton.

1954. 'Is a structural dialectology possible?', *Word*, 10: 388–400.

Woolard, Katharine A. 1998. 'Simultaneity and bivalency as strategies in bilingualism', *Journal of Linguistic Anthropology*, 8 (1): 3–29.

Wright, Sue 2004. *Language policy and language planning: from nationalism to globalisation*. Basingstoke: Palgrave Macmillan.

Yip, Virginia, and Matthews, Stephen 2007. *The bilingual child: early development and language contact*. Cambridge University Press.

Youssi, Abderrahim, 1995. 'The Moroccan triglossia: facts and implications', *International Journal of the Sociology of Language*, 112: 29–43.

Zentella, Ana Celia 1997. *Growing up bilingual*. Malden, MA: Blackwell.

Author index

294

Places and languages index

Subject index

accommodating multilingualism, 193, 198, 200, 212
acculturation, 12, 200
Arabisation, 16, 115, 117–19

bilingual
    children, 144–45, 149, 168, 181–82, 224, 232, 240, 242
    competence, 158, 180
    continuum, 158
    development, 147, 162, 168
    education, 47, 61, 109–11, 118, 122, 233, 235, 244
    education programmes, 126
    education system, 122
    mode, 167
    natural, 139
    processing, 164, 166–68
    programmes, 122, 129, 150
    regular, 139
    speech, 162, 230
bilingual first language acquisition (BFLA), 145
Bilingual Model of Lexical Access (BIMOLA), 158, 167
bilingualism
    balanced, 110
    childhood, 217, 226
    elite, 217, 234
    societal, 204
    subsequent bilinguals, 41
    subtractive, 151
biliteracy
    development, 258
borrowing, *see* language borrowing

Castilianisation, 19, 110
code-mixed, 244

code-mixing, 173, 177, 179, 181, 186, 190, 211
code-switched, 244
code-switching (CS), 79–80, 96, 120, 144–45, 147, 154, 158, 164, 173–81, 186, 189–91, 196–98, 204, 211, 223–24, 230, 246, 258
codification, 39
cognition, 153, 170, 172, 199, 229, 252, 262–63
cognitive
    factors, 167
    mechanisms, 190
    practices, 248
    processing, 159, 164
Common European Framework of Reference for Languages, 159
communicative
    behaviour, 227
    competence, 160–62, 229, 236
    identity, 194
    needs, 24, 161, 193, 227
    repertoire, 257
    skills, 228
Competition Model of Bilingualism, 164, 166
complementarity principle, 157, 191
corpus planning, 40, 79, 111, 113, 123
creole, 50, 103

diglossia, 51–53, 59–60
discourse strategies, 162
Dynamic Model of Multilingualism (DMM), 171

education
    system, 21, 83, 85–86, 110, 125, 229, 240

303

educational
  needs, 143
  system, 242, 245, 254, 261
English, 125
  as an international language, 130
  language learning, 124
  as a second language, 125
  speakers, 127
  spread of, 58, 94, 99, 101, 123–24,
    130, 132
ethnic group, 42–43, 50, 56, 60, 65,
    70–71, 75, 82, 84, 88, 244
European Directive of 1977, 66
European Language Portfolio (ELP), 261
European Schools, 150, 240

factors (that favour/hinder
    multilingualism)
  attitudes, 45–46, 51, 54, 59, 79–80,
    85, 88, 91, 105, 108, 111, 116,
    119, 126–28, 131
  Christianisation, 16, 18, 99, 108, 111
  colonialism, 27, 94–97, 106, 131
  colonisation, 12, 15–16, 18, 21, 27,
    32, 34–35, 93, 95, 98, 108, 131
  conquest, 12–13, 15, 18, 21, 35,
    93, 108
  crusades, 16, 93
  demographic developments, 36
  displacement, 30
  dynastic politics, 21
  economic inequalities, 36
  economic influence, 15
  economic power, 18
  education, 12, 21, 35, 62, 130
  federation, 25–28
  globalisation, 45, 93–94, 97–99, 124,
    132, 201, 214, 217, 220, 228,
    242, 245, 254
  immersion, 150
  intermarriage, 12, 30
  internationalisation, 45, 64, 80, 94,
    97, 99, 129, 132
  language ideology, 46, 48, 102
  language of administration, 15,
    22, 34
  language policies, 45, 47, 55, 57,
    60–61, 82, 160
  linguistic minority, 30
  literacy, 35–36

mass expulsion, 30
migration/immigration/emigration,
    11–12, 29, 32–35, 43–44, 47, 58,
    62, 64, 71, 80–81, 90, 93, 126,
    138, 147, 160, 220
mobility, 30, 45, 64, 130
movement of people, 30, 32
multinational state, 71
nation building, 68–69, 101, 109,
    116, 119–20
national unity, 36
nationalism, 68–69
occupation, 13
pluralism, 85, 91, 112
political dominance, 15
political unity, 29, 36
population changes, 30
population movement, 30, 32
postcolonialism, 34, 93–94, 132
printing, 20, 35
recognition, 63–64, 68, 71, 78,
    80, 106
recognition of minority
    languages, 127
recognition of minority rights, 62
religion, 16, 18, 90
remigration, 29–30
resettlement, 12, 29–30
slave trade, 30
status planning, 111, 113
trade, 16, 18
transfers, 131
travel, 105
Family Language Policy (FLP), 212–20,
    224–27

Hispanics, 127

identity/identities, 146, 160, 176, 180,
    194–95, 197–204, 206–13, 220,
    228, 240, 242, 244, 247–48, 253,
    258, 262
intelligibility, 41
interlanguage, 230
intersentential switch/switching, 178
intrasentential switch/switching, 178

language/languages
  accommodation, 152, 193, 196, 201,
    207, 213, 220, 227

acquisition, 102, 136, 138, 140–43,
    146–47, 150–53, 155, 158–59,
    167, 175, 227
  simultaneous, 142
  subsequent, 142
  third language, 153
  trilingual, 145
additional, 21, 101, 132, 141
of administration, 13
affiliation, 258
alternation, 200
attrition, 140
awareness, 146, 167, 182–85
behaviour, 64, 106, 144, 157, 159,
    186, 216
borrowing, 79, 100, 120
choice, 54, 145–46, 148, 172–73,
    194–95, 198–200, 224, 227
classical, 40
colonial, 28, 35, 50, 93–96, 104–107,
    113–15, 119, 123, 131–32, 151
communication, 139
community, 34, 43, 66–67, 139, 141,
    143, 148, 224–25
competence, 66, 135, 153, 157–59, 173
contact, 32, 141, 146, 180, 186, 258
crossing, 176, 203–204
death, 34
development, 142, 144–45, 149,
    168, 226
differentiation, 145
dominance, 146, 159
dominant, 65, 92, 102–103, 109, 111,
    148, 208, 222–23, 236
education, 15, 19–21, 47, 66, 91, 231,
    242–43
education policy, 241
education system, 47, 150, 154
endangerment, 68, 258–59
environment, 259
ethnic, 50, 54
evolution, 258
family policies (FLP), 213–20, 224–26
first, 21, 40–41, 48, 55, 59, 122, 136,
    145, 245, 249
foreign, 98, 135, 138, 153, 207, 226,
    236–37, 241–42, 245, 256, 261
global, 99–100, 124
heritage, 43, 213, 215–18, 220,
    236, 245

home, 42, 50, 150–51, 222–24, 227,
    231, 233–35, 240, 244
immigrant, 43, 66–67, 83, 91, 126
immigrant communities, 71
indigenous, 32, 34, 45, 60–61, 93–94,
    106–11, 113–15, 119–21, 123,
    126, 132, 143, 153, 238
input, 152
of instruction, 83
international, 40, 61, 94–95,
    128, 132
language mixing, 167, 175
learning, 51, 98, 127, 129–30, 152–
    54, 165, 167–68, 221, 230–31,
    256, 261
legislation, 47
loss, 214
maintenance, 14, 47, 65, 87, 90–92,
    214, 216–17, 220, 244
majority, 199–200, 214, 218, 233–34,
    236–37, 240, 242
majority language, 53, 57, 63, 66–67,
    69, 71–72, 82, 106, 125
majority language English
    speakers, 126
minorities, 19, 34
  indigenous, 44, 55, 68, 150
  new, 150
  non-English, 126
minority, 148, 150, 198–200, 216,
    219, 227, 228–29, 233–36, 238,
    242, 258
minority language, 43, 46–48,
    53–58, 63–67, 71–73, 80, 92, 110,
    127, 130
minority language rights, 68
mixing, 146, 154, 173, 177, 224
national, 23, 38–41, 47, 51, 54,
    56, 60, 94, 105, 113, 120–22,
    241–42, 249
national official, 55
official, 21, 23, 25, 28, 32, 38–40,
    50, 54, 59, 61, 83, 88, 94, 96–97,
    107, 109, 120, 152, 241
planning, 28, 45, 68, 82, 107, 111,
    219, 243, 258
planning policies, 68
policies, 19, 94, 96, 104, 109–11,
    117–18, 120–21, 191, 212,
    215, 243